INVENTORY MANAGEMENT FOR COMPETITIVE ADVANTAGE

Smart, strategic inventory management delivers competitive advantage, yet Inventory Turn trends suggest that little seems to change. Sustainable improvement through increasing control of systems and processes generates savings that can, in turn, be invested in growth initiatives. Inventory is not something that just concerns planning, production and finance. By working to better understand and control their inventory-related processes, everyone can drive improvements that will harness inventory's potential to become a source of sustainable competitive advantage.

Unlike other guides to inventory management, this book is not only aimed at planners or inventory managers, but details the impact, both direct and indirect, that all functions have on inventory. It is rich in practical tools that can be clearly implemented, including a detailed purchasing strategy and guide to error management. It is also rich in best-practice cases that further show how to implement these methodologies in a real-world context.

This book is essential reading for any manager or executive looking to boost their organisation's competitive advantage, as well as students of inventory management, production and operations management.

Keith Jones is a consultant in inventory management and project data analysis with 40 years' experience, primarily in the chemical industry, working in roles from R&D Chemist to Commercial Director. In his consultancy work he harnesses his experience of working in R&D, production quality control, purchasing, finance, customer service, production planning, IT project management, supply chain project management, data analysis, inventory management, sales, market research, warehousing and logistics. The breadth of his experience has given him a unique perspective on inventory management that is applicable across all industries.

INVENTORY MANAGEMENT FOR COMPETITIVE ADVANTAGE

Including a Practical and Effective Purchasing Strategy for Managers

Keith Jones

Routledge

Taylor & Francis Group

LONDON AND NEW YORK

First published 2020
by Routledge
2 Park Square, Milton Park, Abingdon, Oxon OX14 4RN

and by Routledge
52 Vanderbilt Avenue, New York, NY 10017

Routledge is an imprint of the Taylor & Francis Group, an informa business

© 2020 Keith Jones

British Library Cataloguing-in-Publication Data
A catalogue record for this book is available from the British Library

Library of Congress Cataloging-in-Publication Data
A catalog record for this book has been requested

ISBN: 978-0-367-44289-7 (hbk)
ISBN: 978-1-003-00923-8 (ebk)

Typeset in Bembo
by Apex CoVantage, LLC

TO CAROL AND MAM

CONTENTS

CONTENTS

ACKNOWLEDGEMENTS

In 1989, my wife, Carol, saw a programme on BBC2 about the Open University Business School. That fateful Saturday morning set in motion a chain of events that changed my life. Now, 30 years of support and encouragement later, here I am having written a book. What can I say but – thank you darling.

I have had the good fortune in my career to work with many good people, too many to mention here but my thanks go to them all. Without good colleagues and plenty of tea, a book like this could not have been written.

One person I have to mention though is my very good friend, Gino Francato. He took the time to read my initial drafts and subsequent modifications. His insights and feedback proved invaluable and helped make this the book that you read today – Grazie mille Gino!

Finally, I have to thank Amy Laurens at Routledge for having faith in the book and Amy, Alex Atkinson and Gabriele Gaizutyte of Routledge and Nancy Moses of Apex Covantage for their patience and support in bringing about its publication.

PREFACE

In any organisation, very few employees will take the time to read, let alone understand, the annual report. Those that do, even when they look closely, would only be able to find a few references to inventory. Usually, those references will include:

- A value for inventory at the end of the reporting period. There will often be a breakdown with values relating to raw materials, work in progress and finished product.
- Some reference to having policies relating to obsolete and slow-moving inventory.
- Occasional measures showing either Inventory Turn or Days of Inventory.
- Occasional values assigned to new provisions made in relation to inventory (having applied policies referred to above).

Of course, for most employees these will just be numbers with little meaning. For most employees, inventory will be the physical stuff that they buy, sell, move or moan about because the company has too much of, too little of or have unsaleable inventory that should be got rid of and so on. Essentially, these are the practical everyday inventory issues that people have to deal with.

However, closer inspection of annual reports shows that, despite its relative lack of prominence, inventory, especially its value, is not something that can be ignored. By way of illustration, Table 0.1 shows the inventory values for 20 global companies (mostly chemical).

As you can see, the values are large – extremely large for companies like Company C, Company D and Company I (a total of nearly \$33 billion in 2017). These are values that simply cannot be ignored.

Of course, the initial reaction to high levels of inventory is that you should manufacture less. Indeed, this is often the directive from the business executive – what can be seen as a knee-jerk, though understandable, reaction. The problem is that as instructions cascade down the hierarchy, exceptions begin to develop such that short-term improvements prove not to be sustainable, and the cycle begins all over again, resulting in the same directive having to be repeated time

Company	2016	2017
A	129	129
B	1614	1289
C	11461	16047
D	10537	12144
E	8855	7720
F	2029	2255
G	2675	2655
H	292	343
I	7363	16992
J	1404	1509
K	121	144
L	1344	1073
M	1125	1469
N	811	1026
O	237	315
P	147	171
Q	1620	1833
R	42	51
S	891	924
T	5176	7231
TOTAL	**57874**	**75321**

Table 0.1 Inventory values (expressed in USD millions) for 20 companies.

and time again. The problem is that the process does not change in a fundamental way, and without fundamental change the outcomes will always be the same.

So, whilst the amount of cash tied up as inventory is quite significant, managing it in a sustainable way is clearly not a simple as you might think.

Of course, whilst any particular inventory value can seem high, it is important to know how this relates to the size of the company. Here, a useful measure is Inventory Turn. Put simply, if you sell inventory with a cost of sales of £1000 per annum and have inventory valued at £200, the Inventory Turn is 5 (£1000 divided by £200).

Table 0.2 shows Inventory Turns calculated from the annual reports used in Table 0.1.

Whilst an average is quoted for Inventory Turn, it is significantly skewed by the levels of inventory reported for companies such as Company C and Company I.

Figure 0.1 shows the distribution of Inventory Turns, and it is clear that there is a significant grouping between 3 and 6.

From Table 0.2, it is very evident that there is a considerable variance from one company to another and, indeed, historical analysis for any company will show that Inventory Turn varies from one year to the next.

| Company | Inventory Turn | |
	2016	2017
A	7.9	8.4
B	5.4	8.2
C	4.0	4.0
D	3.9	4.3
E	2.4	1.7
F	5.0	4.9
G	6.2	5.0
H	3.4	3.3
I	5.1	3.8
J	4.7	4.7
K	3.2	3.4
L	5.9	6.1
M	9.5	10.0
N	15.2	14.5
O	4.0	3.5
P	6.6	7.7
Q	4.7	4.5
R	11.7	12.9
S	4.5	5.1
T	9.6	12.6
AVERAGE	***5.5***	***5.7***

Table 0.2 Inventory Turn calculated from annual reports.

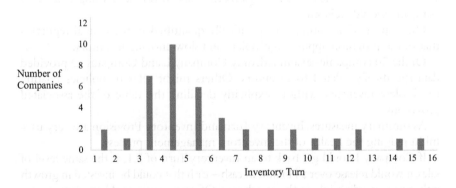

Figure 0.1 Inventory Turn distribution 2016 and 2017.

Figure 0.2 shows Inventory Turn from 2009 to 2017 for five of the companies listed in Tables 0.1 and 0.2. For these particular companies, there does not appear to be any sustainable and positive change in Inventory Turn. Indeed, the only patterns appear to be either of deterioration (Company D, Company E and Company I) or cyclical (Company L and Company O).

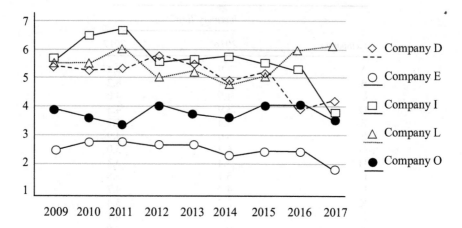

Figure 0.2 Inventory Turn 2009 to 2017.

No doubt there will be many reasons to explain both the variations from year to year for a single company, and indeed the differences between companies – the markets they serve, manufacturing capabilities and protocols, currency fluctuations etc. However, there appear to be instances where companies with broadly similar markets have different Inventory Turns (e.g. Company I and Company D fall into this category). The question is, 'Why?'

What is clear is that if sustainable improvements were made a lot of cash would be released back into an organisation, and this is something that every company would welcome.

One aspect of inventory not specifically quantified in the annual reports is that of the provision applied to obsolete and slow-moving inventory.

Of the 20 companies examined, only Company L and Company O provided data specifically related to inventory. Others might refer to policies relating to obsolete inventory without explicitly detailing the value of the associated provisions.

As summary measures, Inventory Turn and Inventory Provision are very useful in judging the health of the inventory management process.

If Company I could get back to an Inventory Turn of 5.1, at the same level of sales, it would release over $4 billion in cash – cash that could be invested in growth rather than standing idle in the warehouse. Of course, you could say that you are no better or worse than your competitors, so the playing field is reasonably level.

However, consider this – if you could *completely* and *sustainably* eliminate inventory-related issues and optimise inventory management, you would end up with:

- Considerably less cash tied up as inventory.
- People spending less time on the issues of the past.

- People spending more time focussing on future growth and development.
- Lower ongoing inventory management costs.

Delivering on these aspects will be a considerable benefit to any company and securing sustainable improvements will put that company ahead of its competitors in terms of process management – in other words, focussing on improved inventory management will have delivered a sustainable competitive advantage.

It is easy to think that looking at other organisations is the route to improved performance, and doing so, no doubt, could be quite beneficial. However, the data seems to challenge some of these preconceptions. For example, Companies C and D can be thought of as best in class certainly in terms of size, but when it comes to the control of inventory, bigger would not appear to mean better.

Some preconceptions are misplaced. You need not necessarily look elsewhere for guidance; answers can be found much closer to home.

Of course, the question still remains – 'How can progress actually be made?' Well, if you want to know the answer to that, then read on.

TERMS

The following are explanations of some of the terms used in this book:

Acid value   The mass of potassium hydroxide in milligrams required to neutralise 1 gram of chemical substance; used as a measure of the remaining acid molecules available to react.

Alcohol   A molecule with a hydroxyl group that can, in turn, react with an acid, such as adipic acid.

Alkyd resin   A chemical product manufactured using a condensation reaction and frequently used in paint manufacture.

Azeotrope   A mixture of two liquids that has a constant boiling point and composition through distillation. This property is utilised in condensation reactions to remove the byproduct (e.g. water).

Batch card   A card that details the product to be manufactured, the forecasted yield, the raw materials required (in sequence) and the quantities of the respective raw materials (see also **Bill of Materials**).

Best practice   When an organisation (or several organisations having similar procedures) has several procedures for dealing with the same topic, with one that will be considered to be the best.

Bill of Materials (BOM)   A list of materials (and associated quantities) required to manufacture the product concerned. See also **batch card**.

Business system   An organisation's computer system used, amongst other things, to process sales orders and purchase orders, generate finance reports. Some will have planning functionality, often referred to as MRP (Material Requirement Planning).

Certificate of Analysis (CoA)   A document presented with a shipment of material showing key test data for each lot of each product

	supplied (often along with the required range) that is designed to confirm that the delivery meets the specification agreed between the organisation (customer) and the supplier.
Changeover time	The time taken to change over from one product to another on the production line or in a production vessel.
Chimney effect	Describes many effects related to airflow, and in this instance is used to describe the effect of airflow over the open end of a vent line causing a slight pressure drop that, in turn, draws air (or vapour) up the vent line, which, in turn, causes solvents and other chemicals to be lost by evaporation.
Condensation reaction	A chemical reaction in which two molecules combine to form a larger molecule and a byproduct (smaller molecule). The byproduct is often removed during the reaction to promote the production of the larger molecule (product).
Consignment inventory	When inventory is held at an organisation's premises and is paid for on an 'as used' basis. For example, whilst a delivery of 100 units might be made to a company, it will only be invoiced for what it has actually used (e.g. 32 units). Although consignment inventory is held at a company's premises, ownership of the inventory remains with the supplier.
Consumable items	A general description (and financial cost centre or cost code) assigned to materials used in the production process not forming part of the Bill of Materials.
Customer Relationship Management (CRM)	A software tool used to record customer visits listing people involved in the visit and any actions arising from the visit etc.
Days of Inventory (DoI)	See **Inventory Turn**.
Economic order quantity (EOQ)	Typically, the quantity of a material that is purchased or produced that minimises the total cost for the transaction (item, shipping, storage, administration costs etc.).
Enterprise Resource Planning (ERP)	An integrated business software system that incorporates operations such as sales, planning, purchasing, goods receiving, manufacturing and dispatch.
Error containment ring (ECR)	A tool designed to define areas that can contribute to controlling and reducing the risk of an error 'breaking out'.

Firm plan — Planning will seek to continually schedule future production over quite a long horizon. However, each week (for example) Planning will issue a firm plan. This is a production plan that should not change.

Goods Received Note (GRN) — A document created that confirms the detail of a delivery received into inventory. Typically, will include the supplier name, items received, quantity received of each item and any comments relating to the shipment.

Inventory count — A count of items and products sometimes referred to as a 'stock-take' conducted at periodic intervals or as a cycle.

Inventory Turn — A measure of inventory that describes how often a level of inventory is sold in relation to the annual cost of sales. For example, if you have a cost of sales value of £1000 and an inventory level of £200, the Inventory Turn would be 5 (£1000 divided by £200). This can be readily converted to Days of Inventory (DoI) by dividing 365 by 5 – giving a DoI of 73 days in this example.

Key performance indicators (KPIs) — Measures companies designate as being critical to monitoring both their performance and progress towards strategic objectives.

Lead-time — The gap between the start and end of a process. This applies whether the process is a sales order, purchase order or production process etc.

Leading indicators — Measures that help to flag potential issues before they happen. In other words, they point to a process showing signs of instability.

Material Requirement Planning (MRP) — A tool/method used to create a plan to manage a manufacturing process, accounting for the raw material, product inventory and product demand.

MDI — An abbreviation for methylene diphenyl di-isocyanate, a chemical used in the manufacture of polyurethane systems.

Merchant goods — Materials that are purchased for resale. They might be rebranded, but do not require any further modification.

Michelin Stars — Michelin Stars are awards that are published annually in the Michelin Red Guide and are awarded for excellence to a select number of dining establishments.

Open-top drums — A type of drum that has a removable lid clipped onto the main body of the drum which is locked in place with a locking ring.

Preferred purchase quantity	The quantity that the commercial team would prefer to purchase in order to benefit from lower prices. In most instances this would override the economic order quantity.
Product	The description given to items sold to customers.
Product inventory account	A financial cost centre. When product is created, the value of the product is added to a product inventory account. When product is sold, the standard cost of the product(s) concerned is removed from the product inventory account.
Production run	Relates to the manufacture of a product or sequence of products using a particular production line, vessel or other resource.
Pro forma	An accounting term sometimes used to describe a process or document that is incomplete.
Provision	An accounting term that relates to the liability carried by an item or process. It is commonly used to assign and categorise items that might be considered un-saleable.
Purchase price variance	The difference between the standard cost and actual cost of a purchased raw material or other item.
Purchase for stock (PFS)	A classification of raw materials or product where a Safety Stock has been set.
Purchase to order (PTO)	'Make-to-order' is a very common term used in the manufacture of products. In other words, if a customer places an order for 'x' units then 'x' units should be manufactured – no more, no less. In much the same way, certain raw materials will be classed as 'purchase to order' where if 'y' units are required for production purposes then 'y' units should be purchased. This can be challenging for purchasing, especially where very small quantities are required or where suppliers have minimum order quantities.
Radio frequency identification (RFID)	Technology that uses electromagnetic fields to automatically identify and track tags attached to objects. The tags contain electronically stored information.
Raw materials	The items that are to be converted to a product.
Raw material inventory account	A financial cost centre. When raw materials are received into stock, the value of the raw material is added to a raw material inventory account. When raw materials are transferred to, and used in production, the standard cost of the raw material(s) concerned is removed from the raw material inventory account.

Reorder point (ROP)

A level of inventory that triggers an action to replenish the inventory of a particular product or raw material.

Safety Stock

A minimum level of individual product inventory that an organisation commits to maintain. It is designed to help an organisation deal with variable demand whilst being able to smooth out production of the product concerned.

Short oil resins

A class of product where the proportion of castor oil fatty acid is less than 40%. When certain short oil resins react uncontrollably, they become gels, and this often manifests itself as a tail on the bubble in a viscosity tube.

Standard cost

The cost of manufacturing a product that incorporates the raw material and production costs. For example, Product A might sell for £30/kilo and have a standard cost of $11/kilo which, in turn, is made up of a raw material cost of £10/kilo and production cost of £1/kilo.

Thixotropic resin

A type of alkyd resin used in the manufacture of non-drip paint – usually white spirit–based non-drip gloss paint.

Tight-head drums

Closed-end drums where the only access into the drum is through a 2-inch (50-mm) and 0.75-inch (19-mm) threaded hole.

White spirit

A petroleum-derived clear solvent often used in surface coatings (paint).

Work in progress (WIP)

The stage in a production process where raw materials are being combined or converted into a product. The value of materials being converted is often held in a work-in-progress account. See also **raw material inventory account** and **product inventory account**.

INTRODUCTION

'All truths are easy to understand once they are discovered. The point is to discover them'.

– Galileo Galilei

My first job was in Research and Development, working on the development of emulsion-based gloss paints. It seems a long time ago now, but in the ensuing years I had the good fortune to work in Production, Purchasing, Finance, Planning, Warehousing, Logistics, Customer Service and Project Management, not to mention dabbling in Sales, IT and Market Research. I guess that for a career, not everyone is fortunate to work in so many different areas of the chemical industry, or any industry for that matter. As I reflected on my career, I felt the urge to write a book, though I guess I am not the first, and doubtless not the last, to have that thought.

The challenge was determining what to write about and where to begin. Whilst studying for an MBA it was evident to me that much of the subject matter contained in the myriad of business books, especially those that relate to manufacturing and the supply chain, was written from an engineering perspective. So to start with I thought that it would be interesting, if nothing else, to write a book from a chemical industry perspective. To help me focus, my wife purchased a notebook so that I could make a start and set out some of my ideas.

I started scribbling with gusto, but initially, nothing coherent came to mind, at least nothing that set my thoughts apart from the myriad of books that were already out there.

As I reflected on my notes and musings, it became apparent to me that in each of those areas where I had worked, there was something that crept up time and again. Whilst finance is never far away in each area, my thoughts lay elsewhere. The common thread was inventory. Indeed, inventory was not just something that featured in each area, but it was often the focus of my activities, be that making it, buying it, moving it, counting it or valuing it.

I decided to write about inventory but not just about forecasting and scheduling. I would write about how each and every function is clearly involved in,

1

and has an impact on, inventory and how, by attending to inventory-related detail, much can be learnt, and companies, as a consequence, made more efficient. The book would help everyone understand the part they play in relation to inventory and how inventory management can be developed into a source of sustainable competitive advantage.

I should mention at this point that I have tried to use the word 'inventory' throughout the book but there are instances where the word 'stock' has been used as it is either more appropriate or reflects common usage.

When it comes to organisational and corporate performance, the dominant measures are financial ones. Cash is seen, quite rightly, by many as the lifeblood of the organisation.

However, one of the problems with finance and cost is that people cannot easily relate their daily activities and routines to value or cost. Nobody sees a purchase price when they are offloading a raw material delivery. Nobody sees the work-in-progress (WIP) account being credited when a production vessel is being charged and being debited when the yield is updated. Nobody sees a sales value when product is being shipped to a customer. Nobody sees the potential for an inventory provision when using a new raw material or developing a new product, and so on and so forth.

However, when it comes to inventory, everyone can relate to it so much more easily. For many companies, inventory is a physical thing. Be it raw material or product, you can see it being moved, imagine packs of product being sold, visualise a production schedule and see the truck full of product leaving your facility; it is something that everyone can relate to.

If you've had a busy day, you might say I moved 'x' units or tonnes of raw material or product. You rarely say that you moved 'x' thousand dollars of raw material or product.

Having decided to focus on inventory as a subject, the question is, how can a company make inventory a source of competitive advantage?

Securing and maintaining a competitive advantage is key to any company's future growth and success. There are many strategic tools that companies will look to use. Tools such as Porter's (1985) Value Chain Analysis and Five Forces Model can be used to help better understand where a company's strengths lie and where the opportunities will be to develop a competitive advantage. This will result in particular market or markets being targeted with specific action on product performance, price and/or service – aspects where the organisation will look to differentiate themselves from their competitors.

When undertaking such a review and developing a strategy, inventory will rarely be considered as a potential source of competitive advantage. Indeed, it is more likely to be considered as a cost – a potential liability that needs to be controlled and preferably minimised.

This view tends to be reinforced by the way in which, as has already been mentioned, inventory is reported. A company's annual report will usually reference inventory value and only make comment on any change in value from the previous annual report.

Against this background, senior executives and management are much more likely to be concerned about achieving a reduction in inventory as this will release more cash into the company because, after all, 'cash is king'.

Few people will look upon inventory as a potential source of competitive advantage. However, as inventory is something that everyone in a company can relate to, it is something that everyone can also influence to a greater or lesser degree. Focusing on those aspects of a function's activities that impact inventory will not only improve inventory management, it will, in turn, improve a company's overall internal processes and controls, effectively developing a positive feedback loop resulting in improved outcomes. When sustained, these improved outcomes will prove to be sources of competitive advantage.

The key is understanding the process and paying attention to detail. An example of this type of approach is given in Case Study 0.1.

Case Study 0.1   British Cycling and marginal gains*

Figure 0.3 shows the number of medals won by Great Britain in each of the Olympic Games from 1992 to 2016.

The improvement from 1992 is quite remarkable. In 1992 Chris Boardman's medal was Great Britain's only cycling medal. However, over a period of 16 years, Great Britain rose to become, arguably, the most successful cycling country in Olympic history. Indeed, this success has also been translated to road cycling, with Sir Bradley Wiggins becoming the first British winner of the Tour de France, to be followed by Chris Froome

	Gold	Silver	Bronze	Total
1992	1			1
1996			2	2
2000	1	1	2	4
2004	2	1	1	4
2008	8	4	2	14
2012	8	2	2	12
2016	6	4	2	12

Figure 0.3 Olympic medals won by Great Britain's cycling team.

winning a further four Tour de France races, in addition to becoming the first British winner of the other two Grand Tours – the Giro d'Italia and La Vuelta. Indeed, 2018 saw the first ever occasion when all three Grand Tours were held by different cyclist from the same country (Tour de France – Geraint Thomas, Giro d'Italia – Chris Froome and La Vuelta – Simon Yates). It should also not be forgotten that during this time Mark Cavendish (the 'Manx Missile') recorded, by 2017, 30 individual stage wins in the Tour de France, placing him second in the all-time list behind the legendary Eddy Merckx of Belgium.

* Marginal gains are about making small incremental improvements in all aspects of a process that, when taken together, will deliver a significant overall improvement.

Such a transformation is quite remarkable, and the obvious question is 'How was this achieved?'

Chris Boardman, in an interview in 2016, talked about how he and his coach, Peter Keen, decided they would deliver results by developing a performance-driven approach, focussing on what would become known as 'marginal gains'. In the mid-1990s Lottery funding became available, and British Cycling was founded.

The meticulous approach and attention to detail transformed the British Cycling team, and the evidence of British Cycling's current ascendancy is there for all to see. Looked at another way, British Cycling, by attending to every detail and working to secure marginal gains, has developed a significant and sustainable competitive advantage over all of its competitors.

Whilst Case Study 0.1 is not an example directly involving inventory, the British Cycling example shows the impact of moving the focus onto the process. In other words, by placing greater emphasis on details of the inventory management process and making marginal gains, the outcome will take care of itself, and inventory management will become a source of competitive advantage for a company.

Where appropriate, case studies based on actual events are included, and most chapters include suggested actions for improvement.

One point I would also make at this stage is that anyone undertaking this approach will need to be patient. Sustainable progress is unlikely to be achieved overnight, and you will need to remain focussed. As you develop a more detailed and comprehensive understanding of the inventory process, improvements will come.

Great emphasis will be placed on trying to be proactive – attending to detail early in the process. It is usually the case that one person can stop a problem from happening, but it takes several people to deal with a problem that has already occurred, and time spent resolving a problem means less time spent adding value.

Paying attention to detail will mean trying to find ways of improving the control of processes, sometimes applying methods and approaches developed in other areas. It does not always mean inventing totally new methods and techniques. Indeed, some of the approaches are evident in everyday life.

A couple of examples are an airline pilot's use of a pre-flight checklist and the increasing use of data recorders (telematics) in cars to monitor driving performance and help improve driving skill.

Checklists

Checklists are used by both surgical teams (pre-op) and airline pilots (pre-flight). If you were told that a pre-op or pre-flight checklist was not going to be used, you would doubtless be very worried. By using checklists, surgical teams and airline pilots are merely following procedures and processes designed to prevent errors and promote best practice. Yet, the value and use of checklists in industry is not fully appreciated. Knowing that they can be useful in preventing errors and promoting best practice and consistency, you have to ask yourself why this is the case.

Telematics

Telematics is an example of monitoring inputs (acceleration, braking, distance travelled, etc.) to help improve driving. Such improvements not only reduce the risk of an accident, but also bring about an improvement in the performance of the car – better fuel economy and reduced wear and tear. In other words, focussing on the process leads to improvements in outcomes.

Translating such approaches to inventory management will be a challenge. Having to devise an appropriate set of procedures and measures for each function or operation will take time. The key thing to remember is that you might not get things right at the first attempt. Introducing controls, procedures and measures is the first step in developing a better understanding of what is going on. Over time, as more data is gathered, systems and processes will be better understood with changes being made that bring about improvement – sometimes minor, but always sustainable.

There will be instances where measures prove to be of little real value. Do not be afraid to abandon or change them, introducing new ones where necessary. This is perfectly normal and should be expected. Persisting with an inappropriate measure is a bit like trying to hammer a square peg into a round hole. There comes a time when you need to pause and reflect as it might be the case that, initially, you did not fully understand the process you are trying to improve.

Layout

The book is set out in chapters that relate to functional activities and covers some of the issues and approaches related to 'paying attention to detail' within that particular function. Everyone, in every function, can play their part attending to detail and improving their processes. Success will not rest on one person's shoulders or on one function. Success will come with everyone working together delivering marginal gains – helping the organisation develop a significant and sustainable competitive advantage.

The structure also means that you do not necessarily need to read the whole book – just read the chapter that relates to you.

British Cycling's success did not happen overnight, but those involved knew that by sticking to their ethos of securing marginal gains success would follow like night follows day.

As you begin to explore the chapters that follow, it is useful to reflect on a quote from Proust:

> *The real voyage of discovery consists not in seeking new lands but seeing with new eyes.*

Reference

Porter, M.E. (1985). *Competitive advantage – Creating and sustaining superior performance.* New York: The Free Press.

1

BACKGROUND

At its most basic, the order fulfilment process is quite simple (see Figure 1.1).

The presumption is that sufficient inventory is in place to meet the order. Multiple orders, as they are received and processed, will ultimately deplete inventory and, unless action is taken, a point will be reached where an order cannot be fulfilled. Of course, there are instances where inventory always appears to be available, examples of which are websites where music and books can be digitally downloaded to your player or reader. Of course, what we really have is the capability to manufacture a product with virtually zero delivery lead-time and zero process time, and that, in truth, has zero inventory.

However, for the great majority of organisations the only way to satisfy any order immediately is by having sufficient inventory to deal with any demand as it arises. In truth, organisations will in all likelihood be unable to achieve this utopian scenario.

The more usual scenario is shown in Figure 1.2.

In the first instance, inventory will clearly be available. However, as the number of orders increases, inventory, at some point, will reach zero. Once reached, if the customer is not prepared to wait, the result will be a lost sale.

Clearly, whether in a retail or industrial environment, no one wants a lost sale. Dealing with this involves manufacturing in advance of a requirement. In other words, organisations (or individuals) will look to anticipate demand and act accordingly. Typically, this will mean either ordering the appropriate quantities or scheduling manufacture. The two scenarios are illustrated in Figure 1.3.

Whilst Figures 1.1, 1.2 and 1.3 might be considered to be too simplistic, the fact that we move from two elements in Figure 1.1 to eight elements in Figure 1.3 clearly shows that having to anticipate demand leads to an increase in complexity.

With most organisations having many products, the whole process of forecasting and inventory management becomes even more challenging leading to a level of complexity that can often only be effectively managed using some form of planning tool.

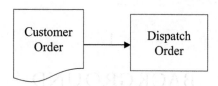

Figure 1.1 Basic order fulfilment.

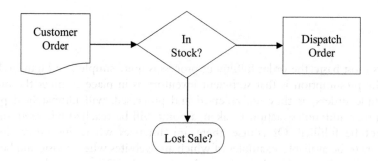

Figure 1.2 Normal order fulfilment process.

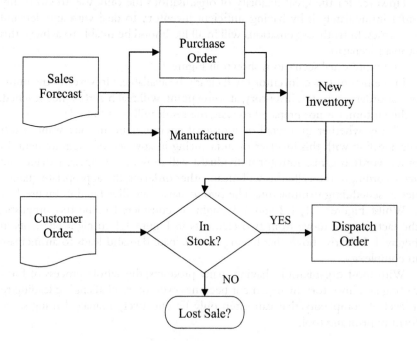

Figure 1.3 Typical order fulfilment using forecasts.

Inventory phases

Few systems are perfect, and the process of inventory management is no different. Taking raw materials and converting them into saleable product sounds quite simple. From this point of view, inventory flow can be fairly easily described (Figure 1.4).

This flow will, in many instances, describe fundamentally what many organisations are doing. However, the simplicity of this flowchart belies an underlying complexity and does not take account of the steps within each phase where people are faced with many challenges and issues relating to 'getting it right'. On closer examination, each step needs its own flowchart in order to properly describe what is involved. The example of raw material (RM) purchase is shown in Figure 1.5.

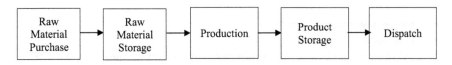

Figure 1.4 Inventory phases.

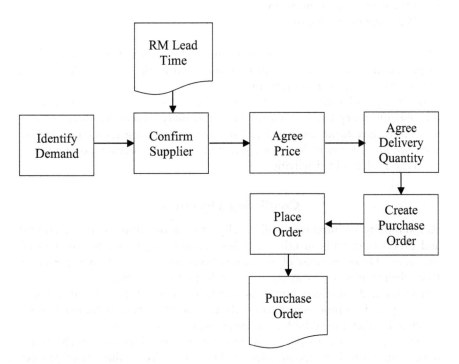

Figure 1.5 Raw material purchase process.

Even this flowchart can be considered to be an over-simplification, and clearly, when considering the other phases, the whole process begins to look much more complex.

Stable equilibrium

When operating efficiently, all processes can be considered to be in a stable equilibrium, requiring little change or intervention. An efficient and stable process will have both raw material and product inventory at optimal levels. However, having so many flowchart elements and, in particular, interfaces between elements, there will always be a risk of instability.

Instability can occur in many parts of the inventory process. Some of the more obvious examples, and ones which most people would be familiar with, include:

- Excess raw material purchase
- Damaged raw material inventory
- Minimum batch size or production run creating more product than required
- Production of rejected product
- Damaged product inventory
- Poor inventory rotation

There are, however, other, less obvious causes of inventory issues that can lead to process instability and ones that, as illustrated in the chapters that follow, involve every part of an organisation.

Instability will invariably lead to either inventory loss or the creation of unusable inventory. Issues that give rise to instability require time and resource to identify, investigate and resolve. Time spent correcting errors and dealing with inventory issues is time that could be better spent focussing on improvements and value-added activities.

Conflicting objectives

Responsibility for inventory will usually sit with functions such as Planning and Production, with all other functions considering themselves as internal customers. However, most of an organisation's functions will, to a greater or lesser degree, play a part in and have an impact on the process of inventory management. A function's impact on inventory will vary, but the small details all add up, and if a process is to run perfectly smoothly, every factor needs to be examined, which means looking at every single function's role.

From an inventory perspective, one can consider the degree to which a function, in its normal operation, adds to the complexity of the whole process.

	Raw Materials		Products		Total
	# Items	Quantity	# Items	Quantity	
Finance	− −	− −	− −	− −	−8
Planning		++		+++	+5
Production		++	− −	+++	+3
Dispatch				++	+2
Goods Inwards	− −	− −			−4
Purchasing		+++			+3
Sales		+	++	++++	+7
Customer Service				+	+1
Marketing	+		++	++	+5
R&D	++		+++	+	+6

Table 1.1 Functional impact on complexity.

One way of illustrating this can be found in Table 1.1. This assesses the degree to which a function impacts on inventory and whether the effect is to either increase or decrease the number of inventory items and/or level of inventory.

The symbols reflect the strength of the stakeholder's inclination (direct or indirect) to either increase (+) or decrease (−) complexity. To summarise each function in turn:

Finance (−8)

One question that can be asked is 'Is inventory an asset or a liability?' Of course, it will depend on your perspective, and Finance's answer might well be 'it depends'.

Whether asset or liability, Finance will view inventory from a cost perspective and see inventory as cash being tied up. Accordingly, Finance's preference will always be to carry fewer items and have a lower level of inventory. With the prominence given to financial reporting, the cost carried by inventory will always come under scrutiny, especially by senior management − hence the strong emphasis on reducing complexity.

Planning (+5)

Responding to demand and requests from internal customers are features of every planner's daily routine. The pressure will always be to ensure that product is available to meet customer demand, and the most obvious way of achieving this is to have inventory in place. This can incline Planning to have more inventory rather than less which might manifest itself as having more items than necessary set to have a Safety Stock.

Production (+3)

In order to keep costs as low as possible, Production will always be looking to either maximise batch sizes or have long production runs of the same product, or both. It will always be more efficient to have longer production runs of the same product rather than production runs that continually interchange product types. This pressure can lead to more, rather than less, inventory being produced.

It should be noted that, whilst never intentional, Production will occasionally produce inventory that is un-saleable – often referred to as rejected or quarantine inventory. If the normal production process is viewed as being in balance, increased complexity pushes the process towards greater instability which inevitably leads to an increased risk of an error leading to the creation of said reject or quarantine inventory.

Dispatch (+2)

Whilst not directly influencing inventory levels, Dispatch will always be looking to have inventory in place so that customer orders can be picked each and every time so that it can ship product to customers on time and in full.

Goods Inwards (−4)

The job of locating raw materials is always easier if you have fewer to find. Consequently, Goods Inwards, whilst having no direct influence on the number and quantity of raw materials, will prefer to have fewer items in storage, as this will aid in managing and locating what is required.

Purchasing (+3)

Purchasing will mainly be responding to demand as determined by the production plan created by Planning. The quantity required of any single item will be set by a combination of the total demand, Safety Stock, minimum order quantity and purchase order lead-time.

The prospect of lower prices will always pressure purchasing to take larger quantities and be tempted by quantity discounts. These can lead to situations where Purchasing will sanction purchase orders for raw materials that might not be required in the short to medium term.

Sales (+7)

Due to its customer focus, Sales will always be looking to have inventory in place to meet customers' demand. Sales staff will usually look to service-level and lead-time measures to support their case, often arguing that business will be lost if service levels are not maintained.

Customer Service (+1)

As with Sales, Customer Service will always prefer to see inventory in place to meet customer orders. The requirement will be more immediate for Customer Service, though, as the customer will have an order to place and will be looking for confirmation of delivery.

Marketing (+5)

Marketing will have a similar view to Sales, though it might be more product focussed in response to a particular marketing campaign. Supporting such campaigns will usually mean that Marketing is keen to ensure adequate inventory is in place.

When new products are designed to replace existing ones, less emphasis will be placed on ensuring that all existing inventory is sold. This increases the likelihood of adding to un-saleable inventory.

R&D (+6)

With a clear focus on improving existing and developing new products, R&D will indirectly always be adding to inventory complexity and increasing the risk of creating instability in the manufacturing process.

From an organisational strategy perspective, functional objectives should be aligned. However, as we can see from Table 1.1, there is a clear potential for conflicting objectives to develop. It is essential that each function understand its relationship with inventory and how it can play in part in minimising complexity and the associated risks.

Measures

Measures, when not properly applied or understood, can result in the very act of measurement being questioned as to its purpose or benefit. Some measures used in the UK public sector fall into the trap of being used merely to compare facilities, differentiating between good and bad performance, rather than being seen as a means of helping to understand the process to which they are being applied. In such instances, the reaction can lead to measurement being stopped, and with it the opportunity lost to better understand the process concerned and the improvements that could be made.

The context within which measures are used is best illustrated by a 'control loop' (Figure 1.6). Where many tools focus on the input and output elements, a control loop shows how all the key elements of a process fit together.

The steps involved in the loop are described below:

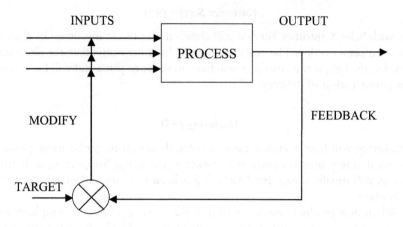

Figure 1.6 Control loop.

Inputs

All processes have inputs, and these will include raw materials, equipment, energy, people etc.

Process

The process is the method by which the inputs come together to produce an outcome. For a car journey, the outcome will be a destination. For a chemical process, the outcome will be a product.

Outputs

The outputs not only include the destination and the products, but also relate to the status of the process at any one point in time.

Feedback

Data from the process and/or output can be used to assess progress. How far are you along the journey to the destination? How is the chemical reaction progressing towards the desired end point?

Target

The feedback data, whether obtained during the process or after the completion of the process, will be compared against a target. In other words, for any data point, where would you expect it to be? This is either a specific target or a target range defined by upper and lower limits.

Modify

Comparing the data points with the target range will determine whether the process is performing as expected. Where a deviation exists – whether minor or major – one or more of the input variables might require modification.

In order to know which inputs to modify and by how much, the user needs to understand which inputs are critical to the control of the process and how they affect it.

Though we might not always be aware of it, we all encounter and use control loops in our daily routines. One example is driving a car, as described in Case Study 1.1.

Case Study 1.1   Car journey

Input

Accelerator and brake

Output

A journey that results in arriving at the destination at a particular time – not early and not late

Target

Having determined the output, there will be an average speed that has to be achieved.

Feedback

Speedometer and clock

Modify

Where the speed has fallen below the average required, the accelerator will be used to speed up. Where the speed is in excess of the average required, the brake will be used to slow down. In both instances an input has been modified in response to feedback (measures) when compared to the target (expectation).

Case Study 1.2 illustrates how a control loop is evident in the control of a chemical process.

Case Study 1.2   Chemical process

Input

Temperature and raw materials

Output

A product that has to be produced within a particular time to a particular specification

Target

Having set the output, the chemical reaction will normally be monitored and compared to expected in-process criteria (targets).

Feedback

Viscosity and acid value

Modify

Where the viscosity and/or acid value fall outside expected criteria, typically either the temperature will be increased/decreased or a small raw material addition will be made to bring the reaction in line with expectations.

In both examples, measures play a key part in enabling the process to be controlled – whether for driving a car or chemical manufacture.

In much the same way, measurement of inventory is key to understanding the underlying processes and in bringing about improvement.

Generally, organisations will have many measures in place, either direct or indirect ones. Two of the most common inventory-related measures will be Inventory Value and Inventory Turn or Inventory Days (also described as Days of Inventory).

Inventory Value

As mentioned previously, having inventory usually represents a significant financial commitment, and placing a value on it is vital. The basis of the calculation can vary with the value being determined, for example, on a FIFO (first in, first out) or replacement cost basis. There are no rights or wrongs. The important thing is to be consistent and to properly understand the advantages and disadvantages of the method selected.

One aspect of inventory valuation that does vary quite significantly from organisation to organisation is that of provisions related to aged inventory. Such inventory provisions are discussed in more detail in Chapter 2 on finance.

Inventory Turn/Inventory Days

Inventory Days equates to the number of days that it would take to sell the whole inventory. If, for example, you have 45 Inventory Days, it means that the inventory should last 45 days based on current sales.

Inventory Turn, on the other hand, measures how many times the inventory will be sold in a year. Using the above example where we have 45 Inventory Days, the calculation of 365 (days in a year) divided by 45 gives an Inventory Turn of 8.1.

The two, in combination, work quite well. For example, where an increase in Inventory Value might lead to knee-jerk actions designed to reduce inventory, Inventory Days or Inventory Turn will help put the change into context. Whilst the Inventory Value might have increased, Inventory Days might not have changed. In this instance, there might not be any need to reduce inventory, as the Inventory Days measure points to an increase in inventory having gone hand-in-hand with a corresponding increase in sales.

This is a simple example, but it serves to illustrate the point that taking a measure in isolation does not necessarily tell you the whole story.

Actions

Issues related to inventory will trigger a number of actions. In many instances, processes and procedures will be developed and implemented that are designed to deal with particular aspects of inventory management. Typical examples include:

- Creating reports to flag expired or aged inventory
- Routines designed to deal with quarantine inventory
- Efforts designed to sell substandard material

What these and many other actions have in common is that they are often reactions to issues and events that have already happened. A report flagging expired or aged inventory is trying to deal with a problem that has already occurred. This is a commendable action; it has to happen and is certainly much better than having nothing in place.

However, the danger is that organisations get wrapped up in focussing on waiting for problems to arise, thereby developing a reactive culture. As a consequence of such actions, inventory goes down, and so the problem is seen to have gone away. The improvement means that focus is shifted away from expired or aged inventory. Whilst successful in dealing with the symptom, the solution does not necessarily deal with the root of the problem of how and why it was created in the first place.

Accordingly, many of the actions suggested in the chapters that follow are designed to be proactive. In other words, they shift the focus away from dealing with problems, placing equal, if not greater emphasis, on preventing or anticipating an issue in the first place.

2

FINANCE

Of all the functions, Finance is the one function that does not directly affect physical inventory. Yet, despite this, its importance in relation to inventory management cannot be ignored. Ultimately, whatever happens to physical inventory, an organisation will be judged on its financial performance. It is from this perspective that Finance has to be considered as a factor in the management of inventory.

Inventory's associated costs are amongst the most significant part of an organisation's costs. Ranging from a raw material purchase price through to the margin generated when sold, virtually without exception, all inventory movements have a financial impact.

The impact of inventory cost is generally managed through what are described as 'inventory accounts' with raw material (RM) inventory account, work in progress (WIP) and product inventory account being the most common. Each physical movement of inventory should be mirrored by a financial transaction relating to one or more of these inventory accounts. The triggering of a financial movement usually arises as a consequence of an interaction with the business system. The main movements that have a financial impact are:

- Raw material receipt
- Product manufacture
- Product delivered to inventory
- Product sales

Each of these movements has an impact on overall inventory value, with their treatment being dependent on the capabilities of the business system and the organisation's policies.

Raw material receipt

With purchase orders placed, each working day will see scheduled deliveries of those particular raw materials. Whilst the raw materials will be placed in storage (bulk storage tanks or warehouse), the processing of the Goods Received Note

19

(GRN) will not only update the business system inventory, but also trigger a financial transaction – an addition to the RM inventory account. The actual value added to the RM account will be determined by the price on the purchase order or on an average price, based on a business system algorithm or the policies operated by the business.

Many organisations will opt to use some form of average pricing or standard cost when dealing with the value of a raw material or product. This will depend on the type of business that an organisation carries out, the fluctuation and frequency of change that might be experienced with raw materials prices, the organisation's preference and the business system's capabilities.

Adopting an average price system will inevitably result in what are described as 'price variances', especially where the actual price of each purchase order changes, as might be the case with materials such as white spirit. However small these may be, they can, if not managed, build up to be quite significant, and consolidating these variances will have a direct impact on an organisation's profit.

A negative balance will lead to an increase in profit, whilst a positive balance will lead to a reduction in profit. The degree to which this impacts profit will depend on the frequency the standard cost is updated and the size of the gap that has developed.

Product manufacture

Each product will have its own specific Bill of Materials (or formulation) listing all the raw materials and associated quantities required to produce a predetermined yield. In response to a demand for a product, a batch will be scheduled for manufacture with a batch card generated that is designed to produce the quantity required.

Flagging the start of the production run will trigger the movement of raw material values from the RM inventory account into the WIP account. As has already been stated, the actual value being moved from the RM inventory account into the WIP account will depend on the organisation's policies and the capability of the business system.

Unless physical inventory movements are tracked with absolute precision, inaccuracies will begin to creep in, which will add to any variances that may have occurred in the raw material receipt stage.

More so in a chemical industry than in engineering, there could well be adjustments made to a production run either during or at the end of the manufacturing process. Whilst they may be small, systems need to be in place to record the physical movement and update the business system so that the appropriate financial movement is triggered. Failure to record such movements will result in a further variance in both the RM inventory value and the physical quantity that the business system thinks is in place.

Product delivery to inventory

When product is received into inventory, the inventory value held in the WIP account will be removed and a value added to the product inventory account determined by the yield of the batch. The value being moved will be based on the product's standard cost held in the business system.

When the standard cost being used does not reflect current costs, the value transferred from the RM inventory account and into the WIP account will result in a non-zero value being left in the WIP account. Whether this variance is positive or negative depends on whether the standard cost understates or overstates the true RM value.

The handling of work in progress and associated credit and debit balances will vary from organisation to organisation and will also depend on the capability of the business system being used. When a reconciliation is undertaken, remaining balances will be reset to zero with the debit or credit being released which will have, as already mentioned, a direct impact on the profit for the organisation.

Where product is held in inventory at batch level, that is, 'lot controlled', the cost records might reflect the standard costs that prevailed at the time the batch was produced. This is a complication that needs to be taken account of when reconciliations are being undertaken.

There will be instances where a product being produced is not suitable for sale and may be classed as quarantine or redundant inventory. The financial treatment of such batches is dealt with in the section 'Provisions'.

Product sales

When dispatched from inventory, the value, as set by the standard cost for the particular batch or batches used to fulfil the sales order, will be removed from the product inventory account.

Where inventory is not lot controlled, an average or standard cost at the time of the transaction will be used. In these scenarios the likelihood of further cost variances will increase.

The inventory value determined using the business system is entirely dependent on the accuracy and consistency of each process step and interaction with the business system.

Inventory count

The inherent instability that manifests itself through such inaccuracies and inconsistencies will require corrections to be applied at some stage. The normal method of identifying and correcting such discrepancies both in terms of value and physical inventory is to carry out an inventory count.

Whilst typically involving warehouse and production functions, the inventory count is often the responsibility of the finance function. This involves organising an inventory count (whether a full physical count or cycle counting) and dealing with the subsequent reconciliations.

The importance of a well-managed and executed inventory count process cannot be overstated. The more accurate the count, the less time that will be spent checking discrepancies arising from miscounting, missed inventory, recording errors, data transposition errors when the business system is updated etc. This means that more time can be spent on reconciliating variances between the inventory level held in the business system and the inventory count. When there is insufficient time to properly resolve inventory variances, the margin for error suffers, with higher discrepancy tolerances being applied – for example, an ideal tolerance might be $\pm0.5\%$, whereas having to be pragmatic might mean a tolerance of $\pm1\%$ or more being accepted.

Having a well-controlled and well-executed inventory count means having comprehensive and documented procedures that cover the four phases of every count – preparation, count, reconciliation and review.

Preparation

As with all processes, planning and preparation are key to delivering a successful inventory count. The preparation stage should typically cover the following:

Locations to be counted

Many organisations will operate an inventory location system. When preparing for an inventory count, a detailed map of all locations will be required to help ensure that nowhere is missed. It might be necessary to have maps covering multiple sites. Once defined, teams will be allocated locations for counting.

Teams required

The inventory count will often be conducted by teams of people. The number of teams will depend on the scope and time allocated for the count. It will be necessary to clearly define the role of each team member – who does the counting, who does the data recording etc.

Auditors

Every count should be audited. An audit serves two purposes – firstly to check that data recording is accurate and, secondly, that the count is progressing as planned. The number of auditors required for the count will, as for teams, be dependent on the scope of the count.

Data recording

Where data is being recorded on pre-printed forms, it is essential that all data recording requirements are included. This should include sections to confirm any auditing activity and data entry. All forms (whether paper or electronic) should be allocated a reference number. This is to aid in the tracking of paperwork and ensure that all forms issued are accounted for – whether used or not.

Increasingly, technology such as barcodes or RFID is being used to manage inventory and for inventory counting. The technology helps to speed up the count, reduces data entry errors and updates information directly into the business system etc., all of which means more time can be spent on reconciliation.

Marking method

When undertaking any count, it is essential that a method is established to confirm that items and locations have been counted. This is to avoid double counting and to aid in the auditing process.

Timetable and inventory count milestones

An inventory count should be treated as a project, and a basic plan should be in place. This means that responsibilities are clearly defined, milestones set and the critical path known from the outset. As with any project, this will serve as a means of ensuring that the count progresses on schedule.

Performance measure

A means of measuring the count performance should be in place so that a count can be compared, not only to a target, but also to previous counts. This will be critical in helping to bring about improvement in the inventory count process.

Count

The count itself has several aspects that require attention and control.

Briefing

As with any project, it is essential to brief all staff so that they understand both their roles and the process(es) they should follow. The briefing should involve all counting teams, auditors and those involved in data entry.

Counting method

All staff should be clear on the counting method, how the data is to be recorded and how inventory is marked to show that it has been 'counted'.

Data entry methods

People involved in data entry will need to understand how the data has been recorded, which types of errors to look out for and, from the record sheets, how the business system should be updated.

The process of counting and data entry is much quicker and more accurate when inventory is 'barcoded'. The use of barcode scanners will often eliminate the business system data entry step. The speed of such a count will also enable the reconciliation stage to be reached far more quickly, thereby affording more time to resolve variances.

Auditing

This is a key part of ensuring that the count is both accurate and on schedule. The auditing and recording method should be clearly defined with checks being made on a random basis for most items. High-value items, however, might be preselected as items to be audited.

Paperwork

Where a paper-based system is being used, with pre-printed forms, it is essential that the location and status of each form is known. For any single form, you need to know whether it has been issued, to whom, whether it has been returned and whether recorded data has been updated into the business system.

Data entry checking

In addition to auditing the data collection, auditing entries onto the business system should also be scheduled and be part of the auditor's remit.

Documentation cutoff

Prior to any reconciliation it is essential that all normal business transactions have been completed relating to the period up to and including the cutoff. These include:

- Goods received transactions
- Returns to suppliers
- Batch cards to confirm raw material use and product added to inventory
- Non-production/sales-related transfers (e.g. laboratory use)
- Damaged or lost materials (e.g. spills)
- Disposals
- Quarantine inventory use

- Dispatch notes confirming product dispatched to customers
- Returns from customers
- Location transfers (both internal and between sites)

Consignment inventory

Where customers hold inventory on consignment, arrangements will need to be made to count the inventory at the customer's site. As with documentation cutoff, it is essential that all transactions relating to the customer's consignment inventory have been processed – shipments to, usage and other physical adjustments that the customer is responsible for (e.g. damaged goods, spills etc.).

Reconciliation

Error tolerance

An error tolerance should be established on a percentage, value and quantity basis.

- Percentage tolerance will help ensure that checks will be triggered for otherwise small quantities of critical and strategic items.
- Quantity tolerance will ensure that errors relating to items with a low value but with a significant quantity variance will be investigated.
- Value tolerance will ensure that items that fall within the percentage tolerance but have a high value will be investigated.

Analysis checklist

Investigating inventory variances will likely be undertaken after every inventory count. Many will follow a similar pattern in terms of aspects to be looked at. Accordingly, a checklist can be put together to ensure that all investigations are consistent in their methodology and that nothing is missed.

Review

Performance

A key part of any process is performance measurement. Measures need to be in place at the outset, and their use will confirm the relative success of the inventory count. The number and type of measures should ensure that a complete picture can be determined for the whole count and should cover all phases and activities.

Inventory count closure

A key part of any project is project closure, where the whole process and associated activities are reviewed to ensure that what went well can be captured and improvement opportunities can be identified.

Improvement opportunities

Improvement opportunities will be identified:

- Through feedback from participants.
- As an outcome of any reconciliation activity.
- From the project closure process.

Checklist update

One outcome of the closure process will be updating of the checklist(s) used during the count. This will ensure that both good practice and improvements are captured and included in future inventory counts.

An inventory count is a complex process with many facets that need to be controlled. Both preparation and planning are key to a successful count, and the use of procedures and checklists will facilitate these activities.

Physical reconciliation

The first step in the reconciliation process is to resolve variances between the physical count and the theoretical quantity held in the business system.

The variances to focus on will be determined by the tolerances in place. It is essential to be consistent in the approach to dealing with variances, and all aspects need to be investigated.

The reconciliation process should, for example, cover the following:

- Has the data been recorded correctly?
- Has the data been entered correctly into the business system?
- Has any data been transposed? In other words, are there any keystroke errors: '39' typed in when it should have been '93'? This can apply not just to quantities, but also to items and batch references.
- Have all batch cards been processed? Have raw materials been 'consumed'?
- Has the product inventory been updated?
- Has any material been taken out of inventory for samples or laboratory use?
- Has any material been damaged, and the loss not recorded?
- Was the correct quantity received into inventory? In other words, was there an error when the business system was updated upon goods receipt or confirmation of the quantity of product manufactured?

- Was a raw material used that went un-recorded? This can occur when adjustments are made during the manufacturing process.
- Was some un-saleable inventory used in the manufacture of the product? Was the use recorded?

The above points are not prescriptive, and there could of course be many other questions that need to be asked, and these might well vary from organisation to organisation. The important point is to put together a comprehensive list that will both aid the reconciliation process and bring about consistency from count to count.

Financial reconciliation

Reconciling physical variances will resolve some, if not most of the financial variance that will have arisen from the inventory count.

Resolving some of the remaining financial variance can be more protracted. There will be financial accounts (e.g. purchase price variance and work in progress) that may hold balances (credits or debits) that will have built up due to cost variances, as discussed earlier in the chapter.

Provisions

During the period between inventory counts, it might be the organisation's policy to apply a provision that will be used to offset any correction that is applied after the inventory count is complete. It should be noted that such a provision, as is the case with all provisions, directly impacts the organisation's profit. By anticipating an inventory variance, an organisation may choose to apply an inventory provision every month so that the financial impact is smoothed. For example, an organisation might take the view that an inventory provision will be required for each inventory count. If this is expected to be, for example, £100,000, the organisation might choose to spread the provision equally over each month in the period between counts. Of course, applying a provision will reduce the organisation's profit for that particular period. It is just a case of either taking the hit at an inventory count or smoothing the impact equally over the intervening period between counts (e.g. £16,666 per month).

Where the whole provision is not required (i.e. the financial correction required is less than the provision that has been built up), the balance released will have a positive impact on the profit for the next reporting period. The likelihood of this happening depends on the degree of prudence that an organisation chooses to adopt.

It is worth pointing out that being able to release a general inventory provision, whilst on the face of it is a good thing, can mask an underlying issue with the costing system. An example of this is given in Case Study 2.1.

Case Study 2.1   Inventory count gain

Background

Over a period of a few years when a company undertook an inventory count there were a few instances where there appeared to be financial inventory gain, despite the physical count showing the usual instances of inventory losses.

Of course, being able to release some or all of the general inventory provision was always welcome, and on the first few occasions the result was just accepted.

Analysis

There is always a tendency to focus on those problems that have a negative impact and be less concerned about those that are seen to be beneficial. However, there was always a niggling concern. It is all well and good to have positive news, but the company needed to understand why.

Scanning the data, an anomaly was spotted in relation to one of the products (Product A), and one raw material in particular. The raw material concerned was available in two forms – expanded and unexpanded. When first manufactured, Product A used the expanded form of the raw material at a cost of £x per kilo with the standard cost of Product A based on this price.

Over time, as demand grew for Product A, the company opted to purchase the raw material in unexpanded form and convert it to the expanded form on site. The unexpanded form cost £y per kilo – significantly less than the expanded cost.

Whilst the benefits were clear from a purchasing perspective, the standard cost of Product A was not adjusted to take account of this lower cost. Consequently, when each batch of Product A was manufactured, the WIP account was being debited by a greater sum than it should have been. This basically means that a negative balance was building in the WIP account that was set to zero at each inventory count. The net effect created this apparent inventory gain in value terms. This meant that where a general inventory provision had been building to take account of expected inventory losses, a significant part of it was not required, thereby resulting in a release of a part of the general inventory provision.

Outcome

Whilst this was a problem that manifested itself at the inventory count, and a sudden release of cash to the bottom line in the month or quarter of the count, there was no real benefit over the longer term. The reason is that the costing error was causing profit to be understated in the intervening months.

In this particular instance, the standard cost was changed resulting in a more normal use of the general inventory provision and slightly higher (and more correct) profit in the intervening months.

Of course, you might wonder what this has to do with the physical count. Well, the answer is very little, but it cannot be overstated how important it is that all physical transactions are matched with appropriate and accurate financial transactions, and where gaps develop, problems arise that need to be resolved. In truth, it also means that until they match, an organisation does not properly understand and control the flow and handling of inventory.

A general inventory provision is not the only circumstance where an organisation will apply a provision. Other circumstances are:

Quarantine inventory

When a batch of product fails to meet specification or a raw material becomes contaminated, some organisations will have a procedure that triggers a provision that effectively writes off the value of the item concerned. Some will also adopt a more prudent approach and provide for the disposal cost of the item(s) concerned.

Expired inventory

Depending on the nature and type of product manufactured, some will have a shelf life. This can vary from days to weeks, months and years. When a raw material or product goes past its expiry date it is deemed unusable and may well trigger a provision being applied. As with quarantine inventory, some organisations will also provide for the disposal cost of the item(s) concerned.

Aged inventory

Irrespective of shelf life, a provision can also be based on the age of the product. Whether this is used will vary from organisation to organisation and depends on the level of prudence it wishes to adopt. For example, when a product is 3 months old, a provision equivalent to 25% of the item's value is applied. At 6 months, a 50% provision is applied, whilst after 9 months, a full provision, including disposal cost, is applied.

When a provision is applied it will have a direct impact on the organisation's profit. Whilst it is normal practice to apply a provision to quarantine inventory, the application of provisions to expired and aged inventory varies from organisation to organisation. It is entirely dependent on the view that the organisation wishes to take.

Of course, when quarantine, expired or aged inventory is recovered (i.e. becomes immediately saleable) the associated provision will be released. This will have a direct and positive impact on profit.

Whilst it does not always follow, a company's attitude in relation to provisions can be taken to reflect its attitude towards the management of inventory. The more rigorous its policies on provision, the more serious the company is about inventory management. Where less rigour is used, opportunities are potentially being missed to monitor an aspect of the effectiveness of an organisation's inventory management process.

Measures

Many measures can be used in relation to the inventory count:

- Purchase price variance
- WIP account
- General inventory provision
- Aged inventory provision
- Quarantine inventory provision
- Expired inventory provision
- Percentage non-zero variances
- Number of items to be reconciled
- Number of items counted

Purchase price variance

Where a standard cost approach is taken, a purchase order with a price that is different from the standard cost will create a purchase price variance. Tracking such variances will help identify any increasing drift which could result from a lag in the final costing of product, which, in turn, could lead to product margins being exaggerated where the product's standard cost is lower than it should be.

WIP account

A key part of the costing process is to ensure that the standard cost of all products accurately reflects the purchase cost of the raw materials. These are a few of the reasons why the WIP account will develop a non-zero balance:

- Raw material standard costs differ (higher or lower) from actual costs – this may be due to missed costing updates.
- Missed transactions.
- Product standard costs differ from actual costs – this may be due to missed costing updates.
- Incorrect Bill of Materials/formulation being used to create the standard cost of a product (Case Study 2.1).

General inventory provision

Built up in anticipation of an inventory loss at the inventory count, tracking the general inventory provision will, in addition to other inventory-related measures, show the financial impact of improvements in the inventory management process.

Aged inventory provision

As with the general inventory provision, tracking the aged inventory provision will show the financial impact of improvements in aged inventory management. Many organisations will choose not to adopt this level of financial prudence. The argument being that a provision is being applied to inventory that is saleable. However, this level of prudence can be seen as showing the organisation's effectiveness in inventory planning and management.

Quarantine inventory provision

As with the general inventory provision, tracking the quarantine inventory provision will show the financial impact of improvements in quarantine inventory management and in production performance.

Expired inventory provision

Tracking the expired inventory provision will show the financial impact of improvements in the aged inventory management process.

Whichever way the organisation chooses to display the data, charts are always useful, as trends can be more easily seen in this form.

In addition to financial measures, the following are typical measures used to track inventory count performance.

Percentage non-zero variances

Where there is non-zero variance, the clear implication is that a transaction has either been missed or erroneously recorded. For some slow-moving inventory, a non-zero variance should not be expected, especially where there has not been any movement since the previous count.

Tracking the data over several inventory counts will show whether any progress is being made. It should be noted that this is not a measure that you should wait for in order to gauge whether actions taken are having an effect, as an inventory count might only take place every 6 or 12 months.

Number of items to be reconciled

This measure shows how many non-zero variances fall outside the percentage, value and quantity tolerances. This helps show whether financial and physical control over inventory is improving or not.

Number of items counted

With any inventory count performance measure, particularly when comparisons are made with previous inventory counts, it is important to put the count into context.

The number of items counted will show whether there is any change from count to count. An increase in the number of items will bring with it an increased risk of errors − errors that will manifest themselves as issues down the line. A decrease in the number of items, especially against the background of growth, will point to an improvement in the management of inventory. Also, the less there is to count, the more accurate the count will be − with a consequent reduction in down-the-line issues.

These are some examples of measures that can be used to aid in not just monitoring performance over time, but also in developing a better understanding of how the whole process works.

The cost of inventory is just as important to manage as inventory itself. In an ideal world, they would mirror each other. In the real world, gaps exist between the two and corrections have to be made.

Narrowing this gap will not only mean that improvements are being made, but that the organisation's control has improved.

Whilst useful in highlighting problem areas, there are a couple of aspects to note with inventory count measures. Firstly, they are not always useful in tracking the impact of changes in a timely manner, as counts tend not take place that often. Secondly, they are usually flagging issues that have already happened and cannot really be described as leading indicators.

Actions

It is important to develop procedures that describe, in detail, each phase of the inventory count.

- Each phase should have a checklist of items to help ensure that what needs to be done, is done (see Appendix 1). The checklist is a dynamic document that can be updated with new improvement opportunities to ensure that the same mistakes are not repeated in the future.
- Procedures and checklists are key tools when it comes to capturing expertise and knowledge that are critical for organisational learning. They also help ensure that consistency can be maintained whoever is engaged in future inventory counts.
- Analysis checklists (see Appendix 2) help ensure a consistent and thorough investigation. This not only means that root causes are established with appropriate corrective actions, but it also reduces the risk of incorrect assumptions being made. As part of the inventory count process, the checklist should always be reviewed and updated where necessary.

3

PLANNING

Given its control over both the production schedule and consequent raw material demand, Planning clearly has a significant impact on inventory. The responsibility brings with it accountability, with Planning usually being the first to be asked when it comes to questions relating to higher than expected inventory levels, extended lead-times and deteriorating service levels.

The planning process, as shown in Figure 3.1, is quite straightforward with a production plan (or schedule) being compiled by taking account of five basic elements.

The initial points to consider for each of these elements include:

- *Customer orders*
  What and how much has the customer ordered, and when do they want it by?
- *Demand forecast*
  In addition to customer orders, are you in a position to anticipate customer demand?
- *Safety Stock*
  Has an internal commitment been made to keep certain products in inventory? If so, what is the quantity of inventory?
- *Current inventory*
  Knowing the overall demand from customer orders, sales forecast and Safety Stock levels, can any of the demand be offset by current inventory?
- *Production resource*
  Where it has been determined that production of certain products is necessary, what resources are available to manufacture those products?

Answers to each of the above questions leads to the construction of the production plan.

Of course, dealing with each element in turn throws up further questions:

- *Customer orders*
  Where several customers require several products, is there a priority?
  How does planning deal with urgent orders?

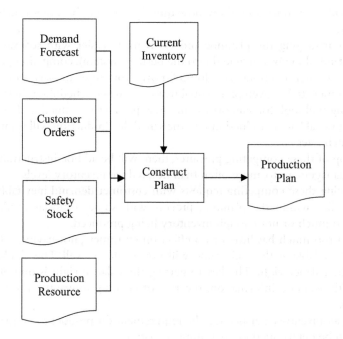

Figure 3.1 Basic planning process.

- *Demand forecast*
  How reliable is the demand forecast?
  How has the forecast been constructed?
  How often is the forecast updated?
- *Safety Stock*
  How often is Safety Stock reviewed?
  What is the basis for setting Safety Stock?
  Has product shelf life been factored into the Safety Stock calculation?
  Are there storage constraints related to any of the products flagged for Safety Stock?
- *Current inventory*
  Is the current inventory in the correct package?
  Is the inventory located across several facilities?
  Is product inventory close to its expiry date?
- *Production resource*
  Are all resources suitable for producing a product?
  Are resources scheduled for maintenance downtime?
  Are there contingency plans in place?
  Has a raw material plan been put in place?
  Have raw material delivery lead-times been taken into account?

These, and other questions, show how quickly planning becomes much more complex.

Whilst managing the planning process is made easier with software tools (either stand-alone or integrated into the business system), competing pressures come from other functions. Sales looks for inventory to be in place and for certain customers to be given preferential treatment when scheduling their orders. Marketing will look for support for any new product introduction. R&D will want to fit trial batch production into the schedule. Production will want maximum batch sizes etc.

On top of these competing pressures, there will be ad hoc instructions from senior management to, more often than not, reduce inventory levels.

Balancing these competing requests with customer demand inevitably leads to instability within the planning process, with some decisions resulting in either too much or not enough inventory being produced.

Whilst too much has little or no effect on customers, not having sufficient product available at the right time will not go down well. The challenge is to get the balance right. The key to getting the balance right is one of accuracy. With accurate information, the risk of creating unwanted inventory is reduced.

From an inventory perspective, the requirement for product to be manufactured can be determined using a simple equation:

Closing inventory = Opening inventory − Customer orders

When closing inventory has a negative value, Planning will act accordingly by scheduling the manufacture of sufficient product in order to fulfil the customer order.

However, every organisation has to work with constraints and uncertainty. Three of the factors to consider are Safety Stock, demand forecast and production resource. Assuming that closing inventory, opening inventory and customer orders are known with precision, the question becomes − 'How reliable is the data for Safety Stock, demand forecast and production resource?'

The degree of confidence that Planning has in the data being used will vary. Taking each factor in turn:

Opening inventory

Whilst a high degree of confidence should be expected, there can be discrepancies − inventory might not be at the level recorded in the business system, there might be expiry date issues or the inventory might not be at the stated location. These are very real issues that usually manifest themselves as incidents when the Dispatch function comes to assemble a customer's order for shipping or as variances at an inventory count.

Customer orders

Under normal circumstances customer orders can be considered to be accurate. The Planning function can only operate on the basis of what it has been told and is unlikely to be in a position to control any issues that will have arisen as a result of order entry – which are covered in more detail in the chapter on Customer Service.

Production resource

The production resource will be predetermined, and again, Planning will have to operate within specific constraints. These will determine which equipment/ reactor will be used for which product and the minimum and maximum production run/batch size that can be accommodated – all of which will be set by Production.

It should be noted that with regard to batch or production run times, the chemical industry is likely to differ from the engineering industry. For example, an engineering company might take 1 hour to manufacture 1 unit of a product. To manufacture 20 units will therefore take 20 hours.

A chemical company, however, might manufacture in vessels with the capability of producing between a minimum and maximum quantity. For example, it might be possible to manufacture 1000 kilos of a product in 15 hours. Where this did not fully utilise the vessel's capacity, it might be possible to produce 2000 kilos in the same reaction vessel. Charging raw materials, discharging the product and the actual process might take longer, but it is likely that producing 2000 kilos will not take 30 hours. It is more likely that 15 to 20 hours will be sufficient.

Whilst process time is unlikely to directly impact inventory, it will impact the planner's decision-making process. Where the opportunity exists to maximise batch sizes, there will be pressure from Production to manufacture the maximum quantity batch size, thereby increasing the risk of producing an excess of inventory.

Safety Stock

The commitment to hold a Safety Stock of product is usually driven by the need to be in a position to fulfil certain customer orders from inventory, rather than having to factor in production lead-times. Typically, the reasons will be one of the following:

* The product is supplied to a strategic customer and having a Safety Stock enables them to respond quickly to their own customers' requirements.
* Short lead-times are required to match or improve on a competitor's offering.

- Inventory is required to offset production constraints where the production plan does not match customer demand.
- Pressure from Sales to maintain inventory of certain products.

The setting of Safety Stock is intended to take account of these aspects and will, if the business system or stand-alone planning software is used, be entered as a specific record for each particular product.

There are, however, a couple of problems with Safety Stock. Firstly, people tend to overstate the need for Safety Stock – either the quantity required or whether it should be applied to the product in the first place.

Secondly, once set up, the figure is rarely reviewed, and this can lead to problems in the long term where the pattern of demand changes.

For example, where demand increases there is an increased risk of a stock-out. Not appreciating the need to respond to this change can prove problematic and carries a considerable risk to future business with those customers being affected and would likely sour relationships internally between Planning and Sales and Marketing.

When demand falls, failing to respond will lead to an increase in inventory and a greater risk of having un-saleable product. This means that setting Safety Stock should not be seen as a one-off event with action only being taken when a problem arises.

A key question when looking to establish Safety Stock for any product is 'Where does it fit in the business strategy?' A way of approaching this is to consider the product life cycle and price profile (Figure 3.2)

Figure 3.2 illustrates phases that a product will go through, reflecting both the sales growth pattern and associated price movement. There will be instances, of course, where products move into the decline phase because the market itself is declining. In these instances, products might not see any price reduction.

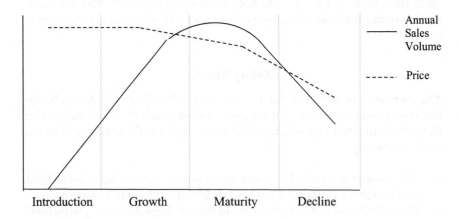

Figure 3.2 Product life cycle and price profile.

However, it is assumed that sales growth decline will be due to competitors driving down prices.

What this means is that profitability will decline, and in order to compete when prices fall a company will need to reduce its cost base.

Oftentimes the difficulty is that organisations are used to healthy margins and profitability and are reluctant to accept the new reality. The approach then becomes one of reacting to circumstances, where a more proactive approach could result in delivering better returns and maintaining market share.

Being proactive means reducing costs as early as possible in the product's life cycle and an organisation, if it is to maintain the product as a viable revenue stream, has to be rigorous in its approach. Part of that rigour involves inventory management.

Having four phases in a product's life cycle implies that there should be four different inventory management approaches. Placing each product (or group of products) on this chart will identify which phase it is in – 'introduction', 'growth', 'maturity' or 'decline'.

For each phase, an organisation can prescribe some actions – examples of which are shown in Table 3.1.

This process begins to show how inventory management can connect to the organisation's strategy and how functions can play their part in supporting that strategy.

Introduction

For products with Safety Stock levels, it is evident that in the introduction phase growth can be rapid, and against this background there is little to be gained by establishing a Safety Stock level. The main focus should be on working with Marketing and Sales functions to establish a forecast against which an inventory build can be planned with scenarios modelled to assess what needs to be done to keep pace with growth. Scenario variance analysis can model different growth rates, manufacturing requirements and production's 'right first time' capability.

Growth

Moving into the growth phase, demand becomes more predictable and customers will have a service expectation and fulfilling this expectation might warrant Safety Stock. There will be less reliance on the market forecast, so the onus on managing inventory and meeting customer demand will shift increasingly to Planning.

Maturity

As the maturity phase is approached, competitors entering the market are likely to look at offering better service and lower prices or that some

Table 3.1 Managing inventory through the product life cycle.

Phase	Aspect	Action
Introduction	Demand	*Rapid Increase*
	Inventory Category	Inventory build
	Planning	Optimal batch sizes. Scenario modelling.
	Forecast	Market forecast
	RFT	Expect up to 90%
	Resources	Identify critical RMs and build inventory
Growth	Demand	*Predictable Increase*
	Inventory Category	Consider Safety Stock
	Planning	Product grouping – reducing lead-times
	Forecast	Sales forecast and customer orders
	RFT	Expect less than 100%
	Resources	Identify critical RMs and build inventory
Maturity	Demand	*Stable*
	Inventory Category	Safety Stock tapering
	Planning	Optimal sequencing and minimum lead-times
	Forecast	Customer orders and historical forecast
	RFT	100% and uninterrupted production
	Resources	Optimise RM shipments. Taper RM inventory.
Decline	Demand	*Reducing*
	Inventory Category	Make-to-order
	Planning	Longer lead-times
	Forecast	None – customer orders only
	RFT	100% and precise MTO
	Resources	Do not stock product specific RMs
		Purchase precise quantities of product specific RMs

customers are unwilling to source exclusively from a single supplier. Meeting this challenge means that aspects such as Safety Stock may well become a necessary feature.

Increased competition means that the control and reduction of product cost will become increasingly important, as this will help either sustain growth in or at least maintain market share.

Whilst Production has its part to play (discussed in a later chapter), from a Planning perspective every aspect should be considered that leads to cost reduction – product sequencing (i.e. scheduling production of several batches rather than leaving it to be dealt with on a batch-by-batch basis), raw material delivery optimisation etc.

Decline

When the decline phase is reached, Safety Stock should be reduced, if not eliminated, and greater focus should be placed on getting the customer to provide longer lead-times. Here, for example, Customer Service can be proactive in calling the customer(s) concerned.

It should be remembered that whenever an organisation commits to having Safety Stock for a product it is making a financial commitment that is equivalent to an investment decision. The scale of the investment might not be significant when compared to new equipment or other asset but, nevertheless, as with any investment decision the organisation will expect a return on the commitment being made.

Looked upon from this perspective it is clear that setting the Safety Stock needs to be a structured process. The value created by the decision should be subject to review. This means that a process should also be in place to review Safety Stock.

Having a detailed process for the setup of Safety Stock, and subsequent review, might seem an onerous activity or even viewed as overkill. However, when errors are made, much time will be spent trying to deal with them, and there will, in many instances, be a financial loss to the organisation. This is on top of, for example, storage costs that might have been incurred in the intervening period between the creation of unwanted inventory and dealing with it.

Demand forecast

In addition to customer orders, the sales forecast is an important source of information when creating a production schedule. Forecasts help to:

- Optimise batch sizes, helping to reduce both downtime and production costs.
- Create more effective and efficient production sequences which can reduce equipment swap-over and vessel cleaning downtime between different products.
- Optimise raw material quantities which can help purchasing take advantage of quantity discounts.
- Optimise raw material delivery scheduling which helps with the management of both resource and warehouse space.

A typical demand forecast can be constructed from four main components:

- Historical data
- Customer orders
- Sales team forecast
- Market overview

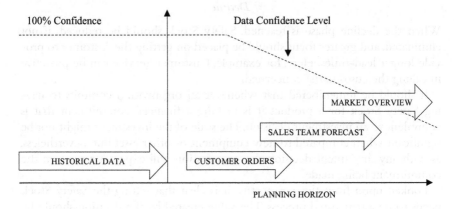

Figure 3.3 Forecast timeline confidence.

The degree to which a demand forecast is used will depend on the planning horizon being used. Figure 3.3 illustrates how, together with historical data, the three main data sources sit in relation to the planning horizon and the level of confidence that a planner might have in the data.

The degree to which the planning horizon extends beyond customer orders will vary. On a day-to-day basis the need for a sales team forecast and/or market overview might only be for an individual product. Of course, greater use of the sales forecast and market overview will be made when preparing budgets or longer-term plans. Whichever the scenario, the lack of certainty (confidence levels) has to be taken account of.

Historical data

This is reliable data source as the demand is known with 100% accuracy and can be used with a high degree of confidence to predict future demand. The key factor to be wary of here is that historical demand might not help you anticipate a sudden change in demand.

Customer orders

Customer orders are a reliable data source where the customer's demand is known very precisely. However, orders with long lead-times can be at a greater risk of being changed (quantity and/or delivery date). It should be noted that having a long lead-time does not guarantee an on-time delivery, especially where the product is make-to-order.

Customer orders might also be received that are required urgently and might not be available when Planning is working on the production schedule.

Sales team forecast

A short- to medium-term forecast provided by Sales helps to identify opportunities to optimise production schedules. One of the main reasons for the forecast is to flag any significant change in demand. A sharp, unexpected increase in demand can lead to supply issues, letting customers down and pressure to change the production schedule. Short-term changes are never welcome, because they disrupt plans already in place with an increased risk of issues arising and the creation of unwanted inventory.

An unexpected drop in demand can result in the production schedule not being corrected and lead to more product being manufactured than is required. If demand remains on a downward path, this could result, ultimately, in inventory being flagged as expired and possibly end up as un-saleable.

The recurring issues are communication and confidence – how accurate and reliable is the Sales forecast, and will Planning be told of any changes?

Market overview

Whilst having less of an impact on short-term inventory management, a market overview is an important part of the planning process because it can highlight potential constraints on manufacturing resources and raw materials.

The key to dealing with the certainty, or rather the lack of certainty, regarding market overviews is to develop a process that can harness experience over time. Overviews should be developed using a robust process where every aspect – process, data, criteria and assumptions – should be subject to evidenced validation.

Expected demand

Another aspect that should also be considered is that of anticipated demand. Often flagged by Sales, anticipated demand can lead to product being manufactured on the basis that an order is forthcoming.

These circumstances carry significant risks, and where uncertainty exists, a clearly defined approval process should be developed. The process should set out criteria and data requirements together with approval authority clearly set out. If a process is not in place, the problem is that any subsequent review of the surplus inventory might not take place for quite a while (when the product is flagged as 'expired') by which time the reasons for its manufacture will have been forgotten.

Clearly, as forecasts have lower confidence levels they need to be treated with a degree of caution. When being completely relied upon, there will be a greater risk of un-saleable inventory being created.

When not being manufactured for Safety Stock, products will generally be considered as 'make-to-order'. This is where an organisation will look to produce exactly what the customer has ordered – no more and no less. Whilst make-to-order can obviously apply to small orders, the approach can also apply to very large orders, as illustrated in Case Study 3.1.

Case Study 3.1   Project-driven orders

Scenario

A part of a large construction project requires 3000 tonnes of Product A. The project is of a type where the organisation's product competes not only with suppliers of similar products, but also with competing technologies.

Supply of the product would be over a period of 7 months.

In addition, Product A has a limited shelf life of 6 months.

Challenge

Projects of the type that trigger demand for Product A do not happen every year.

The quantity required for the project is very specific. Not enough will leave the project incomplete, whilst too much will result in inventory scheduled for disposal.

Action

In order to balance production of Product A with demand, the organisation created a usage forecast that showed how much the customer was expecting to use on a daily basis.

Arrangements were made with the customer to report their inventory of Product A on a weekly basis. Using this information, the organisation could calculate how much Product A was being used by the customer. This data could be compared with the original forecast, and any deviation checked and followed up upon.

Outcome

By setting up and following the routine of checking with the customer, the organisation could accurately predict whether there was going to be a greater or lesser demand for Product A. This meant that not only would a sufficient amount be supplied, but that a surplus was less likely to be created – which would be beneficial to both the organisation and the customer.

Measures

As has been stated, planning is a critical process with regard to its impact on inventory.

The measures that most organisations use to monitor the process are generally focussed on inventory itself, of which the following are examples:

- *Inventory level*
  This is reported as the overall inventory level and/or inventory days. As a 'macro' indicator of the organisation's performance, it tends to lead to more questions being asked.
- *Service level*
  Typically, the percentage of customer orders supplied 'on time, in full' (OTIF). A deteriorating service level can be seen as a failure of the planning and manufacturing process. However, it could be due to a rapid and unexpected increase in demand.
- *Average lead-times*
  This will almost have a direct correlation with service level, as you would expect a deteriorating service level to be mirrored by longer lead-times. However, care needs to be exercised as the customers themselves might be giving the organisation longer order lead-times.

If looked upon as an event timeline, Planning's position is shown in Figure 3.4; the measures described are very much focussed on the 'outcome' stage.

Using outcome-based measures is placing all the focus on reacting to events. Whilst this is necessary, it should not be the only way that measures are used.

If we consider Figure 3.4, in an ideal world decisions made will trigger the desired actions and outcomes – in other words, lead to the purchase and creation of inventory that will perfectly balance the requirements of customer orders, sales forecast and production constraints.

However, such balance is not always achieved, and to bring about improvement measures are needed that will help inform Planning's

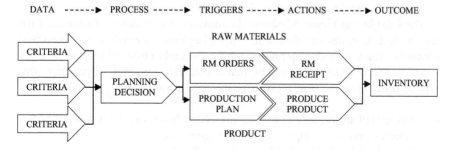

Figure 3.4 Event timeline.

decision-making rather than just require it to react to the impact at some future point in time.

Some examples of useful measures that can inform the planning process include:

- Inventory Turn
- Aged inventory profile
- Production changeover time
- Safety Stock review
- Plan stability/production plan changes
- Forecast accuracy

Inventory Turn

Inventory Turn is a measure that is more often associated with performance at the company or corporate level. However, it has a real value when applied to both products and raw materials.

At the company level, Inventory Turn is generally based on values. However, this is complicated by aspects such as the basis applied to costing (FIFO, batch costing, average cost etc.), as well as possibly having to take account of foreign exchange movements. From the planning perspective, Inventory Turn should be calculated using quantities, as this eliminates all the financial variables.

We have already seen in the Preface that Inventory Turn varies, and certainly calculating it at product level will likely demonstrate considerable variance from one month to the next – effects that are generally smoothed out when looking at annual sales. However, with an Inventory Turn target for the year, it should be possible for planning to determine whether the month-on-month Inventory Turn is going to hit the target. By monitoring on a monthly basis, planning will be better placed to take action to help deliver the target Inventory Turn.

For example, an organisation has a target Inventory Turn of 6.0. The movement in inventory for a new product (Product A) is shown in Table 3.2, together with the cumulative Inventory Turn, where the Safety Stock has been set at 40 units and the typical production batch is 30 units.

A plot of cumulative Inventory Turn is shown in Figure 3.5.

The solid line in Figure 3.5 shows the movement over time of Inventory Turn for Product A, whilst the dotted line (running from November to December) shows the impact of reducing production for December from 60 units to 30 units.

Of course, the argument will be that if you have hundreds of products, this will be difficult to manage. However, aspects to consider are:

- There will always be a range within which Inventory Turn will vary for a product, and an example is given in Figure 3.6.
- A product might be set to have a Safety Stock.
- The pattern of demand could be predictable, linear or irregular.

Table 3.2 Inventory movement and Inventory Turn for Product A.

Month	Opening Inventory	Sales	Production	Closing Inventory	Inventory Turn (Cumulative)
Jan	60	50	60	70	0.7
Feb	70	30	30	70	1.1
Mar	70	75	60	55	2.8
Apr	55	45	60	70	2.9
May	70	55	30	45	5.7
Jun	45	60	60	45	7.0
Jul	45	40	60	65	5.5
Aug	65	100	90	55	8.3
Sep	55	15	30	70	6.7
Oct	70	50	30	50	10.4
Nov	50	65	60	45	13.0
Dec	45	35	60	70	8.9

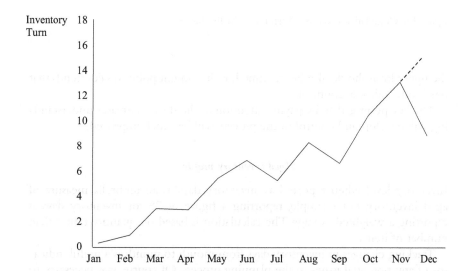

Figure 3.5 Cumulative inventory turn for Product A.

- Production runs or batch sizes may be fixed or varied.
- Obsolete inventory might exist that could distort the data – something that should not be ignored.

By having a preset range within which the Inventory Turn is expected to vary, one need only consider looking at the exceptions as they arise. The obvious course of action is to focus on those that fall below the lower limit. Those above

47

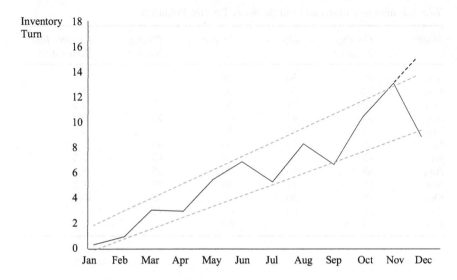

Figure 3.6 Cumulative Inventory Turn limits for Product A.

the upper limit should also be examined, as they might point to sales trends that need to be taken account of.

The key point is that, by paying attention to the detail, a greater understanding will develop, and control of the process will be much improved.

Aged inventory profile

Inventory level when reported as 'inventory days' is an umbrella measure of aged inventory. For example, reporting a figure of 28 for inventory days is reporting a weighted average. The calculation is based on quantity rather than number of items.

Tracking changes in inventory days from month to month is a useful indicator of any potential issues in the planning process. Of course, it is necessary to take account of any seasonal variances, scheduled plant maintenance and holidays etc., as these will distort the figure. For example, ahead of any scheduled plant maintenance, an organisation might commit to producing extra inventory to cover the effective loss of production. This will drive the inventory days figure up but is clearly a planned activity. Similarly, where production is linear (i.e. make the same quantity every month) and demand is seasonal, there will be a variation in inventory days from month to month.

This shows how important it is to understand what the measure is telling you.

Taking an aged inventory profile as shown in Figure 3.7, the average inventory days might be as indicated. What is clear is that this represents an average

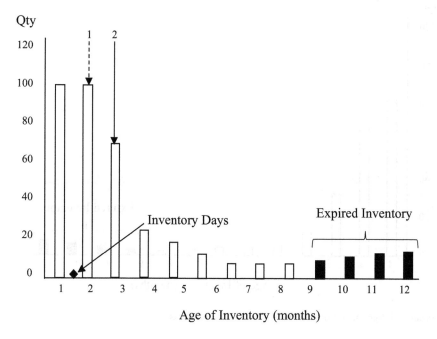

Figure 3.7 Aged inventory profile.

for the whole inventory and that there will be inventory that is aged both less and more than the average.

At any one time, the inventory days figure is a snapshot and does not neces-sarily give any direct pointers as to where any problems might lie. Clearly, in order to deal with any issues, more detail is needed. As an overview, the aged inventory profile can provide the level of detail required.

When displayed as a chart (see Figure 3.7), the degree to which the problem is perhaps more systematic (i.e. a consequence of a less-than-perfect process) is more evident.

The indicators shown in Figure 3.7 (referenced as '1' and '2') are discussed later.

One useful way to further drill down is to separate out the aged profile for Safety Stock and make-to-order products. In so doing, the profile might look like those shown in Figures 3.8 and 3.9.

With regard to Safety Stock products, one might expect there to be two main causes of age-related issues – inventory rotation or a reduction in demand. To a degree, these issues should be fairly easy to resolve.

Where there is strong demand, inventory rotation or easing back on pro-duction should be sufficient. Weakening demand might require further actions

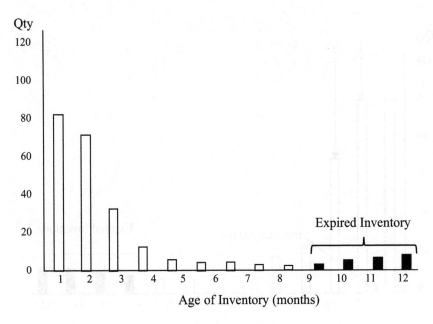

Figure 3.8 Aged inventory profile – Safety Stock products.

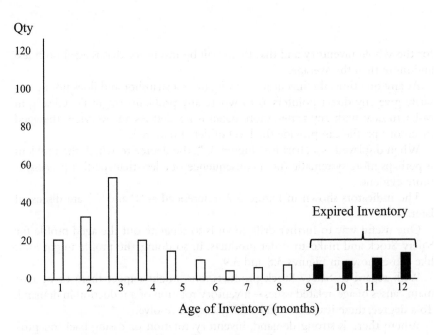

Figure 3.9 Aged inventory profile – make-to-order products.

such as reducing Safety Stock levels or setting the product to make-to-order (and setting the safety stock to zero).

Dealing with expired Safety Stock should be easier in that there should be opportunities to, for example, recover the inventory in upcoming production.

Issues related to the aged inventory profile of make-to-order products will likely prove more challenging to resolve. Quite naturally, initial focus will usually fall on very old product – expired inventory for example. The difficulty though, when focussing on very old inventory is that:

- Customer demand could well have already dropped to zero.
- The customer(s) could have been lost to the competition.
- People will have forgotten why the product was manufactured in the first place.
- Priorities will have moved on and people will not want to be pulled back to deal with what might be perceived to be a planning issue.

A structured approach to addressing the issue of expired inventory will deliver some type of resolution and one or more preventive actions. As the level of expired inventory is reduced (including through disposal) the problem will be seen as having been solved.

It should be noted that, having made a start, there might not be any observable changes in the profile because future expired inventory will already have been produced. Significant progress might not be demonstrated for several months, although improvements in the safety stock age profile should be seen earlier than the make-to-order age profile.

As improvements are made in the aged inventory profile, emphasis should shift from expired inventory to an earlier stage of the profile. For example, the first step might be to look at product older than 3 months, indicated by 'Expired Inventory' in Figure 3.7. Further improvement could see the trigger move to looking at inventory that is older than 2 months (as indicated by '2' in Figure 3.7) and then older than a month (as indicated by '1' in Figure 3.7).

The benefits of moving the trigger point closer to the point of manufacture are:

- Customer demand might not yet have dropped to zero.
- Competitors might be at an early stage in their efforts to become established and the opportunity to respond might still be available.
- People are likely to remember why decisions were taken to manufacture a particular product, which makes it easier to find a better solution for the future.
- Priorities are unlikely to have moved on, and it will be easier to retain people's focus on finding improvements.

51

Selecting a trigger can be done using inventory days, for example, though a tolerance might be needed. For example, if the target is to achieve 28 inventory days, the trigger might be to look at product greater than 35 (+10%) or 42 days (+20%). There are no hard-and-fast rules on this matter. As time goes by, an organisation will develop a better understanding of the inventory management process and will be better able to determine tolerances that are appropriate to their business.

A move to having an earlier review is part of the process of anticipating problems and being able to deal with them in a timely manner. Of course, not many organisations will have reached this stage, and it might seem a long way away, but having this as a goal will drive improvements and, when reached, the organisation will likely have developed a thorough understanding of the inventory management process and causes of unwanted inventory.

Production changeover time

For an organisation, value is created when raw materials are converted into a product. The time that this takes – batch or process time – is always something that an organisation will look to reduce. The time between the finish of one batch and the start of another does not add any value and is one that often incurs a cost. This is also an area that an organisation will look to simplify or shorten in order to both reduce the cost and increase capacity.

Where a production schedule is created, whether sequencing products on a production line or in chemical reactors, changing from one product to another will involve changeover time. A change could entail altering equipment and/ or cleaning a vessel. Both will take time to undertake – a period of production time that is not adding value.

Whilst some changeover time may be inevitable, the duration and type of changeover time are useful measures as they can point to potential inefficiencies in the planning process.

A measure that might already be in place is expenditure on consumable items. 'Consumable items' is often the designation for materials used in the production process, but not forming part of any Bill of Materials. As a financial measure, the definition of what constitutes a consumable item may vary from organisation to organisation, but it would be useful as it assigns a value to part of the changeover process.

Plan stability

Where Production has a clear view of what is expected, it is able to prepare in advance and allocate resources accordingly. When constructing a schedule, the planners will obviously have a view going out many weeks or beyond but might only issue a firm production schedule for the upcoming week.

As Figure 3.10 illustrates, when scheduling production, the longer the planning horizon, the more likely it is that it will be altered. This would be normal

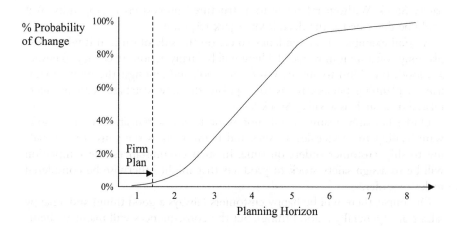

Figure 3.10 Percent probability of change over time.

in most planning environments, though actual planning horizons will vary from organisation to organisation.

Whilst changes are to be expected, there will come a point in time where a firm plan is issued. Changes to the firm plan are unlikely to be welcomed as they will not only be viewed as disruptive, but also risk impacting on service levels for those customer orders dependent on the original plan.

Attention to detail

The inventory event timeline in Figure 3.4 shows that the planning process draws on three main data elements – criteria, demand and resources. In order to deliver optimum outcomes, it is essential to have a high level of confidence in these elements.

Criteria (preset parameters)

There are four types of criteria that impact the planning process.

- Safety Stock – initial setup and review
- Production or batch times
- Production or batch yields.
- Sequencing rules

Safety Stock – initial setup and review

The usual response to service issues is to consider requests to create Safety Stock, and this, over time, will result in more products being classified as requiring

53

Safety Stock. Without reference to a structured process (as in Appendix 3) it could be described as the default knee-jerk response.

A good example of the tendency to err on the side of caution is when new planning software is introduced. There will be many actions necessary to ensure a smooth transition to any new software tool, and amongst the requirements from a planning perspective is to populate the new database with product-related data, such as a Safety Stock level.

Understandably, planners will not want to see a transition to new software leading to service-level issues and being seen as the cause of any failure to ship customer orders on time. In such circumstances, the temptation will be to assign safety stock to products that might otherwise be considered make-to-order.

Of course, there will be happy customers (always a good thing) and a happy sales team (generally a good thing), but the consequences will manifest themselves over time when inventory levels rise to unacceptable levels with consequent increase in problems with aged inventory.

Whilst this might be a very specific scenario, it illustrates the point that without a structured process, control will be lost. Having established a procedure for assigning Safety Stock, it is also necessary to conduct regular reviews of products assigned a Safety Stock in order to anticipate any changes in demand that might warrant a change to a particular product's Safety Stock level (increase, decrease or elimination).

This does lead to the question of which products should be reviewed. In order to answer this question, it should be remembered that what you are looking for is any sign of change. The starting point is to consider the criteria that triggered the setting up of Safety Stock for a specific product in the first place. The review will involve looking at the justification(s) to see if anything has changed. Instances where the existing data varies from the original are those that warrant closer examination. Sales data will be the most obvious starting point, but it should not be forgotten that there might have been strategic reasons why the Safety Stock was set up in the first instance.

Limits, or tolerances, can be set at either percentage or quantity levels, depending on the needs of the organisation.

Production or batch times

Knowing how long it will take to manufacture a product is vital, enabling batches or production runs to be scheduled such that they are complete by the time a customer's order needs to be shipped.

In the first instance this seems to be an obvious requirement and easy to answer. However, this might not always be the case. Case Study 3.2 is an example based on an actual conversation between a planner and production staff.

Case Study 3.2   Production batch time

Background

Planners were looking to improve the production schedule so that resource allocation could be anticipated more easily. In order to bring about this improvement, production batch times were required.

Conversation

PLANNER: *So how long will this product take to produce?*

PRODUCTION: *I don't know. It depends.*

PLANNER: *Well, you must have an idea? Roughly how long?*

PRODUCTION: *Well, like I said, it depends.*

PLANNER: *Depends on what?*

PRODUCTION: *On raw materials and whether we have enough staff available.*

PLANNER: *OK. In an ideal world, with raw materials and manpower available, how long?*

PRODUCTION: *Well, it still depends.*

PLANNER: *Look, I don't mind whether you give me the longest possible time. I will be happy with that, as it will be a starting point. So, what would the longest batch time be?*

PRODUCTION: *It still depends.*

PLANNER: *Will it take 30 minutes?*

PRODUCTION: *No.*

PLANNER: *Will it take 50 hours?*

PRODUCTION: *No.*

PLANNER: *So, the answer will lie somewhere between those two figures. What if I take 20 hours?*

PRODUCTION: *You can if you want. It shouldn't take that long.*

The planner was somewhat perplexed at this point.

Outcome

This conversation revolved around one product. In order to avoid similar conversations in the future, the planner decided to make assumptions. This would be on the basis that, if the assumed batch time was incorrect, it would be challenged by Production, in which case the planner would be supplied with more realistic batch time – a sort of win-win.

Whatever your view of the conversation, it is clear that the planner did not fully appreciate how Production worked, and Production did not understand the value in having an accurate batch time. A lack of understanding often leads to conflict and disagreements, and the moral is clear – you should never assume that just because you see a value in something that your colleagues will have the same view.

As with Safety Stock, the key is to be notified of any changes to batch times. A key routine to capture any changes is the review of a production schedule. When preparing a production schedule, the expectations are that both the predicted quantities will be produced and that the schedule will be completed according to the set timings. Where this is not the case, the cause of any change should be investigated and resolved.

In this way, a focus is maintained on ensuring the detail on production batch times remains accurate.

Production or batch yields

Particularly in the chemical industry, vessels used for the manufacture of products will often be capable of producing yields that vary between a minimum and maximum value. This is determined by the type and size of vessel and nature of the product.

With products set to have a Safety Stock, the maximum batch size will usually be manufactured, whereas make-to-order products might have anything between the minimum and maximum quantity produced.

When materials are blended or subject to a chemical reaction, unlike an engineering scenario, the quantity of raw material charged into a vessel might well be greater than the yield produced. This will be due to either a physical loss through material handling (pump priming, vessel residue etc.) or from the creation of a byproduct of the reaction (e.g. condensation reactions) that requires removal, or a combination of both.

Whichever scenario is the case, the danger is that when an organisation has many products a standard approach develops whereby when a process is designed to deliver a specific yield, an assumed 'typical loss' (perhaps expressed as a percentage) is taken into account. Whilst the figures themselves might be small, being precise is another part of paying attention to detail, and in-process losses should not be set on the basis of typical loss. Data needs to be collected and analysed, with actual losses confirmed.

This exercise is not only useful from an inventory perspective, but also from a standard cost perspective, as it will make sure that those figures are a more accurate reflection of the material cost of a product.

Sequencing rules

Product sequencing and its impact on changeover time has already been mentioned. For any production plan, there will be rules that determine the type and nature of the changeover from one product to another on either a production line or in a chemical reactor. Data relating to changeover times can be put together in the form of a matrix whereby rules can be quickly established for production sequences (e.g. if A follows B, or E follows B, then a particular changeover is required).

Sequencing rules and the changeover matrix need to be both accurate and well understood by the planners.

There will be many ways of reducing changeover time – sequencing products that are the same or similar is one approach.

Whilst the firm production schedule might have a short time horizon, ongoing demand, customer orders and sales forecasts can be used by the planner to take a longer-term view and look to optimise the production schedule.

For example, relying entirely on MRP (Material Requirement Planning) software to construct a production plan might well produce the sort of plan shown in Figure 3.11.

MRP software (whether stand-alone or as part of the business system) might have generated a plan based on customer orders and Safety Stock, driven entirely by dispatch dates and inventory levels. Allocation of batches to reactor vessels (or production lines) will be on a first come, first served basis. In the scenario illustrated, there are 20 changeovers from one product to a different product, as indicated by the vertical black bars.

Switching from one product to a completely different product usually is the most time- and resource-consuming type of changeover.

The planner, through manual intervention, can revise the plan by sequencing the same products to be manufactured together – as shown in Figure 3.12.

Figure 3.12, whilst being for the same products, shows how sequencing can impact changeovers. Following the sequence revision, there are now only

PRODUCTION SEQUENCE

Figure 3.11 Production schedule (MRP).

PRODUCTION SEQUENCE

Figure 3.12 Production schedule (planner).

9 changeovers from one product to a different product. The remaining 11 changeovers are from a product to the same product. This, for chemical vessels, significantly reduces, if not eliminates, the need for cleaning and/or equipment changes.

You could consider the examples in Figures 3.11 and 3.12 to be simplistic, but they do clearly show what planning can achieve. Having fewer changeovers saves both time and cost and increases productivity. The reduction in the number of real changeovers also reduces the risk of errors arising that lead to inventory-related issues. For example, in Figure 3.11, you have to achieve the correct changeover on 20 occasions, whereas in Figure 3.12 you have to achieve the correct changeover on only 9 occasions.

This may seem obvious, but organisations can be set in their ways when it comes to routines and processes, using them because that's the way things have always been done.

Establishing repeating patterns in any production cycle helps build familiarity which, in turn, leads to fewer issues and shorter batch times.

Demand

There are two aspects of demand to consider:

- Customer orders
- Forecasts

Customer orders

It goes without saying that being accurate when creating customer orders is absolutely critical. Not being 100% accurate can lead to problems such as:

- Order entered for the incorrect customer
- Items entered incorrectly
- Quantities entered incorrectly
- Incorrect delivery date

Of course, orders (unless entered by the customer themselves using a portal of some form) will be added onto the business system by trained Customer Service staff. There should be well-defined processes that explain exactly how an order is to be added to the business system.

Of the four main error types, an incorrect customer will have the least impact on the outcome of planning decisions in so far as the correct product and quantity will have been manufactured.

An incorrect item and/or quantity will matter greatly to planners as this can lead to either too much or the wrong inventory being produced. This will then result in the need to schedule manufacture of the correct product and have an adverse impact on the production schedule.

Lead-time errors, on the face of it, might not be too serious from a planning perspective. However, it should not be forgotten that either the customer could cancel their order (which could result in surplus inventory) or a change in the production schedule will be required not only having the potential to impact other customer orders, but any change will carry a risk of a problem arising. This, in turn, could result in unwanted inventory being produced.

Forecast

Typically, there will be two sources of forecast – one from Sales and one from Marketing. Both are dealt with in more detail in the respective chapters, but it is worth pointing out that accuracy and confidence in the data are vital from the planning perspective.

Resources

Planning must take into account four key resources when constructing a production plan:

- Manpower
- Vessel/line capability
- Product inventory
- Raw materials

Whilst much of the data will be stored within the MRP or business system, it is important for planners to know where the data is logged and how it fits into the planning process.

Manpower

Generally, Planning will assume full availability of resources, including manpower, unless told otherwise. Inevitably, there will be occasions where manning levels are not at 100%. This can be due to planned and unplanned absences – holidays (vacation), training, sickness, personal issues etc.

The impact of planned absences can always be anticipated and discussed with Production well in advance. Depending on the circumstances, it might, for example, be possible to cover planned absence with either overtime or contract staff.

The impact of unplanned absences will always be more difficult to assess. The key here is to develop contingency plans and, in so doing, understand the limits of what is possible.

Vessel/line capability

Production will often be inclined to want production lines and reactor vessels producing maximum quantities all the time. However, customer demand might not warrant this, and Planning will need to know what the minimum production run or vessel capacity will be for every product.

Whichever options are taken by Planning, it is essential to know what each production line or reactor vessel is capable of producing. For any number of reasons, it is unlikely that every product can be produced everywhere and, indeed, having such capability might not necessarily be a good thing. It is likely to encourage random allocation of production and give customers and Sales an unreasonable expectation of what is possible.

Product inventory

Accurate control of product inventory is an essential part of the resources phase. This means that a high level of confidence is required in product inventory records held in the business system. It goes without saying that if the data is incorrect, the MRP system will be making inaccurate assessments of what needs to be manufactured and by when.

Raw materials

Equally, accurate control of raw material inventory is also an essential part of the resources phase. As with product inventory, this means that a high level of confidence is required in raw material inventory records held in the business system

Whilst much of the focus has been on product, raw material inventory should not be forgotten. As important as it is to fulfil customer requirements, an organisation should also be equally concerned about the scheduling of raw material deliveries.

Whilst supplier terms, delivery quantities, pricing and lead-times are dealt with by Purchasing, the raw material delivery schedule will be entirely driven by Planning, though it will be based on the combination of inventory records and data provided by Purchasing.

Those aspects vital to product inventory management are no less important for raw materials. Minimum and maximum delivery quantities are the equivalent of batch sizes. Safety Stock levels (and associated triggers in the business system) are equivalent to reorder points (or quantities). The number of suppliers is equivalent to number of production lines or reactor vessels capable of producing a product.

These similarities between product and raw material mean that equivalent actions can be taken. The same rigour, as applied to products, should also be applied to raw materials.

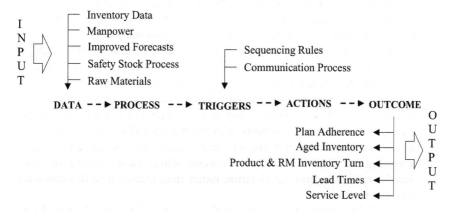

Figure 3.13 Planning process: inputs and outputs.

Summary

As with any process, there will be considerable focus on the measurement of outputs. For Planning, as already mentioned, these could be aged inventory, adherence to plan, service level and lead times. Figure 3.13 shows that these are very much output focussed.

To bring about improvement, attention should focus equally on detail, especially those points of detail relating to the process inputs. Some examples are shown in Figure 3.13.

Actions

The focus for the Planning function is on ensuring that all the input data is accurate, and that processes and procedures are in place to deal with the issues that come into play when determining what and how much is to be produced.

- Create a process for dealing with setting Safety Stock. An example is given in Appendix 3.
- Create a process for dealing with the review of Safety Stock levels at the product level. An example is given in Appendix 4.
- Create an anticipated order pre-approval checklist and process to deal with requests to manufacture product(s) prior to receipt of order. See Appendix 5.
- Review the accuracy of forecasts, because it is essential to have confidence in them when planning over the short to medium term – when customer orders are not the only source of demand data. Each of the sources – customer orders, sales forecasts and market overviews – are dealt with in the later chapters on Customer Service, Sales and Marketing, respectively.

- Ensure data is available on vessel or production line capacities – both minimum and maximum. Data needs to be checked and validated to ensure that the organisation has not drifted into an inefficient state.
- Ensure data is available for all product changeover combinations. Without data, there will be little chance of identifying new opportunities and new techniques that help to reduce changeover times and cost.
- Establish adherence to plan measures. Where plans are being disrupted, the instances need to be reviewed and actions taken. For example, if a single, strategic, customer places orders with short notice that causes a firm plan to be changed late in the day, set some capacity to one side and arrange a weekly call with the customer to double-check their demand. In other words, try and control the situation rather than leaving it to the customer to force you to react.
- Establish Inventory Turn measures for each individual product and raw material. The points to remember are that upper and lower limits should be set and that what you are looking for are instances where the Inventory Turn falls outside these limits.
- Review raw material purchase order quantities – any change in product demand needs to be communicated back to Purchasing.
- Purchasing needs to review its purchase order quantities as 'purchase to make' needs to be precise. In other words, if the demand is for 1.5 kilos, purchase 1.5 kilos – do not purchase 5 kilos or 25 kilos.

4

PRODUCTION

Whilst Planning has considerable responsibility with regard to inventory management, it is very much a data-processing activity. Production, on the other hand, involves actual handling and movement of inventory.

In relation to inventory, two areas of significance are capability and execution. Capability means understanding what available resources (equipment and manpower) are capable of, whilst execution means being able to convert raw materials into product correctly and 'right first time' (RFT) each and every time.

Not getting it RFT during execution has several consequences:

- Un-saleable product has been produced.
- Customers might be let down.
- The production schedule might need to be changed.
- There is the potential for financial loss.

Any financial loss has significance as it directly affects profit. A £10,000 loss of raw material means profit is reduced by £10,000, in addition to any disposal costs that may be incurred.

Production activities can be split into three phase – preparation, execution and delivery, as shown in Figure 4.1.

The relative simplicity of the flowchart belies the complex nature of the whole process. The phrase 'right first time' is often used when talking about the manufacturing process, and the very fact we have this phrase points to the fact that organisations generally, and Production in particular, does not always get it right first time.

From an inventory perspective there are two questions to be considered by production:

- Can all production be right first time?
- What are the optimum productivity levels?

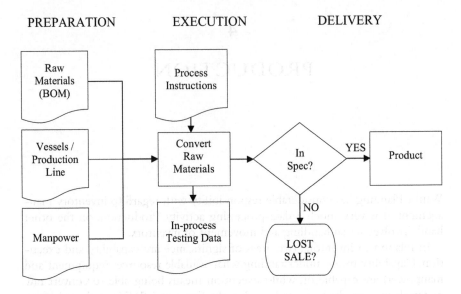

Figure 4.1 Production activity flowchart.

One of the main measures of production performance is the RFT percentage. The conversion of raw materials to product is the stage when value is being added. Failure to deliver saleable product means that not only has value *not* been added, but also a cost has been incurred. Indeed, the cost is not limited to the raw materials, as there will be a need to recover the product, or at worst dispose of it.

Ensuring that Production gets it 'right first time – every time' is vital, which brings us back to the preparation and execution phases. The treatment of these phases is no different to that seen in Planning or any of the areas to be discussed in the chapters that follow.

Production clearly has a part to play, but it also needs to have complete confidence in those elements not entirely within its control – specifically the Bill of Materials and process instructions.

The main elements of the preparation and execution phases will have several aspects and questions to consider:

- *Bill of Materials*

   Does the Bill of Materials clearly identify the raw materials required and the associated quantity?
   Is the Bill of Materials current?
   Are there any new raw materials that have special handling requirements?
   Are there any potential raw material supply issues?
   Is there any re-blending of quarantine or off-spec inventory?

- *Vessels*

  Is the reactor vessel or production line capable of producing the required product and quantity?

  Have any changes been made to the equipment since the product was last produced?

  Does the vessel have a validated maintenance record in line with recommendations?

- *Manpower*

  Are there sufficient people available to manufacture the product?

  Are all plant operators fully trained?

  Have staff been briefed on new products?

  Do all plant operators understand the health and safety requirements and are certain to use necessary safety equipment?

- *Process instructions*

  Are detailed process instructions available that fully describe all the steps and actions necessary to produce the product?

  Does the product have any aspects that are new or different?

  Are process control charts easy to use and understand?

- *Conversion process*

  How will the conversion process be controlled by the production operatives?

  If a new product, will there be any R&D support to monitor initial production.

  Are there any new in-process testing requirements?

  Are there any product-specific parameters that have to be adhered to (e.g. sequence of raw material addition)?

These are fairly obvious questions, but when considered they invariably lead to further questions.

In Production, as in all departments, there is always a risk that inappropriate assumptions will be made – often unknowingly. These can give rise to instability in the production process that will lead to an increased risk of problems arising.

Problems associated with manufacturing product RFT are often put down to raw materials. However, in many cases this could not be further from the truth.

In order to deliver RFT every time, it is necessary to look more closely at all aspects of capability and execution.

Preparation

Taking each of the three stages from Figure 4.1 in turn – vessels/production line, manpower and raw materials (BOM):

Vessels/production line

Often an organisation will have more than one production line or vessel, and it might be possible to produce a product on one or more of these.

It is essential to know what each of these vessels is capable of producing, both from a processing and quantity perspective. This impacts planning decisions, and consequently, has a direct impact on inventory.

Each vessel or production line will have design limits relating to, for example, temperature, pressure, material tolerance (e.g. corrosive materials), mixing capability, maximum run–rate, capacity etc. There are many design parameters, with some production lines and vessels being designed specifically to manufacture particular products. Most of these features will dictate the suitability of the vessel or production line with regard to manufacture of specific products.

However, when it comes to inventory it is evident that many organisations using vessels to produce batches of product do not always manufacture as much as the vessel is capable of producing. Case Studies 4.1, 4.2 and 4.3 are examples based on actual events and illustrate how organisations can drift into accepting that 'what has always been done must be the correct way of doing things'.

Case Study 4.1 Emulsion manufacture

Background

Water-based paints like vinyl silk and vinyl matt paints are generally based on water-based emulsions (vinyl acetate being a typical monomer). An organisation producing such paints also produced the polyvinyl acetate (PVA) emulsions used in their manufacture.

They had two production vessels, each producing batches of around 4800 litres.

The emulsion manufacturing process involves drip-feeding monomer into the reaction vessel at a set rate ('x' litres per minute). The monomer is pre-charged into a 'monomer' hopper with the quantity specified in the BOM.

An obvious question?

A production chemist was walking round the PVA unit one day, and whilst looking at the emulsion manufacturing vessels he noticed a metal plate on each vessel stating that the capacity was 6500 litres. Approaching the plant supervisor, the conversation went like this:

PRODUCTION CHEMIST: *Why is the batch yield only 4800 litres when the vessel capacity is 6500 litres?*

PLANT SUPERVISOR: *Because the monomer hopper can't hold any more.*

PRODUCTION CHEMIST: *So, if we had a bigger monomer hopper, we could increase the batch size?*

PLANT SUPERVISOR: *Yes.*

Outcome

Working with the plant supervisor, the production chemist directed the engineering department to design and fit a collar onto the monomer hopper to allow more monomer to be charged. This resulted in batch sizes being increased from 4800 litres to 6500 litres – an increase in yield of 35%.

Of course, batch times did increase slightly, but the overall run-time did not increase by 35%, and there was a net increase in capacity of over 20% for what was a very little outlay.

Comment

Organisations often get used to doing things because 'that's how they've always been done', and it shows that asking simple questions can sometimes deliver significant improvements.

The inventory benefits of such improvements were threefold:

- *Planning could bring down lead-times.*
- *Sales growth could be accommodated without needing to invest in new resources.*
- *Processing costs were reduced.*

All of this came from asking a simple question, and the moral is that you should keep your eyes and ears open and not be afraid of asking what might seem to be a 'silly' question.

Case Study 4.2   Multi-stage condensation reaction

Background

A chemical plant had several vessels used for the manufacture of products from condensation reactions. The vessels ranged in size, being described as 3-tonne, 5-tonne and 10-tonne vessels.

One of the products – Product A – was manufactured in two stages, the first of which was a condensation reaction, whilst the second stage did not produce any byproduct.

Vessel capacity

Vessel capacity is often quoted in litres, where organisations, more often than not, refer to the capacity by weight. In other words, the capacity is quoted as 'x' kilos or tonnes rather than 'x' litres.

When this view becomes engrained in the organisation, opportunities can be missed to produce considerably larger batches.

Review

A production chemist decided to review maximum yields and factor in each vessel's nameplate capacity.

In one instance, the production chemist noticed that Product A was set to deliver a yield of 2700 kilos (after a 300 kilos byproduct loss) when manufactured in the 3-tonne vessel. As a two-stage process, the byproduct was created entirely in the first stage. This meant that an opportunity to increase the yield was available.

Outcome

It was a simple calculation – scaling the 2700 kilo yield up to 3000 kilos. An increase of 11.1% meant that the first-stage charge would now be 2222 kilos, with a yield of 1889 kilos, which when the second stage charge of 1111 kilos was added gave a yield of 3000 kilos.

The increase did not result in any significant increase in the batch time, which meant that, as in Case Study 4.1, a threefold benefit was seen. In this particular instance, there was no requirement to modify the equipment, so productivity was improved at no additional cost.

It is surprising that inefficiency pervades so many organisations, large and small, whether well-established or not. Recognising that inefficiencies exist can not only reflect an organisation's attitude towards attention to detail but also presents an opportunity to gain a competitive advantage.

Thinking in terms of weight rather than volume can unknowingly hamper an organisation when it comes to recognising inefficiency, and this is evident when it comes to a product's density, as is illustrated in Case Study 4.3.

Case Study 4.3   Density

Background

Returning to the organisation in Case Study 4.2, each of the vessels was referred to by weight – 3-tonne, 5-tonne and 10-tonne vessels. (Organisations that sell product by weight tend to think of their production capacity in terms of weight.)

The products processed were blends. This means that a charge of 5000 kilos would deliver a yield of close to 5000 kilos.

Review of batch yield

If a production vessel has a nameplate capacity of, say, 5000 litres, manufacturing a product with a density of 1.00 would allow a charge of 5000 kilos and a yield of up to 5000 kilos (dependent on the nature of the reaction and whether expansion needs to be taken account of at elevated temperatures).

Over time, the organisation had broadened its product portfolio such that the density of products ranged from 1.0 to 1.25. However, being used to thinking in terms of weight, the batch yield for every product was still set to 5000 kilos.

Thinking in terms of volume immediately begs the question – why, for a product with a density of 1.25, produce 5000 kilos? In a 5000-litre vessel, should it not be possible to charge 6125 kilos?

Outcome

The review resulted in batch sizes being increased for all products with a density of more than 1.00, with yields being increased by up to 25%.

The three case studies are examples, based on actual events, of opportunities that presented themselves and demonstrated that an organisation does not always need to invest in order to increase production capacity.

Manpower

Whether for the firm production plan or for the longer term, planning needs to be made aware of any changes in manpower resources. People are as vital as raw materials in putting together a schedule, and the plan needs to take account of availability.

Planning will also have to balance demands from Customer Service and Sales, and, on some occasions, will need to know whether there is scope for either overtime or having additional resource made available. Working with Production is critical so that the competing pressures are not only balanced with available resource, but also that Production understands where the demand is coming from.

Clearly, where resourcing is the cause of Production's failure to meet a plan, it points to a fault within the planning process whereby resource availability might have been overestimated.

Whilst a production line's or vessel's capability is known very precisely and does not vary (a 5000–litre vessel does not suddenly become 4800 litres one week, and 5200 litres the next), the same level of certainty cannot be said for manpower. In order to move towards greater precision and control, the production plan needs to be more than just a sequence of products (as illustrated in Figures 3.11 and 3.12). The firm plan, as issued, will require the completion of many steps, and those steps need to be completed by set times – effectively a project plan, though perhaps better described as an activity sequence.

Creating an activity sequence will give clarity to all concerned of exactly what is required. With limited resource and multiple production lines or vessels, this might well mean operators working on more than one vessel at a time. An example is shown in Appendix 6.

Of course, having sufficient manpower on its own is not enough. Plant and vessel operators need to have an understanding of the process for which they are responsible.

In order to maintain skills and expertise, training is essential – both accredited and refresher. Best practice will evolve over time, and for a company to maintain and improve its performance it is essential that best practice is not just talked about, but actually enacted.

In a competitive environment, the pace at which best practice is adopted is often why performance gaps open up between organisations and how a business can suddenly find itself unable to compete effectively.

Raw materials (BOM)

The firm plan presented to Production will not only list the products to be produced and the vessels or production lines to be used, but also the quantities scheduled for production.

Each product will have a Bill of Materials (BOM) that details the individual raw materials and quantities required.

Whether collected directly or assembled by the Goods Inwards staff, it is normally Production's responsibility to ensure that what is put together or charged is precisely as specified in the BOM. It is an obvious prerequisite, as the formulation will have been designed by R&D to create a product with specific properties.

Along with the BOM there will be a set of manufacturing instructions that detail when and how each raw material is to be added, and how they should be processed.

For the final product to be within a predetermined specification, the raw materials need to have been charged accurately and the processing instruction followed precisely (see next section).

In the chemical industry, most BOM will list raw materials by weight, though some will be charged using volumetric methods. The transfer of product by volume usually applies to liquids stored in storage tanks.

In an ideal world, storage tanks would stand on load cells whereby it is possible to see the weight of product held in the storage tank. Similarly, the reactor vessel itself could be on load cells so that the quantity being charged can be tracked.

Ensuring accurate charging of liquids controlled by volume is essential. Case Study 4.4 gives an example of dealing with some issues that can arise when charging by volume.

Case Study 4.4   Charging material by volume

Background

A chemical manufacturer produced products ranging from polyesters to alkyd resins. A range of the alkyd resins used in surface coatings were based on soya bean oil, a material that was delivered and stored in bulk.

From the storage tank, soya bean oil was transferred into a liquid hopper that held the charge for the upcoming product.

Whist pre-charging made for more efficient use of the reactor, it was still, nevertheless, important to charge the required materials accurately.

Review

On checking the actual method of charging into the liquids hopper it was found that a 'dipstick' was used.

Whilst more typically found in a car engine as a means of checking the level of oil, this particular use had a dipstick graduated to show how much volume was in the liquid hopper. It was marked off in units of 20 litres, so if the required charge was 1650 litres, you would fill the hopper to between the 1640- and 1660-litre marks.

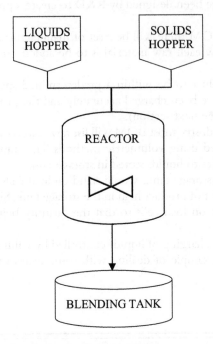

Figure 4.2 Basic chemical manufacturing setup.

The first problem was that the hopper was not lit, and that it was difficult to see the relevant marks. This would often result in slight over- or under-charging.

The second problem was that the soya bean oil was stored at an elevated temperature of around 60°C. The dipstick was graduated on the basis of liquids being at 20°C. The temperature difference meant that charging 1650 litres at the higher temperature resulted in less material being charged by weight.

Outcome

The first problem was solved by the creation of a small clamp that could be fixed to the dipstick. It was powder coated in white to make it easier to see.

The second problem was solved by the creation of a table that, following a requirement to check the temperature of the soya bean oil in the liquid hopper, showed the required adjustment (in litres).

Both of these actions improved charging accuracy with the result that process variances were virtually eliminated.

Of course, Case Study 4.4 might not be quite how many organisations dispense liquids, but it illustrates the point that you need to check everything to ensure that accuracy is maintained.

Such attention to detail is designed to reduce the risk of a problem occurring that results in un-saleable inventory.

Any organisation undertaking this approach will often unearth practices that might otherwise have gone un-noticed, which, when corrected, will further advance the cause of continuous improvement.

Execution

There are three aspects to consider in the execution phase:

- Process instructions
- Conversion process
- Dealing with problems

Process instructions

We have seen how assembling raw materials has to be done as precisely as possible, with accuracy being the key word. Failure to be precise will undermine the manufacturing process once it starts.

As soon as the manufacturing process begins you are effectively moving further away from the raw materials and closer to the final product. The further you are on this path, the more difficult it is to recover the situation should any problem arise. Maintaining precision and accuracy is vital, and this applies equally to the processing stage.

For any and every process, it is essential that plant operators have the tools and knowledge necessary to control the conversion process and deal with any problems that arise. Key to the control of any process will be the process instructions. Process instructions should precisely describe each step of the process, setting out how raw materials should be added, equipment should be operated, when any in-process testing is required and enable the operator to track the process against expectations.

Particularly with chemical reactions, tracking and controlling progress is a vital part of ensuring that the product meets the final specification. When creating the process instructions, it is important to ensure that the correct parameters are being measured. For each parameter being measured, there should be an expected range or target that should help show that the process is under control.

The assumption is that the parameters being tested are always going to be the most appropriate ones. However, as with other aspects of any organisation's operation there will be practices and procedures that have changed little over time – again, an example of 'this is the way we've always done it'. However, whilst the controls might well work in most instances, it does not mean that they cannot be improved upon. Case Study 4.5 is an example of in-process testing being reviewed and changed in order to bring about improvement in product quality.

Case Study 4.5 Alkyd resin manufacture: in-process testing

Background

The production of alkyd resins is a polymerisation process involving a condensation reaction run at temperatures in excess of 200°C. During the process, the viscosity of the product is measured and should increase during the reaction until it reaches a point where the reaction is deemed to be complete (allowing for any continued reaction during any cool-down).

Review

When producing alkyd resins for use in decorative coatings, it is essential that polymerisation results from the condensation reaction rather than crosslinking of polymer chains. The product's acid value is measured to show that the polymerisation results from the condensation reaction.

Viscosity is also measured to track both the degree and rate of polymerisation.

Prior to a review, the control chart was as shown in Figure 4.3, with only viscosity measured. With accurate charging and allowing for the fact that soya bean oil is a natural product, there should not be a significant variation from batch to batch in terms of what should be expected.

Data from previous batches was collated, and Figure 4.4 was produced showing that the viscosity measurements were expected to be within minimum and maximum limits and that anything outside these limits could point to a problem.

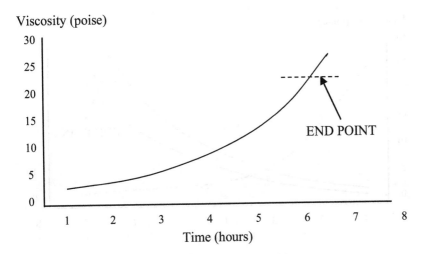

Figure 4.3 Viscosity/time control chart.

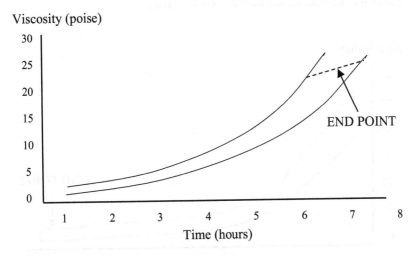

Figure 4.4 Modified viscosity/time control chart.

After appreciating that polymerisation needs to be achieved through the condensation reaction, an acid value test was introduced and added to the control chart, as shown in Figure 4.5.

The measurement of both viscosity and acid value were clear indicators of the progress of the polymerisation process. It was also evident that the two were in fact correlated. This led to the introduction of the control chart shown in Figure 4.6 and a move away from the reaction 'end point'

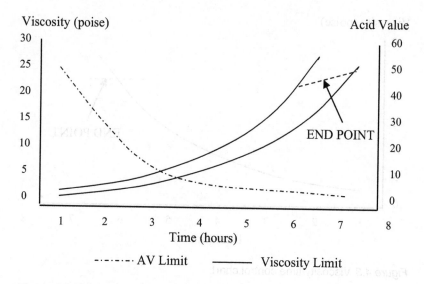

Figure 4.5 Viscosity/acid value/time control chart.

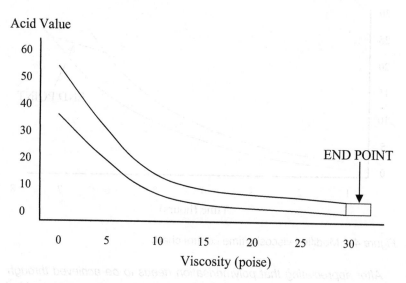

Figure 4.6 Viscosity/acid value control chart.

being entirely based on viscosity. This heralded a new approach in the organisation to the control of condensation reactions, with the 'end-point box' representing a much more appropriate target.

Whilst time mattered, the use of a viscosity/acid value control chart became more important and useful, as it gave a clear indication of any problems and at a much earlier stage.

Outcome

At the outset, the RFT percentage was around 95% and the process time varied between 16 and 22 hours.

After the control chart shown in Figure 4.6 was introduced, RFT reached 100% and process time variation was reduced to between 15.5 and 16.5 hours.

The move from the control chart in Figure 4.3 to the control chart in Figure 4.6 demonstrated the value of gathering data such that a better insight into the state of the reaction at any one time was developed. Having such an in-depth understanding and approaching control in this way meant that consistent run times and product quality were a natural outcome. Having complete control of the process meant that deviations could be identified early. Spotting deviations early means that intervention will be much more effective and much more likely to deliver a successful outcome.

Case Study 4.5 shows how important it is to have process documentation that describes exactly what is required and exactly how the process should be controlled.

When new products are introduced, the onus is clearly on R&D to prepare process instructions, with Production providing guidance on any constraints that might apply. In order to bridge the scale-up gap, R&D need to understand precisely the factors that matter and how things will differ when manufacturing larger batches.

When new products are introduced, processing instructions need to incorporate best practice and, where Production has made improvements in the control of processes, such improvements should also be reflected in the control procedures used in the development laboratory.

It is, of course, essential for any new product introduction to involve both Production and R&D in the design of processing instructions. But it should not be the case that Production has one way of doing something and that R&D has another.

In order to reduce the risk of problems arising and substandard inventory being produced, it is vital that R&D completely understand the processing characteristics *before* the manufacture of the first batch.

Whether initial batches are supervised or monitored by R&D staff varies from organisation to organisation, but it should not be forgotten that when new BOM and processing instructions are designed R&D is making a prediction on how the process will perform and, unless scale-up aspects are properly understood, risks will exist.

Generally, monitoring and reviewing production of well-established products falls within Production's responsibilities. New products, however, are dependent on R&D, and those new products involving new processes have a greater risk of something going wrong.

Reducing risk is vital and having a consistent method of controlling processes is vital. This is why it is important for Production and R&D to work closely together.

Case Study 4.6 gives an example of an assumption being made by R&D that caused a problem in several production batches before it was resolved.

Case Study 4.6   Antioxidant addition

Background

An organisation was charged with developing a product for use in cellular foam production. With the colour of the product being a critical parameter, an antioxidant was incorporated into the BOM.

The process instructions were typical for products of this type, with the reaction being carried out at a temperature in excess of 200°C.

First manufacture

Having been produced satisfactorily in the laboratory, and as the organisation had long experience of producing similar products; the scale-up was from around 5 kilos to 16,000 kilos.

First production batches were, at first glance, within specification; however, it was noticed that there were black specks in the product. This resulted in the customer refusing to accept the first deliveries. The seemingly small problem had affected nearly 80,000 kilos of product.

Having not been able to resolve the problem, manufacture of the product was abandoned.

Second attempt

A few years later another opportunity presented itself to supply the customer concerned. On this occasion, a project team was established to review the opportunity and see if the 'black speck' problem could be resolved.

In order to try and establish the cause of the problem, every aspect of the process was reviewed, including a detailed review of raw material used in the process.

Close examination of the technical data sheet for the antioxidant being used showed that there were recommendations on the conditions under which the antioxidant should be added – it should not be added above 80°C in acidic conditions. Above this temperature and in acidic conditions, the antioxidant would degrade (causing black specks).

A review of the existing process instructions showed that the antioxidant was to be added along with other items at the beginning of the process and that the mix should be raised to a temperature in excess of 200°C. One of the ingredients in the polyester was adipic acid.

Having identified the issue with the antioxidant, the BOM sequence was altered to have it added as the final item. The processing instructions were changed so that, having completed the main reaction, the product was cooled to 80°C before the antioxidant was added.

Outcome

Adopting the modified raw material sequence and new processing instructions immediately eliminated the 'black speck' problem.

The benefits of attention to detail are perhaps never as apparent as they are in production. Quarantine (un-saleable) inventory cannot be ignored, and resolving such problems is time-consuming and carries a potentially significant cost.

Adopting methods that focus on accurate charging of raw materials and improved process control will reduce the number of production failures. This, in turn, will lead to a reduction in the level of quarantine and unwanted inventory.

Improved performance also reduces the amount of time and resource needed to resolve problems and, at the same time, reduces production cost and increases capacity. If you are not producing un-saleable inventory, then you are producing added-value inventory.

Case Studies 4.5 and 4.6 illustrate how gathering data leads to a better understanding, and improved control of processes which, in turn, will lead to fewer inventory issues.

Conversion process

It is often the case when organisations have problems with products that the finger of blame is pointed at the raw materials. Many suppliers will be able to recall instances where they have been summoned by an organisation to explain the problem with a raw material, when in truth over 99% of production problems will be due to the process.

Recognising that this is the case is the first step in bringing about sustainable improvement in any production department's RFT performance.

Having worked on the 'preparation' areas (BOM, vessels and manpower) attention has to be focussed on process control. It goes without saying that all conversion processes require process instructions, control methods and plant operators who are capable of carrying out the required activities with precision.

In the first instance, plant operators will be presented with process instructions with which they may or may not be familiar. Either way, familiarity should not be assumed. Each product scheduled for manufacture should be treated as a project and those involved briefed accordingly.

There will likely be several parameters that have to be controlled during the conversion process. These will range from temperature to flow-rates, pressure, and mixing rates etc.

Processing instructions should specify each of the critical control parameters with the levels to which they should be set and how they need to vary. This is a prerequisite that will enable production to execute the process correctly. What is effectively being produced is a sequence of activities (similar to the activity sequence in Appendix 6) and, indeed, some process instructions will be written in this way.

If we take a step back, we can see that what we have is a project plan – albeit smaller than might be expected with a bona-fide project. However, a project is what it really is, and therefore it should be treated as such. If project management principles are applied to this scenario, we can more clearly see that every operator has to clearly understand their role, every task understood, responsibilities clearly defined and that tasks will be expected to be completed by a particular time.

Of course, when there are multiple batches or production runs of the same product, the tasks may well be part of a repeating pattern.

Where different products are manufactured on the same line or different vessel (as in Figures 3.11 and 3.12 and Appendix 6), the repeating pattern will be replaced by, potentially, an ever-changing sequence of tasks.

The repeating pattern has a number of benefits, some of which were touched on in the chapter on planning. An irregular pattern with a number of different types of tasks is inevitably going to introduce scenarios that carry with them a greater risk of errors.

Mitigating some of the risks can be achieved by optimising the production plan (Figures 3.11 and 3.12). However, some changes cannot be avoided. It is therefore essential that they are recognised, and that staff prepare for them. Team briefings are the means to go through the production plan in detail, highlighting new features, critical milestones and key challenges.

Appendix 7 shows an example of a planning meeting template. This is just an example, but it illustrates the types of points that need to be communicated, with a focus on highlighting areas of potential risk.

When companies operate 24 hours a day, manpower will be organised into shifts. When processes or production lines are continuing to operate, a structured approach to shift handover needs to be in place. The shift changeover is an opportunity to remind operatives of the new features, critical milestones and key challenges, in addition to an update on the state of progress against the production plan. An oncoming shift represents a significant change, and the importance of maintaining effective communication cannot be overstated.

Appendix 8 is an example of what a shift handover form might look like. In addition to communicating progress against the plan, it is an opportunity to reiterate the need to pay attention to detail.

The assumption is that critical process parameters will be maintained at the prescribed level without variation. However, the vagaries of the production process, environment and the degree to which control can be exercised sometimes means that some variation is inevitable.

Case Studies 4.1 and 4.5 are two very different types of polymerisation reactions and illustrate the challenge faced with monitoring some types of reactions. The condensation reaction in Case Study 4.5 is relatively straightforward, as the reaction can be monitored in two ways – acid value and viscosity. Emulsion manufacture (Case Study 4.1), on the other hand, is very difficult to monitor. Indeed, in my experience (albeit in the 1970s and 1980s), there was no test available to track the polymerisation process. All you could do was ensure that the monomer and associated initiator were being added at the prescribed rate. Emulsion manufacture is a process where the charging of raw materials has to be absolutely accurate and process instructions have to be followed precisely.

If complete control has not been achieved un-saleable inventory might be created. In such instances, many organisations will have charged specific individuals with the responsibility for resolving those issues. In the chemical industry this might be a production chemist.

Access to the production chemist will be fairly straightforward during normal working hours, but outside those hours the production chemist might be on-call. Outside normal working hours, access might be erratic and could result in delays in dealing with a problem.

In addition to refining process control documentation and creating a structure to communicate the plan (Appendices 7 and 8), it can be useful to create a troubleshooting document. Such a document offers the opportunity for plant operators to take immediate action to resolve a problem. As has already been said, the earlier that action is taken, the more likely it is that there will be a successful outcome.

(*Author's note: As a young production chemist I was on-call 24 hours a day, Monday to Friday. Obviously, I had no desire to be woken up at 1 o'clock in the morning to deal with a production problem. I therefore set out to improve process control and create a troubleshooting document that enabled production staff to deal with issues within specific parameters. Over time, improvements were made such that I could confidently sleep uninterrupted!)*

Some organisations are reluctant to consider the use of troubleshooting forms citing that they need someone with appropriate technical expertise to give advice. Clearly there is a knowledge gap between production operators and technical staff, but a troubleshooting document is a means of helping to bridge the knowledge gap and enable action to be taken earlier than it otherwise would be.

When committing to creating a troubleshooting document, an organisation will often find that its understanding of a process is much improved. Whilst limits can be established that determine whether the operator can act or needs to refer to technical experts, considerable time is saved, and outcomes are improved. Indeed, a consequence of developing a troubleshooting document is that the number of problems is reduced.

Nowadays, you do not have to look far for evidence of the time saved, with people often resorting to 'Google' to try and resolve a problem before they resort to a technical expert.

Of course, the production process is the perfect illustration of a control loop (Figure 1.7). Some of the types of elements are illustrated below:

- *Inputs*
  BOM, vessel/production line, manpower, process control instructions, temperature, flow rate, pressure, agitation speed etc.
- *Process*
  The conversion process/chemical reaction
- *Outputs*
  The status of the reaction/production run at any one point in time
- *Feedback*
  In-process test results
- *Target*
  In-process control charts, final product specification
- *Modify*
  Temperature, flow rate, raw materials, pressure etc.

An understanding of the way control can be exercised by varying one or more of these controls is a necessity if the desired outcome is to be delivered.

Dealing with problems

Aside from dealing with problems as they arise, organisations are likely to have records and results from production runs or batches going back a considerable time. Rather than waiting for problems to arise, one option is to review past production and look to spot trends and resolve persistent problems.

When faced with many tens, if not hundreds, of products it might be difficult to know where to start. Of course, a product or group of products could be picked at random. However, linking the selection to the product portfolio in a more structured way would link the approach to the organisation's strategy.

Figure 3.2 showed that all products have a life cycle, with price often decreasing as the product moves to maturity and decline. Under normal operating conditions, it might be expected that the level of production failures for any single product will be at their highest when the product is first introduced, with a reduction likely over time – hopefully to zero. Figure 4.7 illustrates how the rate of production failures might fall as the product matures. By the time a product reaches maturity and decline, problems should have been ironed out, with yields at their maximum and process costs at the lowest.

Alternatively, another approach is to select those products that have the lowest RFT percentages. Within this category, it is, again, a case of determining which criteria to apply – those products of strategic importance or those products in the maturity/decline phase that do not have 100% RFT.

The ideal scenario is to resolve the problems during the introduction phase. Whichever method is adopted, the important thing is to make a start, and if a structured approach has been used to make the selection, all the better.

As an example, a tool that could also be used to make the selection would be the growth share matrix as developed by Bruce Henderson in 1970 for the Boston Consulting Group, better known as the 'Boston box'.

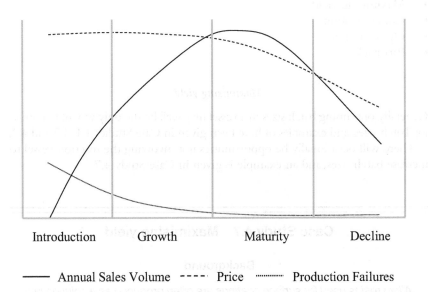

| Introduction | Growth | Maturity | Decline |

——— Annual Sales Volume ---- Price ·········· Production Failures

Figure 4.7 Product life cycle, price profile and production failures.

This tool is designed to help an organisation understand where its products sit within their markets and aid in the development of strategies.

Using this tool, an option might be to focus on 'cash cows' and/or 'stars'. There will be good reasons to focus on both, but either way, the important thing is to make a choice.

Whichever tool or approach is used to make the selection, both provide a connection to the organisation's strategy and logic for the selection.

Each improvement will build a better understanding of the processing of products. As each product is dealt with, there will be a small incremental improvement in RFT performance. As greater understanding develops, it will also become possible to extend improvements across product groups, thereby accelerating the positive changes in RFT.

Delivery

The final part of the production process is putting the product into the appropriate packaging. Boxes may be more of a feature in engineering and retail industries, but in the chemical industry bottles, 25-litre kegs, 25-kilo sacks, 200-litre drums, 1000-litre intermediate bulk containers (totes), 1000-kilo sacks and bulk storage tanks are more common.

From an inventory perspective, there might not seem to be much that needs to be done. However, there are clear opportunities to influence inventory in a positive way:

- Maximising yield
- Contamination
- Optimal filling
- Part packs

Maximising yield

Generally, optimising batch sizes in a vessel may well be the only way of maximising batch sizes, and examples of have been given in Case Studies 4.1, 4.2 and 4.3.

There will occasionally be opportunities not involving the reaction vessel to increase batch sizes, and an example is given in Case Study 4.7.

Case Study 4.7   Maximising yield

Background

Alkyd resins used for surface coatings are often produced as a solution in a solvent (e.g. white spirit, xylene). The contents of a reactor vessel, once the conversion process has been completed, will be transferred into a blending tank that will have been pre-charged with a specific quantity of solvent.

When in the blending tank, adjustments would be made in order to bring the product's viscosity within the product specification.

The procedure when making viscosity adjustments was to take a sample, measure the viscosity and add some solvent. This would be repeated until the product was within specification.

With the practice of needing to make several adjustments in order to bring a product to its viscosity specification, the tendency was to produce product at the top end of the viscosity specification. A further aspect was that the product had a solids content specification (e.g. 64–66%), and that this practice would tend to produce product at between 65% and 66%.

Review

Plotting the viscosity and analysing historical batch records, there was a clear grouping of products, as illustrated in Figure 4.8.

From a specification perspective, this distribution is perfectly OK. However, a product at a viscosity of 8.5 poise and 65.5% solids would still be within specification at a viscosity of 7.3 poise and 64.3% solids. The only difference is the quantity of solvent. In other words, adding more solvent would still produce a product within specification, but the yield would be bigger.

What is also clear is that there is a relationship between viscosity and solids content, and that this could be easily established.

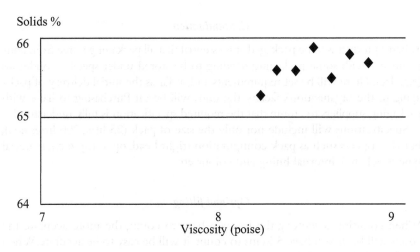

Figure 4.8 Scatter plot for viscosity/solids.

An exercise was therefore undertaken to confirm the viscosity/solids relationship for every product. This resulted in new instructions being issued where, rather than several adjustments being required, a predetermined quantity was calculated related to the viscosity of the first sample. Whilst the products were still within specification, the yields were suddenly increased by around 1%.

Outcome

Whilst 1% does not seem very much, for the main product that the organisation manufactured, yields were increased by 160 kilos per batch. Five batches per week equated to 800 kilos. From a value perspective, solvent at 20 pence per kilo was instantly converted into product at 65 pence per kilo at no extra cost or investment.

The outcome for the single product in Case Study 4.7 equated to an annual profit of £18,000 and, more importantly, would be consistently achieved every year – a good example of sustainable improvement.

Whilst this example is very specific and not many chemical companies will manufacture products in this way, it does serve to illustrate that opportunities will be available at every stage of a process.

From an inventory perspective, increasing yields in this way helps to accommodate growth without incurring any expense.

Contamination

When a product is to be packaged, it is essential that all packaging is free from contaminants, with some packaging needing to be stored under specific conditions (e.g. dry). There will be set requirements and, as far as the initial delivery of packaging to the organisation's facility, the onus will be on Purchasing to liaise with packaging suppliers to ensure that the required specification is fully understood.

Specifications will include not only the size of pack (25 litre, 200 litres etc.), but also aspects such as pack configuration (tight head, open top etc.), material type (steel etc.), internal lining and colour etc.

Optimal filling

When counting inventory, the less you have to count, the more accurate the count will be. If you have 5 items to count, it will be easy to be accurate. When you have 500 items, it is not quite as easy.

Anything that helps to reduce the number of items to be counted will help make inventory management a little easier.

Some chemical companies tend to have a standard approach to the filling of packages. Taking a 200-litre drum for example, products might be filled to 200 kilos as a matter of routine. New products will be set up to be sold in drums containing 200 kilos because that is what the organisation has always done.

At the time of writing, some online retailers have a less than glowing reputation for matching content with packaging. Their systems seem designed to over-compensate, and many users will have examples of inappropriate packaging (much larger than required for the item(s) ordered).

In the chemical industry, the challenges are less complex, and yet some organisations still fail to appreciate that there are mismatches between contents and drum capacities. For example, a typical drum will have a nominal capacity of 200 litres, but, taking account of the manufacturer's drum dimensions, the true volume can be anything up to 218 litres.

Organisations will, however, always look to fill to 200 litres, and those that produce by volume will probably be filling to this level for each of their products. The situation becomes clouded by the fact that many organisations will produce and sell by weight.

Over time, many organisations fail to account for the variation in the densities of their product range and consequently fail to fill drums optimally.

Case Study 4.8 illustrates an instance where variable densities were recognised and acted upon.

Case Study 4.8   Density and drum filling

Background

An organisation manufactured a range of products that were supplied to customers in four main types of package:

25-litre kegs
200-litre drums
1000-litre intermediate bulk containers (IBCs or totes)
Bulk tanker

Over time, the packaging had become standardised at 25 kilos for a 25-litre pack, 200 kilos for the 200-litre drum and 1000 kilos for the IBC.

Amongst the many products the organisation produced was one (Product A) that was filled to 200 kilos. This product had a density at 25°C of between 1.19 and 1.21.

Review

A supply chain specialist, having become aware of the variation in density from one product to another, pondered the question as to why most products were filled to standard quantities but a couple of products were filled to 230 kilos in the standard 200-litre drum.

Focussing on Product A, the specialist made a simple calculation which showed that, by volume, 200 litres of the product concerned would weigh 240 kilos.

The specialist knew that the product was filled into drums at or around room temperature (which meant that there was no expansion to take account of) and that production did not have any reason for limiting the fill to 200 kilos.

Given that there seemed to be no real reason for having selected 200 kilos, other than 'that's the way it's always been done', the specialist undertook to introduce a new item with Product A being filled to 240 kilos in a 200-litre drum.

Having carried out the relevant filling tests, the new pack size was introduced. It was a complete success.

Outcome

The success of this approach was reflected throughout the product range with many new pack sizes being introduced. From a financial perspective, there was a reduction in the amount of packaging purchased, equating to saving around £50,000 per annum. Whilst this was a significant benefit, there were many others:

- *Vessel capacity*
  Applying the same logic to vessel capacity saw some batch sizes being increased by 25%, with a consequent reduction in product cost.
- *Shipping costs*
  Generally, full shipments were determined more on the basis of the number of drums a vehicle could handle, rather than by any weight limit. This meant that a shipment of 80 drums (16,000 kilos) was increased to 19,200 kilos. This led to a reduction in shipping cost.
- *Drum storage*
  Being able to store more of a product in a drum meant effective storage capacity by weight was increased.

There were other benefits, but the impact, having incurred no additional cost, was not only significant but also sustainable.

The overall impact on inventory of the action undertaken in Case Study 4.8 was threefold:

- Whilst vessel capacity was increased, the number of packs to be filled for the same quantity of product was reduced. This would slightly lower the risk of a pack filling error, which might add to un-saleable inventory.
- Albeit a slight reduction, having fewer packs to count during a stock count inevitably leads to improved accuracy.
- For the same quantity, less space was taken up in the product warehouse, which makes management of that stock a little simpler.

It can be easy to question the inclusion of aspects like this and their less obvious connection to inventory management. However, as stated at the outset, bringing about sustainable improvement is about attention to detail – and this means detail in all its forms.

One interesting point arose following the actions taken in Case Study 4.8. The specialist decided to share his findings with two of the organisation's suppliers, as both were supplying similar products. Interestingly, one supplier implemented a change almost immediately whilst the second supplier seemed reluctant to act. You might well ask 'Why? Isn't it obvious?', but the second supplier showed that resistance to change can manifest itself in surprising ways.

Part packs

In the chemical industry, the supply of product in drums or similar package is commonplace. Equally commonplace will be the manufacture of those products in vessels designed to produce specific volumes.

The vagaries of batch manufacture and the slight variations that arise usually mean that it is extremely unlikely when scheduling to produce 5000 kilos, that exactly 5000 kilos will be produced.

If packed into drums each containing 200 kilos, the outcome will be 24 drums each containing 200 kilos and 1 drum containing less than 200 kilos – a part pack.

For an organisation with products manufactured in vessels (of whatever size), the manufacture of part packs is something that can prove difficult to avoid.

Add to this the problem of dealing with the part pack and forgetting to take any opportunity to recover the part, or that the product concerned is not manufactured very frequently, part packs can become a problem that spirals out of control, with the consequential adverse impact on inventory.

Methods of dealing with part packs will fall into one of four types.

- Disposal
- Sell
- Recover/re-blend
- Eliminate/reduce

Disposal

If there is pressure on space and relative lack of progress, then disposal can be the quickest and easiest option. Of course, this has a cost and is in addition to product cost. Whilst not being part of physical inventory, it is part of the overall cost of inventory management and cannot be ignored.

Sell

Selling part packs is an obvious thing to do, but this might not as easy as it sounds. Sales might not welcome this, as it might be perceived that the organisation was selling some form of sub-standard product.

Whilst this might not be the case, perceptions are difficult things to change.

As is often the case, there is no single solution to the problem, but there might be a combination of approaches, such as:

- When a customer purchases a single batch of product, and it is only manufactured for them, the original quote should be for the supply of the whole batch, including the part pack.
- Some customers might be happy to work with the organisation and take part packs on a regular basis. Given that the disposal option carries a cost, it might even be useful to offer incentives such as a price discount.
- Where a product is sold in drums containing 200 kilos it is usually easier to sell a large part pack (e.g. > 150 kilos) than it is a small one (e.g. < 50 kilos). If a part cannot be avoided, the batch yield should be adjusted to ensure that a large part pack is created. This approach can sometimes mean reducing the batch yield slightly, but from a cost perspective this can be a beneficial change.

What should also be remembered is that selling any part pack means that it will not require further handling within the organisation. Whilst it might not be possible to sell the part for every product type manufactured, progress can be made.

Recover/re-blend

Adding a part pack from a previous batch into a subsequent batch is a way of ensuring that value can be maximised for the part. Re-blending, however, might not be the simplest of processes. It might not be possible to re-use the original pack, the residue in the pack will effectively be lost and/or the part might need to be heated in order to remove the product easily from the drum.

It will also distract production staff from the main task of manufacturing product.

Whilst only a slight change to the standard process, it does introduce a risk that can lead to the whole production batch being classed as un-saleable. When looking to pay attention to detail, the introduction of any non-standard step will lead to an increased risk, however small, and this is something to be avoided.

Eliminate/reduce

The goal with any recurring issue is to prevent it from happening again. This should obviously be the goal with part packs. If elimination is the objective, then the focus is on accuracy, and this means, for example, a production run designed to deliver 5000 kilos should deliver exactly that – nothing more and nothing less. Batch production in a vessel is unlikely to deliver such a level of accuracy.

When the production sequence is changing from one product to another it is almost inevitable that a part pack will be produced. Case Study 4.9 gives an example (based on actual events) of an approach taken to significantly reduce the level of product ending up as a part pack.

Case Study 4.9   Part pack reduction

Background

An organisation manufactured product in batches and packed the products mainly into combinations of 25-litre kegs and 200-litre drums. Product A was manufactured in batches of 5000 kilos with six batches being made each month. The pattern of demand was such that five of the batches were scheduled to produce drums containing 200 kilos and the remaining batch kegs containing 25 kilos.

Each month would see five drums containing less than 200 kilos (averaging 175 kilos) and one keg containing less than 25 kilos (averaging 20 kilos).

Whilst some was recovered, over 12 months around 40 drums and nine kegs were added to un-saleable inventory.

Review

As with any problem, the first and arguably the most important step is to define the problem. For part packs, the initial problem was defined as reducing the number of part packs. This almost immediately made people think in terms of yields, accurate charging and possible equipment modification.

As data was gathered, it became clear that, if there was no action, around 11,000 kilos of Product A would end up in part packs in a 12-month period. The question was asked – 'How can we reduce this figure?'. From this point, the problem was redefined as 'How can we reduce the quantity of Product A that ends up in part packs?'.

Having redefined the problem, other options came to the fore. Knowing that six batches were manufactured each month (split between drums of 200 kilos and kegs of 25 kilos). The suggestion was made and adopted to think in terms of having each batch of 5000 kilos producing both 200-kilo drums and 25-kilo kegs. In other words, on completion, 21 drums would be filled off, followed by the remainder being packed in 25 litre kegs. This meant that if there was a part pack, it would always be one in a 25-litre keg.

Outcome

At the outset, the quantity of Product A that ended up in part packs equated to around 2.98% of production. Implementing the proposal of splitting the fill for each batch between both drums and kegs, reduced this figure to 0.4%

When six batches could be sequenced, it was possible to avoid creating a part pack for each batch and that only one would be produced – equivalent to 0.07%.

In quantity terms this meant that around 11,000 kilos contained in part packs dropped to between 240 and 1440 kilos.

Case Study 4.9, whilst only applicable to a small number of frequently made products, showed both what could be achieved and how useful redefining a problem can be.

Changeover

Changeover is an activity that takes place when one production run or batch has been completed and preparation needs to be made for the next run or batch.

When the next batch is of the same type as the one that has just finished, the changeover will probably be minimal.

When the next product is different the changeover will be more complex. The complexity will vary according to the nature of the products being manufactured. For example, when products are pigmented, a vessel will need to be cleaned. This is to avoid the first product contaminating the second product and affecting the colour. The colour difference can determine the type of changeover with, for example, moving from a blue product to a purple one might not require the same type of changeover as moving from a black product to white one.

Such differences will affect not only the cost, but also the time taken. This is important information for the Planning function, as this will determine what can be achieved during a normal production week.

Whilst the materials used in the changeover process will often be classed as consumable items, there will be occasions when inventory items will be used. It is therefore important to control the changeover process and to treat it in the same way that a product would be:

- There will be a material requirement (be that raw materials or equipment or other type of material).
- It will require resource (manpower, equipment).
- There will be an output that will require an action (storage, treatment or disposal) both in terms of quantity and type.
- It will take time.
- There will be a method.

These are all characteristics of product manufacture and a changeover should, accordingly, be dealt with in the same way, including having appropriate documentation.

Measures

Paying attention to detail does place an onus on an organisation or function to design measures that focus on an earlier stage in the overall process

Measurement will play a key part in bringing about control of the various input elements. Therefore, in addition to the usual production measures such as yields, plan adherence and RFT percentage, other measures that monitor performance earlier in the process should be in place. Examples of such measures and controls include:

- Team briefing records
- Accreditation records of process operators
- Charts displaying planned and actual training events
- Structured forms for shift handover
- Control charts designed to give an early indication of any problem

Summary

With responsibility for the conversion of raw materials into product, Production has one of the most significant parts to play in inventory management. When things go wrong, it is often visible to the whole organisation, with an impact ranging from failure to fulfil a customer's order, having to reschedule the production plan through to having to explain the increase in stock provision.

Reflecting these responsibilities, performance will typically be measured on the basis of what has been achieved – RFT percent, adherence to plan, yields and capacity utilisation.

Every organisation will want production to run 'perfectly' which means getting it not just 'right first time' but 'right first time, every time'. Striving for perfection is a challenge, but one aspect that helps work towards this goal is paying attention to detail.

Paying attention to detail means making sure that all the inputs are under control. Many inputs have been addressed in this chapter, and Figure 4.9 shows how they fit into the typical flow of events in the production process.

Any action that improves the production process will have a direct and beneficial impact on inventory – reducing un-saleable product and increasing capacity, thereby either helping production scheduling, accommodating growth or both.

When problems arise, the natural reaction of many organisations is to assume there is a problem with the raw material, whereas in the majority of cases it is a problem with the process. Whilst the knee-jerk reaction is to summons the supplier to chastise them, suppliers should be involved and engaged in solving the problem as they can bring their expertise and can often be viewed as a free resource.

Actions

Production is a challenging area to address. It is important to appreciate that there will not be any magic bullet or overnight success. Improvements will take

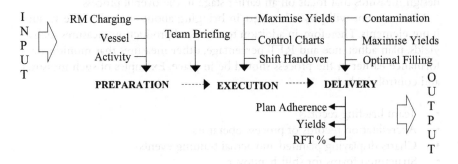

Figure 4.9 Production process: inputs and outputs.

time, and having data will be key to making progress. Some examples of actions are to:

- Create an activity sequence so that everyone knows what needs to be done and when it needs to be done by. Creating a sequence will show up any manpower availability issues. Anticipating such issues enables Production and/or Planning, to resolve the problem in a measured and constructive way. This is a proactive process and ensures that decisions are measured rather than reacting to events that have already occurred.
- Create a template agenda/checklist for a planning meeting. Communication is one of the key methods of paying attention to detail. With any organisation, a team will likely be involved in all production processes, and everyone needs to be part of the process.
- Create a standard shift handover form. Again, this is a key part of the communication process.
- Create a troubleshooting document. It can take many forms, but the basic format is – 'If this, do that'. Many household instruction manuals will have troubleshooting sections to enable the user to deal with some of the more common problems. There is no reason why this approach cannot be adopted in the production environment. It is also a useful way of helping to bridge the knowledge gap between technical experts and plant operators.
- Review vessel capacities in order to identify opportunities to increase batch sizes.
- Review pack fill weights in order to maximise the fill quantities.
- Where applicable, set up systems for dealing with part packs.

Reference

Henderson, B. (1970). *The product portfolio*. Boston: The Boston Consulting Group.

5

DISPATCH

Inventory, specifically product inventory, is something that Dispatch manages on a daily basis.

The main activities of the dispatch process are shown in Figure 5.1.

The essence of the process is quite straightforward and might only vary if there is more than one type of method being used to store and ship product to customers. For example, an organisation might ship product to customers in the form of packages or in bulk. The differences in activity flows between these methods are shown in Figures 5.2 and 5.3.

Whilst they differ, the issues related to the processes are the same and can lead to inventory being adversely affected. For Dispatch, two issues to focus on are accuracy and damage.

Accuracy

Accuracy issues, especially for products being shipped by pack, come in two forms – making accurate selection(s) of product and accurate recording of transactions.

Customer orders when due for dispatch will trigger the creation of selection lists. These will detail the products, quantities, the lot numbers to be compiled in order to fulfil the order and any special instructions or requirements that need to be taken account of.

Storing multiple products, especially in similar pack types and multiple lots for the products themselves, increases the risk of errors being made.

Some errors will be picked up on by the customer when they do not receive what they expected. In these instances, there may well be a cost associated with correcting the error, for example, collecting an incorrect product from the customer and delivering the correct product(s). The inventory will be corrected, but there will have been a period of time (days, weeks or longer) where the inventory will be incorrect. If, however, the error relates to the lot number(s), this error might not be picked up until a stock count is undertaken, or when staff go looking for a lot number that is no longer available.

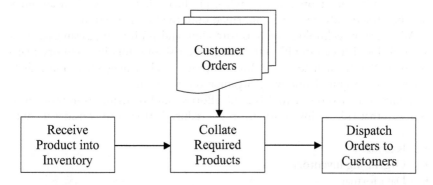

Figure 5.1 Dispatch process.

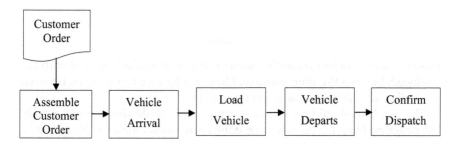

Figure 5.2 Order fulfilment for product stored and shipped in packs.

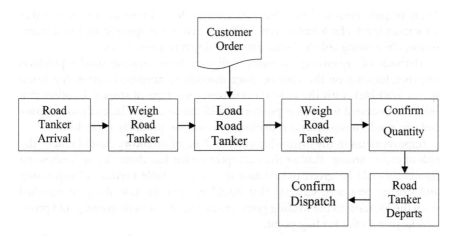

Figure 5.3 Order Fulfilment for product stored and shipped in bulk.

Lot numbering errors can arise when product is being 'picked' for an order, or when the details are being confirmed onto the business system.

Advances in technology, such as barcoding and RFID tags, mean that tools are available that can significantly reduce the risk of errors in inventory management. Whilst such tools can both improve stock management and reduce the resource required, not every organisation uses them.

Whichever method or tool is used, effort should be made to improve processes so that risks of inventory errors are reduced. Aspects to consider include:

- Resource
- Organising inventory
- Data format
- Data processing
- Briefing
- Plan review

Resource

Resource does not just mean the number of people available to deal with the workload, but also the time available. There is a balance to be struck between assembling an order too slowly and too quickly.

The emphasis should not be on getting people to do things more quickly, but rather enabling the process to be done more easily. One example would be changing the warehouse layout.

Organising inventory

Many organisations will have business systems that support inventory stored at a location level. The location can refer to a general or specific area in a warehouse, often being able to locate products down to pallet level.

Methods of organising inventory will vary from locating similar products together, locating on the basis of usage through to random location (i.e. using spaces available), with the only criteria being the type of storage location that might be required for certain products (cold, warm etc.). A lack of process control can result in organisations drifting into storing products at random.

Improvements in the organising and handling of inventory should reduce the risk of errors arising. Rather than accepting what has always been done, some thought should be given to selecting the most suitable method of organising and storing products. Criteria that could be used include distance travelled from the location to the loading point or storing the most frequently sold products nearest to the loading point.

Case Study 5.1 gives a simple example of not only reducing the travel distance, but also eliminating a safety hazard.

Case Study 5.1   Loading hazard

Background

An organisation had grown over many years and had gotten into the habit of loading trailers with drums and pails on pallets in the location shown in Figure 5.4.

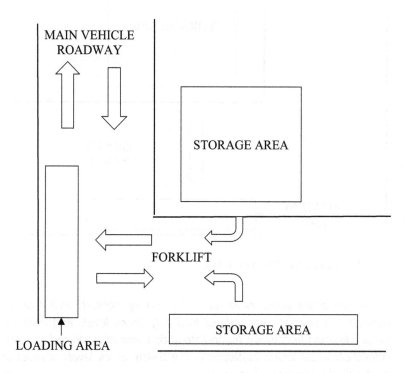

Figure 5.4 Loading area map.

Review

Aside from the travel distance from the two storage areas, there was a significant hazard, as the loading area was on the main roadway for vehicle delivering raw materials and the forklifts loading the trailer (in the loading area) crossed the roadway on a frequent basis.

When reviewing the area, it was evident that the need for storage area had resulted in a solution that had not been properly assessed for hazards.

However, with the levels of inventory that prevailed, a new configuration would prove problematic.

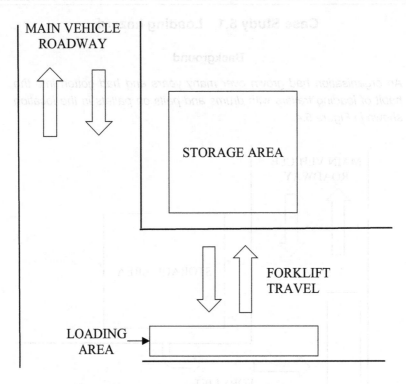

Figure 5.5 Revised Loading Area Map

A review of the products stored in the two highlighted storage areas showed that several were subject to Safety Stock levels that were no longer deemed necessary. Immediate action was taken to reduce, and indeed eliminate where appropriate, the Safety Stock levels of most of the products stored in these areas.

Very quickly the inventory levels reduced to the point where all of the inventory could be consolidated and stored in a single area. This allowed the loading area to be moved to the location shown in Figure 5.5.

Outcome

Having moved the loading area, the risk of a vehicle collision on the main roadway was eliminated, whilst the travel distance between the storage area and the loading area was halved, effectively reducing the time taken to load a trailer.

Relocating a loading area is not always an option for organisations, but Case Study 5.1 illustrates that there are many aspects that can be considered for change. The outcome might not have been significant in the scheme of things but, for the forklift driver, it reduced the number of distractions and this, in itself, helps to reduce the risk of damaging inventory or making a loading error.

Distractions can often lead to issues, in particular safety-related ones, and therefore need to be taken very seriously. Whilst safety was the focus in Case Study 5.1, the benefits were not limited to an improvement in safety.

Data format

One of the key connections between the business system and the dispatch process is the creation of selection lists, and subsequently, dispatch notes. These are the documents that display both what should be picked for an order and then precisely what is being shipped to the customer.

The documents will display details including:

- Customer name
- Customer address
- Customer delivery address
- Delivery required date
- Products required
- Quantities of each product
- Lot numbers required for each product.
- Any special instructions related to either the order or customer, or both.

The format of the document is important. It needs to clearly display all the requirements and display data in a format that is consistent and quick and easy to interpret.

Aspects of formatting that need to be considered are:

- Layout
- Font type
- Font size
- Document size
- Document colour
- Print colour

The emphasis is on clarity, and the ink type is just as important as the overall layout.

Selection lists, in particular, need to be documents that are easy to read and interpret.

Data processing

Any activity involving a keystroke or written note will always be open to the risk of an error being made. This applies to all areas of the organisation. In the sales order process shown in Figure 5.6, there are three points at which data transfer occurs, two of which occur during dispatch.

Assuming that the first data entry step is correct, attention needs to be given to selection list modification and business system update.

If we refer back to the control loop (Figure 1.7), in order to ensure that the output is correct either a step in the process needs to be automated or there has to be some form of validation.

Barcodes and RFID tags offer opportunities to automate parts of the data transfer activity and improve data transfer accuracy. However, not all organisations utilise these tools and alternative solutions are required for data validation.

Handwriting inevitably varies from individual to individual, and this can be problematic if the individual updating the business system is not the same one that added manual data onto the selection list.

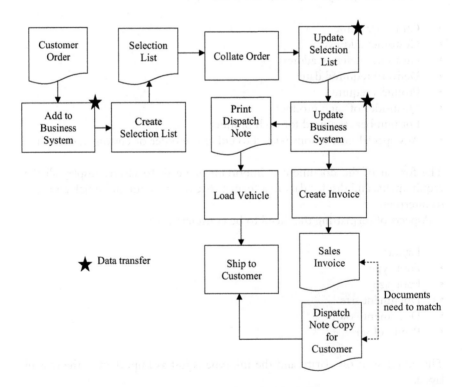

Figure 5.6 Sales order process (with data transfer points flagged).

Where manual data entry is common practice, rather than allowing complete freedom to add the data, selection lists should be designed in such a way as to bring some consistency in manual data entry.

When updating the business system, it is likely that lot numbers will be uniquely linked to a product or item code. This means that the combination needs to exist for data entry to be allowed. This will help minimise instances of data entry errors.

Using selection lists to 'pick' an order and updating the business system before creating the dispatch note carries a keystroke-error risk, but where changes are not required, a single keystroke might be all that will be required to confirm that all details are as printed on the selection list.

Any interaction with the business system has to be treated with the utmost care. It is likely that, at some stage, anyone carrying out such interactions will be subject to an interruption. Interruptions are a distraction, and distractions can lead to errors. Whilst particularly important to deal with when it comes to safety, recognising the part played by distractions (see Chapter 13) is equally important, as they can lead to data translation errors, thereby affecting inventory.

Briefing

When preparing for any activity, having a clear understanding of the task ahead is essential. Where Production has a production schedule (or plan), Dispatch should have a plan of daily or weekly shipments.

For any plan to be effective, the people involved need to prepare for the tasks that need to be carried out and deal with any nuances that might exist with certain shipments.

At the start of every day, the team need to be briefed on the workload and, in particular, on the specific challenges that might be faced. Rather than putting total reliance on individuals to pick up order-specific instructions, they need to be collated for the briefing so that everyone is aware and therefore prompted to pay attention. Other aspects will include circumstances where a product scheduled for selection might not be available until very shortly before dispatch.

For organisations that export products overland, amongst the many points that need to be attended to is appreciating that not every driver will speak their language. Rather than putting complete reliance on 'hoping for the best', an organisation can, for example, prepare a template of standard questions and instructions, and create copies in all the languages that dispatch is likely to encounter. An example is given in Appendix 11. Of course, this type of document can include a basic site map and can be tailored to deal with different types of loading (e.g. loading road-tankers).

Using such a document will help overcome language barriers encountered with some drivers, ensuring they understand health and safety instructions, and aid in the effective handling of the dispatch process.

Having such tools will improve communication, reduce confusion and avoid frustration – all of which can otherwise lead to mistakes.

Plan review

Similar to plan adherence in Production, Dispatch will have a prescribed schedule to ship each day. Having completed the data processing of each shipment, it should be possible to compare the expected shipment (down to lot number level) with the actual shipments.

Where there are differences, these need to be explained. Unless they are planned, differences can point to inventory issues that, if unresolved, will lead to further problems at a later date.

Whilst the number of shipments per day, for some organisations, can run into many hundreds, the important point is that only the differences need to be identified and investigated. There is no need to review each and every delivery. Indeed, an organisation might well be able to create a tool that would just list the differences.

This might well seem an onerous task, especially when introduced, but over time, a better understanding will develop of the causes of dispatch problems and improvements will be made.

An example of a report is given in Appendix 9. Reviewing dispatches within a day of dispatch is a way of not just addressing problems when they are fresh in people's minds, but also a way of being able to deal with any issues that are identified *before* the shipment arrives at the customer, and in particular *before* product is used by the customer.

When adopting this approach, it might well be the case that variances are down to previous errors that would not have shown up in a variance report. This does not detract from the value of the report, as it will likely identify discrepancies well before any stock count.

Where a briefing is held, having a review is a natural conclusion to the whole process.

Damage

Aside from having accurate management of the dispatch process, avoiding damage is also essential. Damage leads to loss of material, cleaning costs, not being able to ship a complete order and might even require an interruption to the production schedule to deal with any shortfall.

Damage to products in storage is not always accorded the importance that comes with a customer complaint or production failure. However, damage does represent a failure in the inventory management process and action should always be taken to address it. The causes are many and varied, and some of the typical ones include:

- Package not stored correctly
- Incorrect forks (on a forklift truck)
- Packs left in a hazardous area
- Forklift over-loaded
- Working conditions (slippery surfaces)
- Inappropriate use of forklift

There will no doubt be other causes, but the above are typical for many organisations. Whilst some might be put down to 'human error', and this is something that solutions rarely address successfully, it is more a case of not paying attention to detail. If the issues are approached from this perspective, some different solutions can present themselves.

An example is given in Case Study 5.2.

Case Study 5.2   Damaged drums

Background

An organisation manufactures product that is typically packed into drums. The drums are usually stored as four drums to a pallet.

The pallets are stored outside, with multiple pallets being stacked both on top of each other and columns in front of each other (as shown in Figure 5.7).

Review

Occasional damage occurred to drums in the middle and back of the 'pile'.

It was noted that there were occasions when forks of different lengths were attached to the forklift truck, and this meant that they were longer than the pallets being used. This resulted in them 'poking out' – see Figure 5.8.

When the longer forks were being used, drums directly behind the pallet being placed in position were open to damage. There was a reliance on the driver knowing that the forks were longer.

Having opted not to purchase a standard pallet for use in all storage areas, pallets of different sizes were used. This meant that, whilst most were of a standard size, some were bigger, and some were smaller. The standard and smaller-sized pallets did not pose any problem. However,

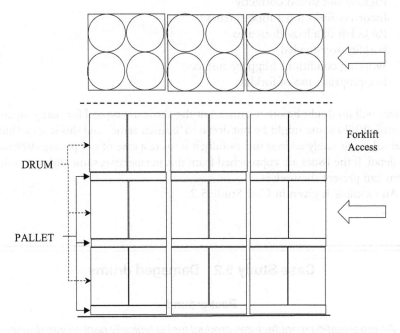

Figure 5.7 Drum storage layout.

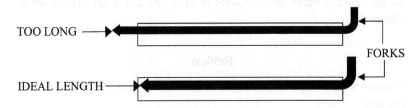

Figure 5.8 Fork lengths and position in pallets.

the larger pallets occasionally damaged the drums behind the pallet when being placed in position.

This problem was sometimes exacerbated when drums could not be tightly fit onto the pallet, as might be the case with open-top drums with ring closures. Whilst this was not generally a problem on-site, it did become a problem when these types of drums were being packed into a container for shipment by sea.

In order to address the problem three courses of action taken:

- *Training*
  Regular training reviews were introduced to ensure that forklifts were being driven and used correctly.
  In order to overcome the problems associated with different pallets, pallet recognition sessions were introduced, with regular reviews such that drivers would routinely identify larger pallets and deal with them in the appropriate manner.
- *Fitting of forks*
  The use and fitting of longer forks became the subject of a controlled process – one that required their immediate removal and replacement after each occasion of their use.
- *Loading pattern*
  The loading pattern for open-top drums was altered in order to reduce the risk of damage in-transit. The original and new loading patterns are shown in Figures 5.9 and 5.10.

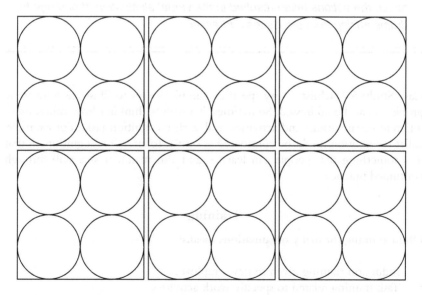

Figure 5.9 Original loading pattern.

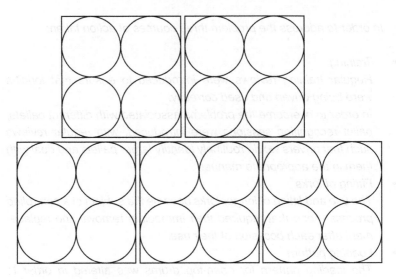

Figure 5.10 New loading pattern.

Outcome

Although slightly reducing the number of drums being shipped in a container, the actions taken resulted in the virtual elimination of damage to drums arising from the issues addressed.

Case Study 5.2, whilst a very specific example, serves to illustrate how some problems can be addressed. Sometimes, it involves thinking how other, quite different organisations and activities deal with recognition tasks. For example, pallet recognition might be considered as similar to aircraft recognition, in that it is something that people can learn – and also maintain as a skill through continued practice.

Training

Often, training for many organisations means:

- Induction training given to new employees
- Task training related to specific work activities
- Ad-hoc training, such as for health and safety or for new processes and procedures

Table 5.1 Examples of training and activity times (estimated).

Activity	Training Time	Activity Time	Training Type
Sales order entry	1 week	51 weeks	One-off
Forklift driving	2 days	51 weeks and 3 days	One-off
Cycling Grand Tours	40 weeks	9 weeks	Ongoing
100-metre sprint	50 weeks	6 minutes	Ongoing

- Development training where an employee is looking to transition to a role with greater responsibility

Each training type can be viewed as one-off, whether the training lasts a day, month or year etc. Whatever the circumstances the ratio of training to undertaking the particular activity is quite low.

It is useful to reflect on totally unrelated areas and how the 'training-to-activity' ratio varies as people strive to be the best. Table 5.1 gives some examples of time spent training, the type of training and time spent on an activity being trained for.

I should emphasise that these are just estimates to illustrate the scale. For example, an athlete might compete in around fifty 100-metre races over the course of a year. It might be more, it might be less, but point is the scale – all of the competitive races will not add up to days and weeks.

For those activities requiring peak performance and a high level of consistency, there is a much greater emphasis on training for the activity. Of course, companies are unlikely to want to move to such high 'training-to-activity' ratios, but adopting regular refresher training sessions can help improve, and maintain, performance levels.

Special conditions

Other aspects related to dispatch involve the storage and shipment of products under special conditions. Most common is a requirement for temperature control. This could range from storing products at very low or ambient temperatures through to storing and shipping at higher temperatures. An example would be shipping thixotropic alkyd resins in bulk which needs to be at between 60°C and 70°C.

Inventory needing to be stored and shipped under specific conditions needs to be dealt with very carefully. There will be an increased risk associated with the shipping stage as this will often be outside the organisation's direct control. Confidence has to be established and the organisation needs to consider how it would deal with issues that arise with products that arrive in poor condition.

Sometimes it is necessary to appreciate that risks cannot be completely mitigated, and those aspects with the greatest level of risk should be identified and plans put in place to deal with the issue should it ever occur.

Measures

As has already been said, paying attention to detail does place an onus on an organisation or function to design measures that focus on an earlier stage in the overall process

Measurement will play a key part in bringing about control of the various input elements. Therefore, in addition to the usual dispatch measures, schedule adherence, damaged packs, other measures and methods that help control performance at an earlier stage in the process should be in place. Examples include:

- Team briefing records.
- Accreditation of forklift operators
- Evidence of instructions in different languages

Summary

The shipment of product is the final stage of the organisation's inventory management process, and Dispatch has an important part to play. As the last main activity, dispatch errors happen at a stage when there is less time to respond, and the consequent risk of failing to fulfil a customer's order is very high. In addition, there could be consequences such as having to reschedule the production plan through to having to explain the increase in stock provision.

Reflecting these responsibilities, performance will typically be measured on the basis of what has been achieved – schedule adherence, damaged packs etc.

Every organisation will want the dispatch schedule to be completed without error. Striving for perfection is a challenge, and great strides towards this goal can be achieved by paying greater attention to detail. Ultimately, this means that an organisation will be making sure that all inputs are under control.

Many aspects and measures have been addressed in this chapter, and Figure 5.11 shows how they fit into the typical flow of events in the production process.

When a problem occurs during dispatch, it is all too easy to start pointing the finger at an individual or group of individuals, when, in all likelihood, it is a case of the organisation not having prepared well enough for the activity and not having a culture predicated on paying attention to detail.

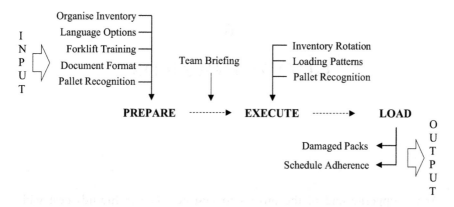

Figure 5.11 Dispatch Process

Actions

In keeping with the theme of paying attention to detail and focussing on inputs, the following actions are suggested for Dispatch:

- Check and modify selection lists notes to include a standard format for data entry. An example is given in Appendix 10. Whilst not completely eliminating errors, it does go some way to standardising the format, and this type of approach does tend to lead to fewer keystroke errors.
- Review the location system and give consideration to re-organising where necessary with a view to simplifying activities for Dispatch staff.
- Establish training routines that focus on particular aspects of the dispatch process, for example pallet recognition. Ensure that training records are maintained and reviewed.
- Set up daily briefing meetings with clear agendas.
- Create multi-language templates to deal with drivers who might not speak your language to ensure that key aspects of the collection process (including health and safety) are covered.
- Create a process to ensure that all selection list discrepancies are reviewed.

6

GOODS INWARDS

At the opposite end of the process to Dispatch, Goods Inwards deal with the receipt of all raw materials. Most deliveries will be required by Production, though there will be instances where the product is to be re-labelled for onward sale.

As with the dispatch process, the essence of the Goods Inwards process is quite straightforward and is illustrated in Figure 6.1.

For some organisations, the items being received will need to be handled in one of two ways. One will relate to deliveries of products in pack form (or on pallets), whilst the other will involve receiving product in bulk and discharging it into a storage tank. The outline processes for each are shown in Figures 6.2 and 6.3, respectively.

In both instances, details will be updated into the business system using data recorded on a Goods Received Note (GRN). This document will be used later to match the invoice received from the supplier.

Whilst the details are likely to perfectly match for packed items, there may well be some slight differences with deliveries of materials in bulk. For example, a GRN for a bulk delivery might indicate a delivery quantity of 23,040 kilos. If the organisation looks to validate this quantity by weighing the road-tanker before and after discharge, the received quantity might not precisely match the GRN.

In these instances, an organisation will usually have a tolerance outside which they will query the supplier's data. For example, a received quantity of 23,000 kilos (a variance of 40 kilos) might be acceptable, whereas a quantity of 23,140 kilos where the variance is 100 kilos will be flagged to the supplier

As with dispatch, though, whichever shipment type is being received, the main issues will be related to accuracy and material loss.

Accuracy

When deliveries arrive on site, there are two aspects to consider:

- Is the delivery as expected from the original purchase order?
- Has the business system been updated?

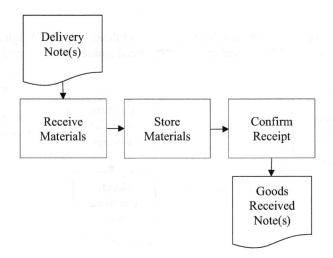

Figure 6.1 Goods Inwards (receiving) process.

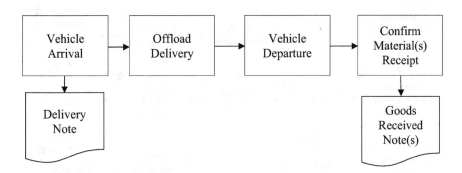

Figure 6.2 Goods receiving process for packed items.

In the first instance, it is necessary to know which deliveries are expected to arrive on a particular day or week. Purchase orders, as required by the production plan, will dictate what is expected to arrive. Where they are created in the business system, it should be possible to create a report that shows which deliveries are expected and when – in effect a Goods Inwards plan.

During the goods receiving process, there are several instances where data is used or transferred. Five such instances are marked with a star in Figure 6.4.

Each instance involving a keystroke is an opportunity for an error to occur and impact raw material inventory, as well as creating a potential mismatch between the GRN and the supplier's invoice.

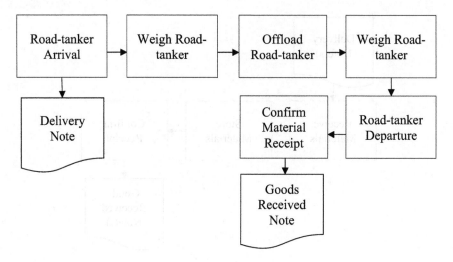

Figure 6.3 Goods receiving process for bulk items.

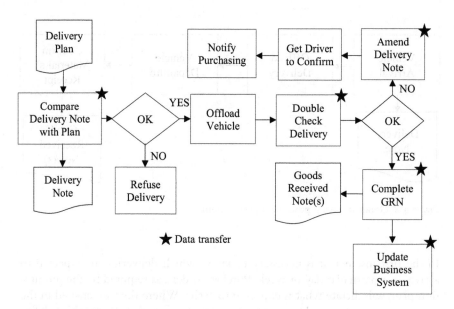

Figure 6.4 Goods receiving process.

All materials should be purchased against an agreed specification. In some instances, suppliers will agree to supply test data for the delivery, often referred to as a Certificate of Analysis (CoA).

Checking the CoA is either the responsibility of the Goods Inwards staff or the Quality Control department. There will be some instances where an organisation will commit to sample and test the material being delivered prior to offloading. There are no hard and fast rules regarding the need for sampling or submission of CoAs. Some industries are more rigorous than others in this regard. For many organisations it is more a question of trust and confidence in the supplier. Does the organisation trust the supplier to supply material within specification each and every time?

This will clearly depend on many factors, cost being one, but also the relationship that an organisation has with its suppliers.

Whichever approach an organisation chooses, there is clearly potential for an adverse impact on inventory, both from a raw material perspective and, more importantly, from a product perspective when things go wrong.

Case Study 6.1 provides an interesting example on what can go wrong and where the responsibilities lie.

Case Study 6.1   Out-of-specification raw material

Background

An organisation produced Product A which required substantial quantities of Raw Material A. To minimise cost, the organisation handled the product in bulk.

The supply of Raw Material A was subject to being within a predetermined specification. The agreement with each supplier was that it would commit to providing a CoA to confirm that the material was within specification.

After receiving and using a delivery of Raw Material A from a supplier, a batch of Product A was produced that failed to meet the required specification.

Review

All aspects of the process were investigated, and it was found that Raw Material A had been delivered out of specification, and that this was the cause of the problem with Product A.

Further investigation showed that the organisation had, in accordance with an agreement with the supplier, been supplied with a CoA. On checking the CoA, it was found that one of the key test results was actually outside the agreed specification.

This posed two questions:

- *Why had the supplier shipped the product when it was not within the agreed specification?*
- *Why had the organisation accepted the delivery when, according to its procedures, the CoA should have been checked?*

Outcome

For a delivery valued at around £3000, the problems with Product A gave rise to a cost to the organisation of around £65,000 when including the disruption caused to production. Whilst the cost was recovered from the supplier, the issue illustrates how simple oversights on the part of both the supplier and the organisation can occur that can have serious consequences.

Finding answers to the two questions was no easy task, in that procedures were already in place that appeared to have little scope for improvement. The first question also serves to illustrate the importance of working with reliable and trustworthy suppliers.

The case study shows that the role of Goods Inwards can go beyond the main activities of offloading and moving the delivered items into storage. Procedures related to the receipt of some items need to be consistently and accurately followed each and every time. Failure to do so can have an impact on inventory that can go way beyond material loss or simple damage to packs.

Material loss

The impact of material loss on inventory will vary both in quantity and significance. For example, the loss of 5 kilos of a catalyst can have more of an impact on production scheduling than losing 1000 kilos of an item where the inventory level will rarely go below 10,000 kilos.

Loss of material generally falls into five categories:

- Damage to packs
- Uncontrolled issue
- Design
- Unrecorded use (production and laboratory)
- Poor practices

Damage to packs

The subject of damage to items is covered in the chapter on Dispatch.

Uncontrolled issue

Uncontrolled issue is where, for example, a raw material is being pumped into a vessel and the quantity that should have been dispensed is overshot. It might be possible to correct for an overshoot, but there is a risk that this might not be possible, and inventory will need to be disposed of. The risk is greater if other materials have already been charged into a vessel.

Where material is being transferred from a storage tank, meters can often be preset with the required quantity and, unless the meter fails, the correct quantity will be charged. The key phrase here is 'unless the meter fails'. To avoid such an eventuality, meters, as with all other production equipment, need to be regularly maintained and recalibrated.

Design

There can be instances where flawed design can result in problems related to inventory. Case Study 6.2 is an example of design flaws that were not picked up until problems occurred.

Case Study 6.2   Inventory in storage tanks

Background

An organisation purchased white spirit which it required for the manu-facture of surface coatings. The white spirit was delivered in bulk, with road-tankers being discharged into storage tanks.

Inventory counts were carried out every 6 months, and there was a consistent inventory loss for white spirit. Whilst it ran into many thou-sands of litres, it was deemed not significant given the overall quantity purchased – over 3 million litres.

On one occasion a batch of product, when mixed with the required quantity of white spirit, was found to be contaminated with water. This was not catastrophic, but it was perplexing.

The production chemist decided to investigate the matter.

Review

In addition to checking the cooling water pipes used in both the reac-tor and 'thinning tank', the production chemist decided to review the whole system which included looking at the white spirit storage tanks (Figure 6.5).

Close examination of the tanks showed that, when constructed, a vent line was incorporated at the top of each tank and that this vent (4 inches in diameter) was open to the atmosphere (see Figure 6.6, 'A').

As the vent line was not covered (Figure 6.6, 'A'), and as the storage tanks were not under cover, whenever it rained rainwater would enter each of the storage tanks.

Because water is not miscible with white spirit and has a higher specific gravity, it collected at the bottom of each tank. Over time it accumulated

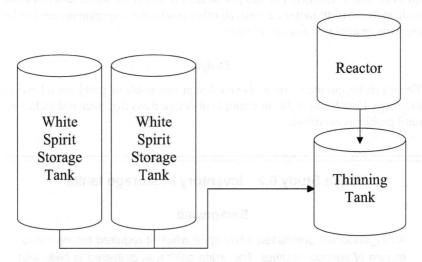

Figure 6.5 Basic design of 'feeds' into thinning tank.

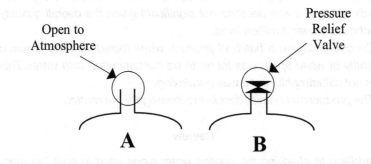

Figure 6.6 Tops of white spirit storage tanks.

118

to the point where it started to be drawn into the system and into the thinning tank, thereby resulting in the contamination seen.

The immediate remedy was to install a pressure relief valve at the top of each vent (Figure 6.6, 'B').

With regard to the loss of inventory, the production chemist also 'walked the line', and in so doing noticed that part of the line was buried. A pressure check was carried out on the buried section and an immediate loss of pressure was seen. This meant that the line was leaking.

The line was sealed off and replaced by a new overhead line.

Outcome

The installation of pressure relief valves not only prevented water ingress, but also eliminated the 'chimney effect' that would have resulted in significant loss of white spirit through evaporation.

The replacement of the buried line saw over a 98% reduction in white spirit losses.

In the UK, white spirit carries excise duty, because it is considered a potential fuel. Where organisations use white spirit for industrial use, they can claim exemption from paying the duty. As part of the exemption, organisations have to account for all purchase and use of white spirit. Periodically, HM Revenue and Customs will visit to review the organisation's records and, where material cannot be accounted for, the organisation has to pay duty on the quantity lost.

In Case Study 6.2, the financial saving from a huge reduction in inventory loss was supplemented by not having to pay over £2000 per annum in excise duty.

The work undertaken to deal with the white spirit problems triggered a similar review of all storage tanks, and other instances of poor design were identified and corrected. Sometimes solving one problem highlights, and solves, similar problems – ones that had been there all the time but had 'slipped under the radar'.

Unrecorded use

Batch production of chemical products will sometimes require additions of small quantities of materials needed to ensure the product meets the required specification. Accounting for such adjustments is a critical part of the process of paying attention to detail not only from an inventory perspective but also from a cost perspective.

Where adjustments are expected, process instructions and/or Bills of Materials should incorporate features in the documentation that direct operators to record the details of each adjustment.

Another source of possible unrecorded use is of materials required by R&D. Applicable to both raw materials and product, the quantities required by R&D might, in the scheme of things, be considered small. However, it is important that R&D appreciate the part they can play in maintaining data integrity with regard to inventory – a role that is discussed in more detail in Chapter 12.

Poor practices

An organisation will have many procedures and practices, and those overseen by Goods Inwards will be no exception. As with Dispatch, there will be procedures that describe how to manage inventory on a FIFO basis, thereby ensuring inventory rotation. This is particularly important when it comes to products with a limited shelf life.

Of course, having procedures is one thing. Executing them properly can be quite another. Inventory rotation is something that is quite common to many organisations, indeed all of us will be familiar with shelf life and the importance of inventory rotation when it comes to food storage.

Inventory rotation for raw materials, however, is not always quite so straightforward.

Not all raw materials will need to be strictly controlled – product in storage tanks is a fairly obvious example of a scenario where inventory rotation is effectively presumed to be happening, but a degree of mixing is almost inevitable. However, there will be raw materials that have a shelf life varying from days to years.

Case Study 6.3 gives an example of a product with a fairly short shelf life and how an organisation dealt with it.

Case Study 6.3   Short shelf life

Background

An organisation, as demand grew, decided to move from handing MDI (a chemical used in the manufacture of polyurethanes) in drums to handling it in bulk. With a fairly short shelf life, from arrival on site the road-tanker's contents had to be used within 10 days.

Review

The organisation, when setting the arrangement up with its supplier, needed to ensure that the quantity being delivered would be used within the timescale required and that it could also accommodate the slight variances that would be found in terms of delivery quantity. For example, a delivery could range from 19,000 kilos to 21,000 kilos. The onus was on the Planning and Production departments to ensure that the plan would consume the correct quantity and that the plan was strictly adhered to.

Outcome

The control being exercised over the whole process ensured that every shipment was dealt with effectively and demonstrated how paying attention to detail could deal with the management of inventory with a short shelf life.

Where there are exceptional cases, an organisation will usually give the attention that it requires. However, where shelf life is much longer (months or years), inventory management is not quite as effective. This is not made easier when one factors in aspects like labelling. Where the organisation's products will be labelled in a similar and consistent manner, raw materials, whilst displaying the same regulatory data, will have labels in different formats. Also, where a pallet of, for example, forty 25 kilo sacks is delivered, the label might only be on the shrink-wrap and not on each individual sack.

Equally, any Goods Inwards label attached to the delivery will likely be as one per pallet, which makes the management of limited shelf life products more difficult, and this is when weaknesses in procedures and practices are exposed.

Briefing

When preparing for any activity, having a clear understanding of the task ahead is essential. Where Production has a production plan, Goods Inwards should also have a plan of daily or weekly deliveries.

For any plan to be effective, the people involved need to prepare for the tasks that need to be done and deal with any nuances that might exist with certain deliveries.

At the start of every day, the Goods Inwards team needs to be briefed on the workload and, in particular, on the specific challenges that might be faced. Rather than putting total reliance on individuals to pick up order-specific instructions, they need to be collated for the briefing so that everyone is aware and therefore prompted to look. Other aspects will include circumstances where a raw material scheduled for delivery is required immediately by production.

For organisations that import raw materials delivered direct, amongst the many points that need to be attended to, it should be recognised that not every driver will speak the local language. Rather than putting complete reliance on pointing at pieces of paper, an organisation can prepare a template of standard questions and instructions and create copies in all the languages that Goods Inwards is likely to encounter. An example is given in Appendix 12. Of course, this type of document can include a basic site map and can be tailored to deal with different types of offloading (e.g. discharging road-tankers).

Such a document will help ensure drivers understand specific health and safety instructions, improve communication, reduce confusion and avoid frustration – all of which can lead to mistakes if left unchecked.

Measures

In many respects, the measures associated with Goods Inwards will be similar to those used in Dispatch. The main types will be:

- Aged RM stock
- Damaged goods
- Team briefing records
- Training records etc.

The Goods Inwards stage is important from a measurement perspective as, in many ways it sets the scene for subsequent stages.

The data gap between actual inventory and what the business systems thinks is there reflects the effectiveness of inventory procedures and processes. Gaps being created at the Goods Inwards stage will only build as materials go through the conversion process. Control of procedures and processes through measurement is therefore vital.

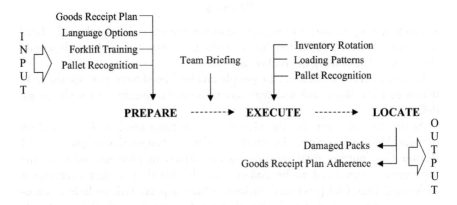

Figure 6.7 Goods inward process.

Summary

Arrival on site is the first instance where an organisation has actual physical control over the handling and management of raw materials.

Problems at this stage will impact Production directly and Customer Service indirectly, so it is of paramount importance that the need for process integrity be recognised at the outset.

Figure 6.7 shows how measures and procedures can be introduced at the input stage to help prevent issues arising, rather than focusing entirely on output-based measures that are reactive in nature.

Actions

In many ways, the actions for Goods Inwards will be similar to those in Dispatch.

- Create a daily or weekly goods receiving schedule so that staff can prepare for the scheduled deliveries
- Review the location system and consider re-organising where necessary, with a view to simplifying activities for Goods Inwards staff.
- Establish training routines that focus on particular aspects of the Goods Inwards processes, for example pallet recognition. Ensure that training records are maintained and reviewed.
- Set up daily briefing meetings with clear agendas.
- Create multi-language templates to deal with drivers who might not speak English to ensure that key aspects of the Goods Inwards process (including health and safety) are covered.
- Create a process so that all goods receipt discrepancies are investigated and acted upon.

7

PURCHASING

Part 1: General purchasing

When it comes to raw materials, Purchasing's role is twofold – firstly, ensure that demand can be met and, secondly, secure the most competitive prices. When considering the process of conversion of raw materials to product, Purchasing is very much focussed on meeting scheduled demand.

At first sight, Purchasing has little impact on inventory, as it will, in most instances be reacting to demand that is dictated by planning actions – as shown in Figure 7.1.

Scheduling a product for manufacture will create a demand for quantities of certain raw materials. This, in turn, will lead to suggested purchase requisitions detailing the quantity of raw material to be purchased and when it is needed by. Purchase requisitions will then be converted to purchase orders and sent to approved suppliers, as determined by Purchasing. These actions are effectively triggered by planning which suggests that Purchasing has little direct impact on inventory. Indeed, for those raw materials where there is a regular and predictable demand, Purchasing's role will focus on ensuring continuity of supply and negotiating the lowest prices possible.

However, there are several aspects of Purchasing's activities that have an impact on inventory:

- Raw material pricing structure
- Raw material lead times
- Minimum order quantities
- Data entry
- Supplier relationship

Raw material pricing structure

From a supplier's perspective, there are clearly cost benefits in shipping the maximum deliverable quantities. Not only are shipping costs optimised, there

124

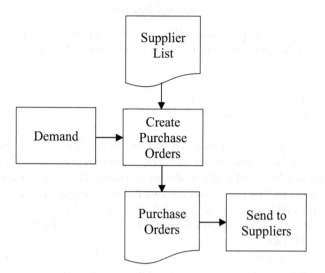

Figure 7.1 Purchasing actions.

will also be lower administrative costs. For example, if an organisation over a 12-month period/ takes 40 deliveries each of 20 tonnes of adipic acid, the cost will be lower for a supplier than shipping 80 deliveries each of 10 tonnes.

Suppliers will offer incentives, usually a lower price, in order to encourage an organisation to adopt an optimal ordering pattern.

In addition to quantity-specific orders, further incentives might be in place to encourage an organisation to order an agreed quantity of material over a 12-month period. For example, in the case of adipic acid, a supplier might offer an organisation a rebate if it orders a total of 1000 tonnes over a 12-month period.

As both types of incentive will result in a lower overall price for a raw material, Purchasing has an obvious incentive to give serious consideration to a supplier's offer.

However, the problem with agreeing to such incentives, from an inventory perspective, is that Purchasing might agree to order a quantity of raw material that could exceed demand. Depending on circumstances, whilst this might only be for a short period of time, the consequent spike in inventory has to be managed.

Whether in the short or medium term, a spike in inventory levels will disrupt the normal routine in Goods Inwards by disturbing the normal equilibrium (e.g. storage constraints) which, in turn, leads to an increased risk of damage or other errors.

The pressure from suppliers will always be there, and Purchasing needs a clear strategy, and one that connects directly to the organisation's strategy. This is discussed in more detail in Chapter 7, Part 2.

Raw material lead times

Following the planning process and the creation of a production schedule, Purchasing will be faced with a set of actions where they will be required to:

- Delay an existing order
- Bring forward an existing order
- Create new purchase orders

The ease with which each action can be processed will mainly depend on the lead-time given by a supplier for each raw material. For example, delaying an order might not be possible if it is already in transit. This can also apply when there is a need to bring a delivery forward. For example, where an order is scheduled for delivery in 14 days, it might not be possible (without disruptive intervention) to bring it forward for delivery in 5 days if the normal delivery lead-time is 11 days.

Similarly, the requisition for a new order might have a delivery date that is sooner than is possible given a supplier's standard lead-time.

This clearly puts a constraint on what can be reasonably achieved when scheduling production and, in general, unless Safety Stock is in place, the pressure on Purchasing is to secure shorter lead-times from the organisation's suppliers.

Of course, there is a balance to be struck between delivery lead-time set out by the supplier and its commercial offering. The importance of a lead-time will depend on the planning horizon and the response time that an organisation will want to offer its own customers. In particular, it is the degree to which flexibility is offered, which, by implication means that a non-standard service is offered. Offering flexibility is not in question but Purchasing needs to be involved in the decision-making process, as having the capability to provide flexibility will be determined, in part, by the availability of raw materials.

Raw material availability means either having sufficient inventory in place or having a supplier's commitment to provide a non-standard service. Both options have the potential to have an adverse impact on inventory by either leading to an increase in the level of inventory or disrupting the existing delivery schedule – and, as has already been alluded to, any change increases the risk of a problem occurring.

Minimum order quantities

Generally, suppliers will have minimum order quantities for raw materials. Some of the reasons for minimum order quantities will include:

- Being committed to supplying large customers, small quantities will be too disruptive.

- The range of packs supplied will be limited.
- Shipping costs for small quantities will be too high and might not always be recovered in the raw material's pricing.
- The customer's demand is too small.

Typically, the way larger suppliers deal with small quantities is through a distributor. This means when receiving raw materials direct from a supplier an organisation might have to purchase a minimum of 5000 kilos, whereas a distributor might be willing to sell 100 kilos. Obviously, costs will be higher for the smaller quantities, but this is better than having to purchase 5000 kilos when only 200 kilos is required.

It is Purchasing's responsibility to establish sourcing options that match demand and minimise excess inventory. This can give rise to conflicts with sales, in that the smaller the quantity, the higher the price, with a consequent impact on the standard cost of the product concerned. In these circumstances, it is not unknown for an organisation to be unwilling to deal with such issues and end up purchasing too much of a raw material simply to avoid the conflict.

If the organisation is committed to paying attention to detail, then these are the types of situations that need to be dealt with. Indeed, it might be appropriate to put together a purchase justification process so that the reasons are well understood and recorded for future reference. This is essentially about exercising control where perhaps there was previously none. An example form is given in Appendix 13.

Data entry

As with all instances where data has to be entered into a business system, there is a risk of keystroke error. Where a planning system is being used it is likely that purchase requisitions will have been created such that keystroke errors in relation to both a raw material's code and the quantity to be delivered will be eliminated.

However, there will be keystrokes at some stage, and there will always be a risk of an error occurring. It is therefore important when a planning system is used that all requisitions and suggested purchase order are checked and signed-off.

Supplier relationship

For any raw material, an organisation's expectation is that a supplier will be able to fulfil its obligations in relation to availability, service and material quality.

In addition to having a structured approach to identifying new suppliers, an organisation's relationship with its suppliers will play a key part in maintaining a balance in the procurement process.

For each raw material, the rules regarding inventory should have been established. Appendix 3 provides a structured and controlled method for justifying Safety Stock for a material. Reference is made in Appendix 3 to 'strategic classification', and this is a key part of the process of managing the rules relating to inventory.

The classification is an output of the purchasing strategy (see Chapter 7, Part 2), and through the purchasing strategy analysis is directly connected to the organisation's overall strategy.

This approach will ensure that an organisation fully appreciates the relevance of each raw material to the organisation, not only from a cost perspective, but also from a strategic perspective. For example, whilst the purchases that account for 80% of an organisation's raw material expenditure will always be important and be uppermost in Purchasing's 'mind', those items used in strategic products will not be forgotten, and despite accounting for very little in terms of cost, they will have the attention they deserve.

Each classification not only helps to determine the approach to the management of inventory levels, but also provides guidance on the approach that can be taken with the suppliers concerned.

Not only is this about maintaining a balance in the supply process and having the appropriate approach for each raw material, but it also shows how supplier relationships play a key part in maintaining that balance.

Measures

We have already seen that purchasing activities play their part in the management of inventory, not only through purchasing raw materials to meet production demand, but also through management of the purchasing process and maintaining a stable equilibrium.

Some of the measures that can be used to assess whether the process equilibrium is being maintained include:

Purchase orders

This represents the level of activity with the premise being that increases in activity levels, unless well managed, will lead to an increased risk of disruption to the purchasing process. This can be as simple as making an oversight in relation to agreeing to minimum order quantities, or not responding to a change in the demand for a raw material. Such issues may well be infrequent and not considered serious, but nevertheless, when they occur, they are symptomatic of a lack of attention to detail.

Purchase-for-stock items

Monitoring the proportion of purchase-for-stock (PFS) items is a measure where an imbalance in the system can be picked up. For example, a range of

8–12% might be considered as 'process equilibrium', and finding a PFS of 15% could imply that process management is not as effective as it should be.

Whenever items are deemed to be stock items, any increase in the PFS figure, by implication, means an increase in inventory level, and this inevitably leads to an increased risk of inventory issues.

Purchase-to-order items

'Purchase to order' (PTO) is the purchase equivalent to 'make-to-order', a term used in relation to product manufacture which is very familiar to Sales, Planning and Production staff. 'Purchase to order' is far less familiar and arguably rarely used. However, it is equally as important as make-to-order, and needs to be monitored in the same way.

Stock-outs

Stock-outs are obviously not what could be considered to be a lead indicator, but they do point to a process that is neither in control nor well understood. All stock-outs should be thoroughly investigated in order to identify the process weaknesses that gave rise to the stock-out so that preventive action can be introduced.

Inventory Turn

As mentioned in Chapter 3, Planning, Inventory Turn is a useful measure not only for products, but also for raw materials. By tracking raw materials in such a way, and working with Planning, Purchasing will be able to determine what action needs to be taken in relation to order quantities and demand patterns for each raw material. Of course, in so doing, Purchasing will be able to assess the impact (e.g. on pricing) of any change in demand and how a supplier relationship might need to change. Generally, when a process is in equilibrium you should expect the raw material Inventory Turn to match the product Inventory Turn.

Summary

Purchasing has both a direct and indirect impact on inventory management. The need for control of the process, as has been illustrated, extends beyond the obvious impact on inventory, stemming from arrangements made to fulfil demand from Production as determined by the production plan.

Supplier relationships and purchasing strategy are useful tools that can help provide a structure to the purchasing process. The purchasing strategy, in particular, will help the decision-making process when other functions look to direct the purchasing function to achieve lower prices by increasing order quantities.

When such pressure is applied, it means that those functions do not fully understand the organisation's strategy and how the activities of each function are connected to the business strategy – including purchasing.

Of course, there are other aspects that can be looked at, such as:

- Placing relationships along the supply chain continuum
- Preventing stock-outs
- Working with suppliers to bring about improvement
- Developing contingency plans
- Developing trust and confidence

The key is recognising that there needs to be a process in place that is both well understood and controlled. Purchasing strategy and activities need to be aligned with the organisation's strategy.

As for maintaining the process equilibrium, there needs to be an emphasis on paying attention to detail and to the creation of measures or lead indicators that assess performance at the input stage of the process.

Figure 7.2 illustrates some of the typical input measures that can be used to control the integrity of the Purchasing process.

Actions

Critical to the success of the Purchasing function is ensuring that all data has been set up correctly and that all raw materials are viewed according to their strategic classification:

- Develop a purchasing strategy, as described in Chapter 7, Part 2 (see also Appendix 14). This should lead to a strategic classification for all raw materials.

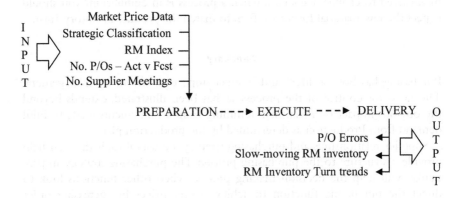

Figure 7.2 Purchasing process and typical input measures.

- Establish lists for all purchase for stock, purchase to order and preferred purchase quantity raw materials.
- Introduce a procedure to control the purchase of raw materials classed as preferred purchase quantity items (see Appendix 13).
- Monitor the number of purchase orders/order lines being processed to track any changes, as these can lead to an overload.
- Monitor the number of purchase order changes.
- From the purchasing strategy confirm the nature of the relationship with each supplier.
- From the purchasing strategy develop contingency plans etc., as indicated by the individual raw material's strategic classification.

Part 2: Purchasing strategy

When it comes to deciding how to deal with any one raw material and associated supplier, there is little available in the form of detailed guidance. The purchasing strategy discussed in this chapter helps to establish a clear and direct connection with the organisation's strategy. Using structured analysis, raw materials are categorised into one of four groups, with each group having its preferred set of actions. These actions are tailored to reflect the relative importance to the organisation of the raw materials concerned. Whilst cost will never be far from people's minds, the purchasing strategy herein described establishes clear actions that aid in the development of supplier relationships, safe in the knowledge that the relationships have a foundation based on, and are directly connected to, the overall organisational strategy.

Introduction

When a business develops its strategy, every function should be aligned to that strategy. There should, effectively, be a cascade of actions from the organisational strategy that provides a framework for each function to develop its own strategy. Each function's strategy should be precisely aligned to the organisation such that everyone working in that particular function will feel connected to the organisational strategy.

It is no easy task to ensure that each function's strategy is aligned to the business strategy, and the problem that Purchasing faces is that it cannot get away from cost being one of the main, and often overriding, factors to consider when developing a strategy.

Whilst cost cannot be ignored, there needs to be an approach that is more closely aligned to, and determined by, the business strategy.

Issues

That raw material prices have an impact on a business is fairly obvious, and most organisations, at some stage, have experienced profit erosion resulting from dramatic price rises. However, significant though price is, a number of other issues need to be considered for any raw material:

Variability in supply

Having more than one supplier of a raw material always carries a risk related to slight variances in the quality of the product being supplied. Organisations will often look to address this through either single sourcing and/or a vendor management programme. Of course, the degree to which this is an issue will depend on the nature of any variability in supply and how critical this is to product performance.

Service level

One of the keys to a smooth and balanced production process is perfect execution of the raw material schedule. This means having 'on time, in full' deliveries 100% of the time.

Continuity of supply

Disruptions to supply are never welcome, and organisations need to work with their suppliers to avoid them.

Supplier relationship

Suppliers need to understand their part in the organisation's business and how best the two can work together not only to support each other, but also adapt to any change in the organisation's strategy.

Procurement cost control

It is essential that all aspects of procurement process costs are controlled – not just price, but raw material storage, handling, transaction, administration and other relationship costs.

Control the agenda

The organisation must make sure that it has a clear understanding of what it wants from a supplier rather than working to the supplier's agenda.

Resource management

Ensure that effective use is made of purchasing resources.

There is little doubt that one of the main challenges is to strike the balance between securing a competitive price and achieving an acceptable and consistent quality. A lower price should not come at the cost of lower or variable quality.

Analysis

In addition to the more obvious elements of profit sensitivity and purchasing profile, a raw material strategic classification needs to be undertaken. What follows are methods for developing a classification, purchase profile and profit sensitivity for each raw material.

Classification

An organisation needs to understand how a raw material is positioned in relation to the overall strategy.

The approach is to firstly determine the proportion of a raw material used in strategic products and deduct the proportion used in commodity products. The steps involved in the calculation are as follows:

- Break the sales forecast for the upcoming 12 months into individual product forecasts.
- Using the BOM for each product, calculate the forecast raw material requirement.
- From the sales forecast, select the strategic products and associated quantities.
- Using the BOM for each strategic product, calculate the forecast raw material requirement.
- Create a table that shows, for each raw material, the percentage required for strategic products and the percentage for the remainder or 'commodity' products.

An example is given in Table 7.1.

Table 7.1 Raw material strategic classification.

Raw Material	Strategic %	Commodity %	Nett
RM A	26	72	−46
RM B	100		100
RM C	58	42	16
RM D	11	89	−71
RM E	69	31	38
RM F		100	−100

Purchase profile

The second step is to establish a purchase profile by considering five factors:

- *Sourcing*
  How many approved suppliers does the organisation have for each raw material? The assumption here is that having multiple suppliers is a good thing and that any variability in quality of a raw material from supplier to supplier has been accounted for by the organisation's technical staff. (Rated as: 1 – 3 or more suppliers, 2 – 2 suppliers or 3 – 1 supplier.)
- *Price*
  How is the organisation's control of pricing described? (Rated as: 1 – strong, 2 – market driven or 3 – weak.)
- *Quality*
  For each supplier, how does raw material quality vary? Is this significant? (Rated as: 1 – consistent and reliable quality, 2 – < 5% of deliveries with issues or 3 – > 5% of deliveries with issues.)
- *Supply*
  How reliable is supply? (Rated as: 1 – 100% 'on time, in full', 2 – > 95% or 3 – < 95%.)
- *Service*
  How easily can supply be obtained if there was an urgent need? (Rated as 1 – local supply available same day or overnight, 2 – supply within 5 days or 3 – special deliveries not possible.)

Each factor is added together to produce a purchase profile score ranging from 5 to 15. An example is given in Table 7.2.

Profit sensitivity

Determine the degree to which raw material price variation impacts on profit. This can be done by calculating the impact that a 5% price change in the raw material price has on the organisation's profit. The data generated in the

Table 7.2 Purchase profile for raw materials.

Raw Material	So	P	Q	Su	Se	Total
RM A	3	2	3	2	2	12
RM B	1	1	2	1	1	6
RM C	2	1	2	1	2	8
RM D	3	1	2	2	2	10
RM E	3	1	3	2	3	12
RM F	1	1	1	1	1	5

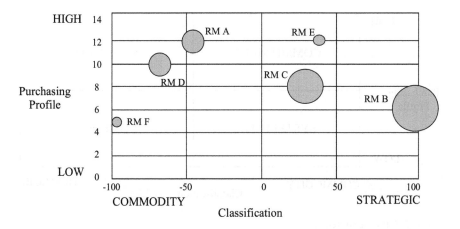

Figure 7.3 Purchasing and classification profile

classification process should be used for the quantity of raw material together with the raw material cost being used when the forecast was being put together.

Examples are: RM A (45), RM B (168), RM C (83), RM D (42), RM E (11) and RM F (10).

These enable the creation of a 'classification/profile' chart where the main axes will be based on strategic classification and purchasing profile score, with the profit impact shown as a bubble. An example is shown in Figure 7.3.

Strategic options

It is clear from any analysis that we should not lump all raw materials together to be treated in the same way. Without a structured approach, a raw material where 2000 tonnes are purchased is likely to be viewed as more important than one where 25 kilos are purchased, however critical the 25 kilos might be. Whilst the significance of cost cannot be ignored, all raw materials need to be assessed in a way that ensures that the purchasing strategy link to business strategy is maintained.

Having developed the material risk profile (Figure 7.3), one can create a two-by-two matrix, splitting the data into four quadrants. This facilitates the development of different strategies which are appropriate for each of the quadrants. The purpose here, as with other two-by-two matrices, is to provide the user with a structure to follow.

Clearly, there will be instances where raw materials do not fall wholly within a quadrant but at the border with another quadrant. In these instances, a judgement will have to be made, but with historical data it will at least be possible to determine which direction the raw material has been going and therefore which quadrant will be most appropriate.

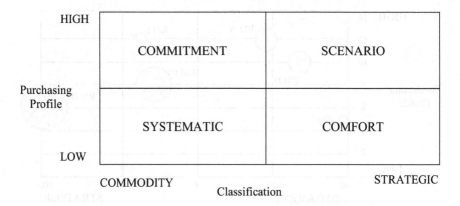

Figure 7.4 Profile strategies.

The basic form of the matrix is shown in Figure 7.4.

Each quadrant will have a strategy with its own set of characteristics.

Scenario

Most materials in this category will carry significant risks, not least of which might be a dependency on a single supplier with no alternatives available.

The strategy for this category is focussed on long-range planning and will include:

- Create long-range forecasts.
- Work with the supplier to develop contingency plans based on worst-case scenarios. This should include a financial assessment of the supplier concerned.
- Conduct a regular review of the inventory-holding policy.
- Enter contractual arrangements in order to secure a commitment from the supplier.
- Use market intelligence sources to work on target prices.
- Continue to review opportunities to establish alternative sources and/or replace the critical raw material with a more readily available one.

Comfort

With a slightly reduced risk, the strategy can be refocussed on:

- Mid-range planning
- Inventory management
- Tracking market prices with targeted support from the supplier.

136

- Risk management based on probabilities rather than worst-case scenarios
- Partnership arrangements to secure commitment for a proportion of the annual demand

Systematic

As products become more like commodities, margins will become tighter. Consequently, greater emphasis should be placed on cost control and cost reduction. This will require:

- A review of each element of the supply chain with a focus on cost reduction and simplification. This should include negotiation methods, planning, ordering, Safety Stock, invoicing and payments etc.
- Work on getting shorter lead-times
- Active focus on securing lowest-cost sources.
- Expansion of the supplier base if target prices are not being achieved.

Some specific examples on cost reduction and simplifying the process will include:

- Using a formula based on feedstock materials to determine the price.
- Having telephone calls to review prices rather than face-to-face meetings which can be time-consuming.
- Limiting the frequency of price reviews. If they were every quarter, move to annual.
- Where an organisation is looking to be loyal to its suppliers, get the supplier to demonstrate that its prices are the lowest or competitive (depending on the objective). In other words, trust the supplier to give you the 'best' price.

Commitment

With regards to commitment, we might find demand falling off and suppliers looking to withdraw from the market, especially if margins are being severely eroded. Against this background the 'systematic' strategy should be supplemented with the following activities:

- Consider withdrawing the product from the market.
- Look to replace the critical raw material with another that is more readily available.
- Enter contractual commitment with a single source, effectively securing support from the supplier for continuity of supply.
- Cost re-engineering of the product and associated process in order to maximise the margin.

In addition to the strategic analysis, it will also be necessary to determine the inventory classification of each raw materials which dictate if the purchase will be made on the basis of:

- A Safety Stock as determined in review with Planning.
- Purchase to order – in other words, if the make-to-order production batch requires 'x' kilos of a raw material, this, taking account of potential waste, is precisely the quantity that should be purchased.
- The supplier's minimum order quantity.

Both the strategic analysis and inventory classification provide a structure for purchasing to follow and a means of translating the business strategy into a strategy for each individual raw material.

Purchasing policy

When developing a strategy, one thing is evident – whatever type of material is purchased, from whatever source, there will be a set of fundamental requirements that will have to be accommodated:

Suppliers

Every effort should be made to work with those suppliers committed to continuous improvement. Service charters and vendor appraisal programmes are useful in setting out the ground rules and enabling a commitment to be monitored.

Quality

The purchasing policy should work towards consistency and standardisation as required by the organisation. This is not about achieving perfection, it is about achieving a consistent standard that is appropriate. You do not need a gold-plated screw where a normal, cheaper screw will work perfectly well.

Pricing

Putting pricing in a strategic context means that attention is not focussed exclusively on the 20% of materials accounting for 80% of the spend. For example, those materials where only smaller quantities are required, but are of strategic significance, will also come under scrutiny.

Logistics

Not only is there a requirement to have materials delivered on time and in full, but being aware of, and applying recommended handing procedures, is of great importance. A late arrival is not the only problem that can occur with a raw material, mishandling the material can also lead to problems with inventory.

Communication

There should be a commitment to communicate with each supplier to ensure that they fully understand not just how the material is used, but also the strategic approach so that when a classification changes – which it will do as each product goes through its life cycle, they understand their part in adapting to the changing circumstances.

Supplier selection

Having identified how we want to deal with raw materials, there remains the issue of supplier selection. The main thrust of the strategy in this regard is that an agenda is being created for supplier selection and relationships, driven by what matters to the organisation.

A purchasing policy is common in many organisations and is a useful tool in setting the minimum standards expected from suppliers, whilst at the same time identifying some of the less tangible elements that form part of the process of supplier selection.

Of course, in most instances, selection can be made on the basis of some specific requirements, but it should be remembered that an organisation is rarely starting from scratch, doubtless having been loyal to some suppliers for a considerable time. Change will not necessarily be easy but having clear objectives will help suppliers understand where the organisation is coming from.

Supplier relationships

Much is written about Customer Relationship Management (CRM), and organisations often have CRM software systems in place to aid in the management of their relations with their customers.

Few organisations place as much emphasis on managing relationships with their suppliers. They will concern themselves only with securing the best prices, and only a very small number will have software systems to aid in the management of their supplier relationships.

From the strategic tool used to analyse purchasing profiles, we can see that as raw materials move from one phase into another, there is a consequent change in the corresponding supplier relationship. This does not, however, necessarily mean that a change in supplier is needed, it merely means that the way that the organisation works with the supplier needs to change.

In as much as the organisation looks to have customer loyalty, the same is true of the organisation's suppliers in that they will also value loyalty. Significant benefits can come from loyalty, not least when material supply becomes 'very tight' (i.e. potentially insufficient supply to meet demand), and it should therefore be the case that changing a supplier should always be the result of a well-considered exercise. Every opportunity should be taken to work with existing suppliers to enable them to understand changing circumstances and work with the organisation as the purchasing profile changes, and whilst the organisation may be a valued customer, the supplier needs to feel equally valued.

Summary

Developing a purchasing strategy that is directly connected to the organisation's overall strategy is vital and enables an organisation to appreciate the position of all raw materials – and not just those that have the greatest impact on profit.

Having a structured approach will provide clarity and guidance in developing a relationship with a supplier and ensure that it is working with the organisation to meet the organisational goals and be able to adapt as the organisation's needs change over time.

Adopting the approach discussed in this chapter is a departure from many purchasing strategies in that some of the emphasis is shifted away from cost by asking the question – 'How does the raw material relate to the business strategy?'

The key aspect is that, as should be the case with all other functions, the purchasing strategy will be directly aligned to the business strategy, all activities will have a clearer purpose and individual staff members will be better able to relate to the organisation's goals.

Of course, as time passes, the strategy will need to be reviewed, and an organisation needs to be aware of the need to respond to changing circumstances and how this might impact not only the business strategy, but also the purchasing strategy. Of course, working with colleagues in R&D, Marketing, Production and Sales will ensure that many of the changes will be anticipated, and appropriate planning can take place where new strategies are required.

Author's note:

When being taken over by another company, Purchasing is one of those functions where there is no hiding from a direct judgement of whether you are any good or not. In other words, you will find that you were either paying too much for raw materials or you were not.

I have twice been in a situation where the company I was working for was acquired by a much larger company. In both instances there were examples of the acquiring company purchasing about ten times as much of a material than we were.

However, my approach to purchasing meant that we were paying the lower price – contrary to expectations.

The purchasing strategy described herein had on both occasions been tested in the most obvious manner, and it had not been found wanting.

8

SALES

The Sales function is focussed on securing sales and developing business opportunities and has a pretty simple expectation when it comes to inventory – ensure that there is sufficient product to fulfil customer orders on time and in full. This might on occasion mean shorter lead-times than those offered by the organisation's competitors.

In this regard, Sales will very much be seen as the internal customer when it comes to inventory. As an internal customer, the role that Sales plays in the management of an organisation's inventory is not that obvious. To identify the part played by Sales, we need to look at the detail of the sales process and how pressures to secure business in a competitive environment can lead to issues with inventory.

Figure 8.1 illustrates the typical sales activity process, revolving around the objectives of maintaining existing business and developing new business opportunities.

In some instances, the sales team will be working in an environment where they have an effective monopoly. Such situations might not be that unusual, especially in those industries that have approval systems in place (that virtually guarantee supply for a period of time that might run into many years) – for example, the defence, pharmaceutical, automotive and aerospace industries.

Outside these types of industries, competition will require the sales team to deal with many issues that either impact an existing relationship or present challenges when developing new business. Some typical aspects are illustrated in Figure 8.2.

Of the typical issues listed in Figure 8.2, service level and product pricing have a connection to inventory.

In order to have a competitive service level, the sales team might want to approach the issue in one of three ways – (1) manufacture product in anticipation of an order, (2) move a product from make-to-order to a stocked item or (3) set up a consignment inventory arrangement with the customer.

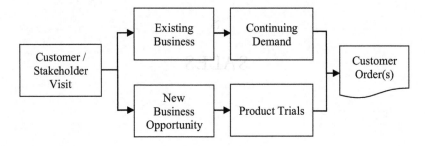

Figure 8.1 Basic sales process.

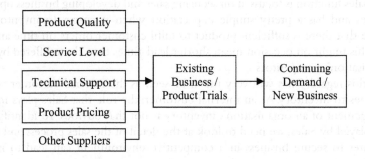

Figure 8.2 Issues impacting existing business and new opportunities.

Anticipating an order

Manufacturing product in advance of an order clearly carries many risks. Firstly, the order might not materialise, resulting in product sitting in inventory with few options available to resell or recover. A structured approach is required that has many of the attributes of setting up an item as a Safety Stock product. As with Safety Stock, a process is required, and an example is given in Appendix 14.

Safety Stock

This has already been dealt with in Chapter 3, Planning, and an example of an approval form is shown in Appendix 3.

Consignment inventory

Setting up a consignment inventory arrangement at a customer is similar to setting up Safety Stock, with the key difference that the inventory cannot be easily sold to other customers. As with Safety Stock, the organisation is making a significant financial commitment. However, having inventory at a customer site means that the organisation is not able to exercise the same level of control as it would when the inventory is located at one of its own facilities. Therefore, in addition to setting up a rigorous process to assess whether it should be adopted, a rigorous system should also be established to administer the system.

Appendix 15 gives an example of a form used to seek approval for the setting up of a consignment inventory arrangement, whilst Appendix 16 illustrates the risks and features of a system that would be used to administer the arrangement.

There will be many reasons for wanting to set up a consignment inventory arrangement (long lead-times, long distances, variable demand, customer retention), but they should be seen as a transition arrangement – even if this transition lasts many years. The competitive environment will change, and the initial arguments in favour of consignment inventory may well become weaker over time.

Product pricing

For product pricing, Sales will put pressure on Production to produce larger batches with lower production costs and for Purchasing to purchase larger quantities of raw materials in order to further drive down standard costs.

We have already seen in the chapters on Production and Purchasing that making or ordering more than is actually required leads to an increased risk of inventory issues. When it comes to Sales, those aspects with the potential to trigger issues include:

- Flexibility
- Minimum batch sizes
- Pricing for failure
- Bullwhip effect
- Certainty

Flexibility

Ideally, organisations would like to be in a position to offer complete flexibility of supply. Flexible response to customer requirements, however, comes at a price, and will often lead to the production/planning process equilibrium being disturbed. Such disturbance invariably leads to an increased risk of issues that could, in turn, result in the creation of unwanted inventory.

It is important to recognise that an organisation may not be able to get away entirely from a situation where, despite Production and Planning being reluctant to, the organisation commits to meet a customer's unexpected demand by changing the firm plan.

Offering flexible response can of course be advantageous and may well be a feature that an organisation wants to be recognised and appreciated for.

However, offering such flexibility comes at a price, and does lead to an increased risk of inventory issues.

To cope with flexibility, an organisation would do well to consider a couple of points:

- Why does the customer need such a rapid response?
- Limit the circumstances where flexibility should be offered.

Why does the customer need such a rapid response?

It may well be the case that the organisation does not fully understand the customer's markets, and that their urgent requirements are predictable. Understanding the process will be key to developing routines that offer some form of control over the demand that enables an organisation to minimise disruption. An example is given in Case Study 8.1.

Case Study 8.1   Erratic ordering

Background

A customer operates in a market where demand can be erratic and unexpected. This leads to contact with the organisation being irregular, often leading to having to make alterations to the production plan.

Review

The customer concerned was a strategic customer, and the one thing that had been consistent during its relationship with the organisation was the erratic ordering pattern.

The organisation, however, did have a sales history, and knew when contact was most disruptive.

The organisation decided, therefore, to accept that there would be uncertainty over the customer's demand, but also recognised that there would be a demand. It was just a case of which product and how much would be required.

Outcome

The organisation decided that they could exercise some control over the situation if they worked with the customer. The organisation and the customer both agreed to set up a process where production capacity would be reserved for the customer's likely requirement and that they would review demand on a routine basis on a Friday morning.

This process had the benefit of limiting the impact on the production plan (in that scheduled production was less likely to be altered, thereby reducing the impact on other customers), and the scheduled contact demonstrated to the customer its importance to the organisation.

Of course, such a routine might not always be required, but working around a customer's routines demonstrates how control can be introduced into the scheduling process.

Limit the circumstances where flexibility should be offered

Reference to the organisation's strategy, together with life cycle data, can help an organisation determine whether offering flexibility is either strategically necessary or comes at too high a cost.

Such decisions, especially when customer specific, should be discussed with the customer prior to implementation so that the customer and the organisation fully understand both perspectives and that alternative courses of action can be explored if necessary.

An underlying objective should always be not to change a production schedule. If this is to be achieved whilst at the same time offering flexibility, an organisation needs to establish alternative ways of managing the issue.

Minimum batch sizes

Some organisations will have rules or guidelines relating to minimum order quantities. Whilst in an engineering context it might be possible, though not necessarily desirable, to have a minimum order of a single item, this level of capability is not always possible when it comes to batch manufacture in the chemical industry. For example, in order to ensure adequate mixing in a 5000-litre vessel, a minimum charge of 1500 litres might be necessary. This would imply either a minimum overall demand or minimum single order for 1500 litres.

Matching minimum batch sizes with customer demand might not be easy, especially when a product is reaching the latter stages of its life cycle. The risk is clear – that the organisation manufactures 1500 litres but only sells 500 litres – ending up with 1000 litres of potentially unwanted inventory.

This is a scenario that has to be managed. Some examples of solutions to this type of problem include:

- Getting the customer to take the whole quantity produced. Whilst this solves the problem as far as the organisation is concerned, this approach merely shifts the problem to the customer, and is perhaps an approach that would not be particularly appreciated by the customer concerned.
- Set a price for the quantity to be sold that takes account of both the loss of profit incurred by the creation of 1000 litres (in the above example) of unwanted inventory, the raw material cost and the cost of disposal. Whilst this will increase the price of 500 litres quite significantly, it will reflect the true cost of producing sufficient product to fulfil the customer's requirement. However, having disposal as an acceptable course of action is not especially desirable.
- Customers and Sales will have to face up to the fact that if an organisation does not want to make a net loss when selling a product, it needs to either set an appropriate price or stop manufacturing the product concerned. Sales should work with the customer to understand the customer's requirement and see if an alternative solution is possible; for example, a different product. The key here is to ensure that both the organisation and the customer understand each other's perspective.

Pricing for failure

Organisations can find that some of their products are difficult to manufacture, resulting in quite high failure rates. This can be for many reasons. For example, not having the appropriate equipment, not having the correct process in place or having a potentially unstable formulation.

Dealing with this can be problematic for an organisation. From an inventory perspective, the objective is to eliminate any risk of failure. Achieving this might require reformulation or investing in suitable equipment and procedures. The difficulty is that organisations, through a misplaced sense of pride, are not always able to recognise that errors may have been made in product design or in appreciating that they are not properly set up to manufacture the product.

Lacking a complete understanding can lead to an organisation accepting that problems will occur and factoring them into their modus operandi. This, of course, means that inefficiency becomes an acceptable trait of the organisation.

It might be that the rewards in relation to the product are very high, but it is unlikely that these risks have been factored into the price. The scenario and issues in that regard are similar to those encountered with minimum orders. The approach to dealing with this type of circumstance is, again, to have a structured process in place. The key here is appreciating that the approach does not necessarily resolve the problem, but it does push the organisation towards a more complete understanding of everything that is involved so that decisions, however pragmatic, are based on data and knowledge.

Paying attention to detail might not, on rare occasions, lead to the goal that the organisation desires. But a structured approach should, at least, ensure that issues are managed more effectively, and that full value is obtained for the product that it sells.

Bullwhip effect

One of the responsibilities of the Sales function is to provide a forecast of demand for the upcoming year. This is usually a requirement of the budget process and may, indeed, go beyond a 12-month period in some circumstances.

When putting together a forecast, the Sales function needs to be aware of what has been described as the 'bullwhip effect'.

The bullwhip, or Forrester, effect refers to an increasing swing in demand, and the further you are down the supply chain the greater the disconnect between an actual market movement and the supply chain response further down the line, resulting in manufacturers' seeing a change in demand that is much greater than is actually the case.

What can be seen as a small variation at one end of the supply chain – perhaps an unexpected additional customer order – can be misinterpreted as market growth, resulting in the manufacture of inventory that is not needed, and that ultimately has to be disposed.

In order to avoid the worst of the bullwhip effect, an organisation needs to have good communication between all functions, but critically, needs to be alert to unexpected changes in demand. Two functions have a key part to play in this regard.

Firstly, Planning needs to have a measure in place that highlights deviations from the budgeted demand and/or historical trend. Whilst the demand itself might be very real, whether it represents a trend or is merely an isolated demand needs to be confirmed, as this will impact the approach to fulfilling the demand. Planning needs to consider whether Safety Stock needs to be established, whether it just needs to meet the exact requirement or whether it should just be happy to allow some surplus inventory once the order has been fulfilled.

The decision taken by Planning will also impact Purchasing and how it should deal with the raw materials involved.

Second, Sales needs to understand what has driven this demand. For example, if demand is the consequence of entering a new market, then sales might be expected to increase month on month for a period of time. In such instances, the Sales function will need to be communicating on a regular basis with Planning, at least until the demand has stabilised.

Should the demand be ad hoc, Sales will need to communicate with Planning so that the demand is seen for what it is, rather than be seen as pointing to a trend.

Of course, these examples are not necessarily precise manifestations of the bullwhip effect. In order to detect a bullwhip effect, the Sales function will need to

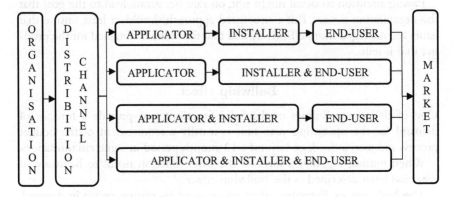

Figure 8.3 Channel gap analysis.

understand the market, together with the position of all stakeholders, so that any spike in demand is well understood and, again, not seen for something that it is not.

With several stakeholders in the value chain, any slight change in demand can see stakeholders over-compensating, with the distortion being greatest when an organisation is quite detached from the market.

A tool that can be used to understand the 'disconnect' with the market is channel gap analysis (Figure 8.3). Here, in addition to the normal distribution chain that a customer will have (e.g. selling direct or through a distribution channel), there will be instances where the organisation will need to have conversations with all the stakeholders that impact on decisions in the market.

Applicators, installers and end-users will have varying degrees of influence on the chain to market, depending on the market they operate in. For example, the end-user might be a consumer using paint or an oil company paying for a construction project.

It is essential that Sales and Marketing fully understand the type of market they are in, who the real decision makers are and whether a change in a customer's demand reflects changes in overall market demand.

As you will have noticed, each of the previous examples focus on an increase in demand. The need for communication, and the part that each function plays, is just as important for declining demand as in this scenario, the risk is greater that the organisation will end up with inventory that it cannot sell.

Certainty

The accuracy of forecasts is often reflected in the degree of certainty that the organisation has in the data that it is using.

Typically, as shown in Figure 8.4, data will be in three groups. Firstly, there will be sales orders. Clearly, these are very real and can, usually, be completely relied upon.

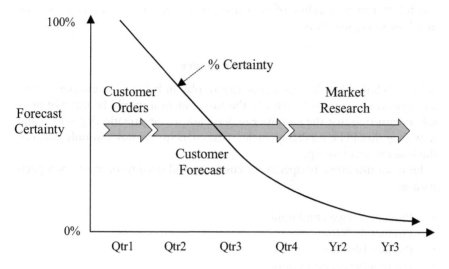

Figure 8.4 Forecast certainty and data source.

Secondly, there will be the customer forecast. Quite often this will be a case of Sales (or perhaps Customer Service) asking customers for their view over the short to medium term.

Beyond the customer forecast, market research will sometimes be used to provide a view over the medium to long term.

The key with any type of data being used to construct a forecast is validation. How reliable is the data source being used? What evidence is there, and how has the organisation validated the assumptions being made when converting raw data into more usable information?

Market forecasts are discussed in more detail in the chapter on Marketing but suffice to say that Sales plays an important part in the validation process. For example, market research can often provide sales leads, and there is a clear need to validate these leads, as they have often been developed on the basis of assumptions made in the data analysis phase.

The degree to which an organisation follows up on sales leads varies quite considerably, ranging from very effective follow-up to totally unwilling. Following up on sales leads is a key part of not just enabling an organisation to grow but helps an organisation to improve its modelling of the markets. Not only will this be strategically beneficial to an organisation, but it will result in further improvements in inventory management which, in turn, will underpin the organisation's competitive advantage over its competitors.

The goal in Figure 8.4 is to increase the certainty levels in the customer forecast and market research stages. Clearly, 100% certainty is unlikely to be achieved, but improvements can be made, and improvements will lead to a much better understanding of the market which, in the long run, can only be good for an organisation.

Customer training

Whilst Technical Service has a clear role to play in helping a customer process an organisation's product correctly, the Sales function should be mindful of its role in ensuring that the customer understands the organisation's products and how they should be used. Supporting customers in this way can only enhance the business relationship.

From an inventory perspective, a customer will need to be aware of aspects such as:

- Product storage conditions
- Product shelf life
- Product labelling
- Lot numbering convention
- Packaging convention (use of colours etc.)
- Ensuring correct product has been used (especially where the customer receives different products in similar packaging – only differentiated by the label)

When it comes to the customer's use of an organisation's products, Sales and Technical Service need to be conscious of the fact that a customer's staff might not have the same rigorous approach to using the product(s). Case Studies 8.2 and 8.3 are examples of organisations not being aware of aspects of a customer's methods that give rise to unintended consequences.

Case Study 8.2   Pack weight

Background

A business's manufacturing operation required the delivery of different types of raw materials in drums. Historically, the raw materials were similar in density and were all delivered in drums each containing 180 kilos. As new products were introduced, the range of raw materials delivered in drums was expanded. One of the new raw materials was di-octyl phthalate (DOP), and this was delivered in drums containing 229 kilos.

After several batches or product containing DOP were produced, it was noticed that the quality was not quite what it should have been.

Analysis was inconclusive, and it was decided to look closely at each stage of the process, from charging to filling.

Review

During the charging stage, it was noticed that where the batch card required a charge of 190 kilos of DOP, the operator was charging a full drum plus 10 kilos.

When questioned, the operator said that they were charging a full drum (assumed to be 180 kilos) plus 10 kilos to bring it up to the 190 kilos required.

The operator was quite surprised to be told that the drum actually contained 229 kilos, and that 239 kilos was actually being charged.

An immediate change was made in the processing instructions to oblige all drummed raw materials to be placed on a scale in order to ensure that the correct charge was being made.

Outcome

There was an immediate improvement in quality, and the change in the process also unearthed a couple of other instances where the '180-kilo' assumption proved to be wrong.

Case Study 8.3   Pack colour

Background

An organisation sold a two-component system to a customer with one 25-litre pack being supplied in black and one 25-litre pack being supplied in blue.

Soon after a delivery the customer contacted the organisation to report faults in their application that they put down to the product.

Review

Following a visit to the customer, it was found that a delivery error had been made and that customer had been supplied with, and used, an incorrect product.

151

When the organisation asked why the customer had not picked up on this at either the Goods Receipt or Production stage, the customer's response was that when using the product they knew that they would need to use one black keg and one blue keg, and this is what their staff were attuned to look for. They never cross referenced the labels or delivery notes with their purchase orders and batch cards.

As with Case Study 8.2, this was an example of people getting into routines and making some critical, if erroneous, assumptions.

Outcome

Whilst clearly an error had been made at order entry, discussion took place with the customer to help them establish more effective raw materials–handling routines in Goods Inwards and Production.

Part of the process was for Sales to go through the handling of the organisation's products and provide a thorough explanation on labelling and what to look out for.

Getting a sustainable outcome is more difficult in these types of circumstances, but it illustrates some of the problems that can arise when errors are made.

Measures and control systems

Developing inventory measures that can be considered as lead indicators might not be so obvious when it comes to Sales. However, some examples are given below:

- Review minimum order pricing.
- List the markets that the organisation operates in and assess the knowledge gap.
- Establish reporting mechanisms that highlight changes in demand.
- Have regular reviews with the Planning function, focussing in particular on changes in demand (both increasing and declining).
- Underpinning Planning's assessment of changes will be the sales forecast. This should accurately reflect not only changes in demand with existing customers, but also new demand within a market or new demand in new market segments.

Quite often, weaknesses in a system will manifest themselves when an organisation adopts a new approach to business opportunities. Whilst it is often a learning experience, there can be, in the first instance, a less than comprehensive approach to planning and preparation.

A thorough approach is essential. For example, when an oil company looks to develop an offshore oil field, there might well be a demand for products such as insulation materials, and the requirement will be for a specific quantity – no more and no less. An applicator will not want to end up with surplus inventory, and neither will they want to find that they are unable to coat the last few pipes of a project. Achieving such precision requires tight control and good communication.

Summary

Managing the flow of information is a critical to the success of any organisation and the Sales function has a vital part to play in that process, especially when it comes to inventory management. Whilst stable demand will lead to a stable system, organisations are always looking to grow, and therefore there will always be change. Functions such as Sales, Planning, Production, Supply Chain and Purchasing need to know about the changes and need to be involved.

The Sales function also has to recognise that driving down the standard cost of a material, whilst desirable from their perspective, can result to an increase in raw material inventory, some of which will be disposed of. The value of this write-off, effectively, is no different to having paid a higher price in the first instance, but what it does do is mask inefficiency. For any organisation, this is something that has to be dealt with.

Arguably, the greatest risk rests with the 'one2one' relationship; that is, the organisation only has one customer for a particular product. In these instances, any unexpected downturn in demand can quite quickly lead to inventory that is no longer required – product and/or product-specific raw material(s). Effective communication and associated actions (e.g. moving product from Safety Stock to make-to-order) should help reduce, if not eliminate, this risk, but nevertheless 'one2one' relationships need careful monitoring in order to avoid the unexpected.

Figure 8.5 illustrates some of the sales process measures that can be used to improve inventory management.

Working with the Sales function in order to develop and implement appropriate measures will not only improve inventory management but will also help the Sales function understand how its activities impact inventory.

Actions

As already alluded to, Sales do not have an obvious impact on inventory. However, as we have seen, many aspects of Sales' activities have an effect on inventory. Ensuring that all aspects are controlled requires actions covering several areas:

- Develop a procedure for establishing Safety Stock for a product.
- Develop a procedure that deals with approval for the manufacture of product prior to receipt of an order.

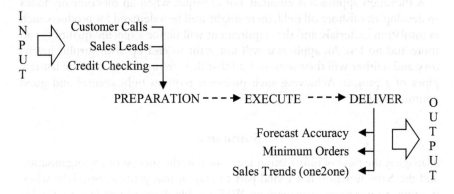

Figure 8.5 Sales process measures (inventory related).

- Ensure that procedures are in place both for the approval of consignment inventory proposals at a customer and for the administration of the arrangement once it has been set up.
- Ensure that forecasts are validated by understanding how the customer compiles its data, and how this fits with market trends. Tools such as channel gap analysis are useful in building confidence in customer and market forecasts.
- Understand the customer's knowledge of the organisation's products and how to process them, as this will reduce the risk of a product being returned by a customer.
- Set up measures to track the numbers (e.g. customer calls, sales leads etc.).

Reference

Forrester, J.W. (1961). *Industrial dynamics*. Cambridge, MA: MIT Press.

9

TECHNICAL SERVICE

When it comes to any product, the manufacturer often knows more about the way to use or process that product than the end-user. In effect there will be a knowledge gap between the two parties. The ease with which this gap is bridged will depend on the complexity of product handling and processing. For example, learning how to heat baked beans in a saucepan is much easier than learning how to process a two-component polyurethane system. Bridging this gap is key to ensuring that a product is processed correctly such that it performs as specified each and every time.

Knowledge gap

Determining the knowledge gap is an important step in developing the appropriate training tools and methods. An example knowledge gap analysis is shown in Figure 9.1.

In general, the bigger and more complex the gap, the more likely it is that Technical Service will be involved. Some day-to-day examples of the type of action related to each segment include:

Low gap/low complexity – user led

Learning to paint, for example, is an activity that the users themselves, with the support of some instruction documents, will undertake. Training can be in the form of looking up a video on the Internet. Whilst there are expert painters and decorators, it is unlikely that everyday users will look for training.

Low gap/high complexity – expert-led individual

An example here is where an experienced car driver looks to gain advanced accreditation or a licence to drive a heavy goods vehicle. The driver will usually have basic skills but further training will be required, and this has to be given by an accredited expert.

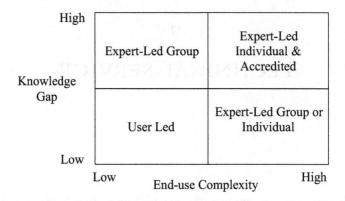

Figure 9.1 Knowledge gap analysis.

High gap/low complexity – expert-led group

An example in this segment will be training to deal with a fire. Often, people have little knowledge of how to do this, but the task will be seen as low in complexity. Training is often undertaken for groups of people led by individual experts.

High gap/high complexity – expert-led individual and accredited

Training to be a pilot might be considered to fall into this category. It is insufficient to have attended training courses, one-to-one training is often mandated and a predetermined level of proficiency is required, evidenced by the issue of a licence. Such is the complexity and need for assurance regarding a pilot's skill, refresher training has to be undertaken with a predetermined level of proficiency required.

In a business-to-business environment, assessing the knowledge gap can be problematic, as can the act of determining the degree of end-use complexity. Over time, an organisation will be able to determine these values more consistently and accurately, though the prudent approach will always be one of assuming ignorance.

Training as a means of bridging a knowledge gap can take many forms. The type of training material used as a resource will also vary and includes:

- Instruction manuals (both paper-based and online)
- Application guidelines (both paper-based and online)
- Instruction videos
- Application videos

- Group training (on- and off-site)
- Individual training (on- and off-site)
- Evidenced training using prescribed assessment methods

As can be seen, bridging the knowledge gap is an important activity, and in a business-to-business environment this task will involve the Technical Service function. The degree to which Technical Service is involved will depend on the phase of the product's use at the customer.

Figure 9.2 illustrates the type of Technical Service involvement in the product introduction process.

The premise here is that whenever an organisation looks to establish new business with either new products or existing products new to the customer, there is a risk that issues will arise.

In an ideal world there will be issue-free trials, followed by issue-free initial use and finally issue-free ongoing use by the customer. Ongoing use reflects the majority of relationships that an organisation has.

When customers have problems using products, many customers invariably look to blame a product, whereas in many cases the cause is the customer's processing of the product(s). Ensuring that a customer understands how to use the product and the importance of controlling the associated processes is a key role for Technical Service, as it will reduce, if not eliminate, the number of reported problems, and also help to protect an organisation's reputation.

Avoiding customer returns is always the goal, as any returned products might be in a state that could prove difficult to recover. This is especially the case if the product is only sold to a single customer.

Technical Service's role in preventing process-related issues effectively revolves around reducing the knowledge gap between the organisation and the customer in relation to the processing and use of the product(s) concerned.

As we have already seen, there are three stages in the use of a product. We will take each stage in turn.

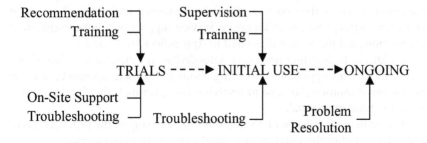

Figure 9.2 Technical Service involvement in a new business.

Customer trials

Whilst Technical Service will clearly have an active part in any customer trial, it should not be forgotten that an important part is to prepare the customer for the trial. Preparation and planning, as with any activity, are key to delivering a successful trial. In this regard, an organisation would be well advised to have a preparatory checklist for any trial. An example is shown in Appendix 17.

Initial use

Depending on the degree of complexity and relative customer knowledge gap, Technical Service may be required to support a customer during the initial use of the new product.

Should support be required, an abbreviated form of the trial checklist can prove useful, and an example is given in Appendix 18.

Ongoing use

Where a customer has been successfully using a product, the need to call on Technical Service will usually only arise when the customer has a problem. In such instances, an organisation may well have logged the issue as a complaint. Whilst the organisation will have an internal procedure to follow, it does not preclude a structured approach to dealing with the issue. Again, a checklist can prove useful, and an example is given in Appendix 19. The value of a checklist is that data is captured and that it captures organisational learning and expertise.

From an inventory perspective, Technical Service is looking to play its part in both ensuring that a customer successfully converts the organisation's product into its own product and, in so doing, prevent the return of product back to the organisation.

Troubleshooting

Through their knowledge and expertise, Technical Service staff are, especially in the customer's eyes, the experts in the field of product application. A consistent approach to the provision of Technical Service support puts great emphasis on preparation, and this is well illustrated in Appendices 16, 17 and 18.

In addition to building their own knowledge and expertise, Technical Service staff have an opportunity to bring about a consistent approach, not only in training customers, but also in resolving issues through the development of a troubleshooting manual.

Most of us are familiar with troubleshooting, as many of the products used at home have within the instruction manual a troubleshooting section.

Having troubleshooting sections is a recognition that, quite often, an issue with a product can often be easy and quick to resolve. More often than not, it will be down to the way that the product is being used or processed, rather than a fault with the product itself.

Creating a troubleshooting manual will prove useful in speedily resolving many of the customer's problems and can be made available to the customer as either a document or on the organisation's website. With help available, 24 hours a day, 7 days a week, simple problems can be quickly resolved, avoiding the need to wait for the supplier's Technical Service to be available. Of course, video clips can also be made available to further aid the customer in taking the first steps to resolve a problem.

What this means is that when Technical Service staff are required to attend at a customer's facility, the customer might well be able to describe any actions that have already been tried, and this can lead to a speedier resolution of the problem.

Having such tools available for customers not only makes better use of the Technical Service resource but also brings about a consistent approach to problem solving.

Measures

Tracking the number of product-related issues is one of the measures that can be used, though it will be necessary to pick out those caused by processing, as these are more likely to be the ones that Technical Service can influence.

As with other functions, the range of measures used should be extended to cover the earlier stages of Technical Service involvement which means focussing on aspects relating to trials and initial use. Some examples are shown in Figure 9.3.

Summary

When handling a product, especially when new to a customer, there will always be a knowledge gap between the supplier organisation and the customer. The size of the gap will vary, and the organisation's approach to bridging the gap will also vary.

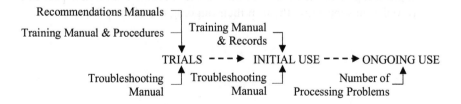

Figure 9.3 Input/output measures for Technical Service.

The approaches will range from reliance on instruction manuals through to comprehensive training programmes. In the business environment, responsibility will lie with Technical Service to ensure that the customer understands how to use the product and understand the parameters that are of importance to the processing of the product.

Simple aspects such as staff turnover can lead to a weakening of the organisation's expertise, and it is vital that the organisation find ways to retain the expertise – and this does not simply mean retaining the people concerned. Preserving knowledge within an organisation is vital for continued success, and a structured approach can aid greatly in both building a reputation as well as in ensuring continuity and continuous improvement. This, in turn, will limit the instances of customers looking to return product that can lead to unwanted or un-saleable inventory.

In performing its role effectively, Technical Service, by focussing on bridging the knowledge gap, and not just problem solving, helps to improve inventory management and builds competitive advantage.

Actions

As with all functions, a structured approach will always be beneficial to an organisation, and Technical Service is no different.

- Develop and introduce checklists relating to customer trials and initial use. When put together by the organisation's technical experts, it is likely that many nuances will be captured, including ones that some of the team might not have appreciated.
- Checklists are one of the key tools in helping to preserve organisational knowledge, and they also bring about consistency in approach.
- Develop product-specific troubleshooting manuals to help customers deal with the more common problems, especially those that might be related to processing issues.
- Establish training records for customers so that the organisation knows not only which customers have been trained, but also which of the customer's staff have been trained.
- Prepare training resources (manuals etc.) for customers. These are an important part of the process of introducing customers to a new product, as well as in supporting them in their ongoing use of the product(s).

10

CUSTOMER SERVICE

Once a business relationship has been established, the key interface between an organisation and its customers will most likely be Customer Service. Of course, many organisations have software platforms that enable customers to place orders directly into an organisation's business system, but many will rely on Customer Service departments to receive the details of a customer's requirements (whether received by post, email or telephone) and transfer that information into the organisation's business system.

Figure 10.1 shows the sales order process beginning with a customer order being added to the organisation's business system. This clearly drives all the other activities in the process leading, ultimately, to order fulfilment.

Accurate order entry is a prerequisite of the process and, unless entered directly by the customer through an Internet interface or customer portal, Customer Service will be responsible for this activity.

If errors are made at data entry, it is entirely possible that the error will not be picked up until the shipment concerned is with the customer. In the worst case, an incorrect product could be used by the customer and cause serious problems.

In order to avoid errors, it is essential that Customer Service has robust routines when it comes to both entry and validation of order data.

As mentioned, customers can place orders in a number of ways with varying levels of detail. An order can be received:

- As a formal purchase order received by post.
- From a phone call with details given verbally to Customer Service. For many organisations, their customers might well vary in their level sophistication. They will range from customers with MRP systems through to ones who phone up and say, 'I'll have what I had last time'.
- As an email to customer service.
- Entered directly through a customer portal.

Whilst each can vary in the level of precision, it is vital that Customer Service, when taking the order, is able to translate the data correctly into the organisation's business system.

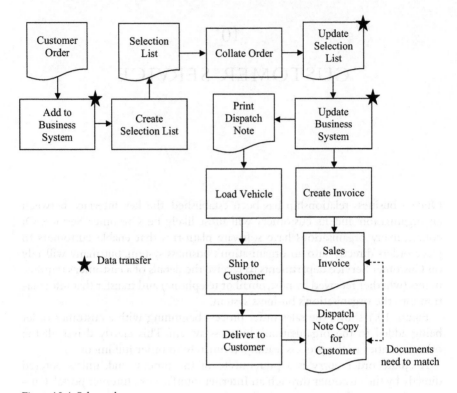

Figure 10.1 Sales order process.

Some industries (e.g. polyurethanes) supply products as two (or more) component systems that have to be mixed in a specific ratio. This added level of complexity can give rise to errors, either on the part of the customer or on the part of Customer Service. An example relating to a customer is given in Case Study 10.1.

Case Study 10.1 Ordering a polyurethane system

Background

An organisation produces polyurethane products, more commonly known as systems. An example might be a product (system) called PU A. Whilst this is the product 'sold' to customers, it is actually sold as two components described as PU A and PU B which are to be blended using a mixing ratio of 1.57 parts of PU A to 1 part of PU B.

Review

One customer did not order the PU A system very often, and it had been noticed that, whilst they ordered both components of the system, they ordered them in an incorrect ratio – 1.75 parts of PU A to 1 part of PU B, when it should be 1.57 parts of PU A to 1 part of PU B. This is a fairly simple transposition error, and errors of this type can and do occur more frequently than organisations would like to think.

If Customer Service took the order as written, then the customer would end up with either a surplus of PU A or insufficient PU B or, in the worst-case scenario, set their equipment to use the incorrect mixing ratio.

Outcome

The organisation, having spotted this error, told the customer about it and also had a checklist created for the particular customer which included checking the mixing ratio they used.

Despite being told about it, the customer repeated the error on two further occasions, but, because of the checklist, the organisation prevented both any problems arising and the creation of unwanted inventory.

Whilst this was a very specific case, it illustrates the difficulty that Customer Service can have when processing this type of customer order. Where a customer makes an error, it might not always be easy to spot those errors when they occur, unless robust systems are in place. The problem serves to illustrate the importance of paying attention to detail.

When processing a customer order, Customer Service has, typically, seven key details to enter into the organisation's business system:

- Customer name
- Customer delivery address
- Product code(s)/description
- Pack type required
- Quantity required
- Delivery date
- Special instructions

As a customer might have multiple products to order, a considerable number of keystrokes will be used to enter the details. Every keystroke has an inherent risk in that an incorrect key could be 'hit'. On a single keystroke, the risk might be very low. If each element required 5 keystrokes, then a typical order might require 30 keystrokes. If 100 orders are processed per day, then this could mean around 3000 keystrokes, and with so many it is evident how the risk of an error is increased. It would not take much for an error to be made that leads to an inventory issue.

Order entry drives the sales order process through to fulfilment, and it therefore needs to be error-free. Developing routines that deliver this goal is not always easy, but some useful approaches include the following:

Customer portals

As already mentioned, customers can use customer portals to enter orders directly onto an organisation's business system. The use of customer portals does not absolutely guarantee that order entry will be error-free, as the customer can make errors. The customer might either order the wrong product or enter the incorrect quantity, or both.

Whilst errors are likely to be the customer's responsibility there is an element of having 'passed the buck' to the customer. In such circumstances, an organisation should not just sit back and say it was the customer's problem. The organisation needs to work with the customer, as they might not appreciate being reminded that they should have 'got it right in the first place'.

Familiarity

Some organisations will have their Customer Service set up such that any customer can place an order with anyone in the department. Other organisations will have Customer Service staff designated to deal with specific customers and their orders. The latter helps develop familiarity with a customer, enabling individual staff to develop an awareness of, for example, a customer's order patterns. This, in turn, can help the organisation query orders from customers that do not fit their usual order pattern. Identifying such issues can avert the creation of unwanted inventory.

Whichever approach is adopted, the organisation needs to appreciate any inherent weaknesses and consequent risk.

Templates

Most business systems will have the capability to create order templates for customers whereby their most commonly purchased products can be displayed on the Customer Service representative's screen. This means that a product is selected and only the quantity needs to be entered. This reduces the number of keystrokes/mouse clicks required, thereby reducing the risk of errors.

Variance reports

Whilst templates have their place in reducing errors at the data entry stage, variance reports can prove useful in picking up errors after the data entry stage.

Typically, when making a comparison, three data sources can be used – historical pattern of demand, budget demand and template products. The activity flow is shown in Figure 10.2.

Running the reports on a daily basis will both highlight potential errors sooner rather than later and establish a control routine that becomes a standard activity.

It is easy to see the adoption of such methods as overkill, but the use of such routines and tools needs to be offset against both the cost and inconvenience of an error and the potential damage to an organisation's reputation.

Part packs

In the chemical industry, Customer Service can have a role to play in dealing with one of the consequences of batch processing – namely part packs. The preferred solutions are, in order of priority:

- Not to produce a part pack.
- Produce as small a part pack as possible.
- Commit the customer to taking the whole batch, including the part pack.
- Sell the part pack.

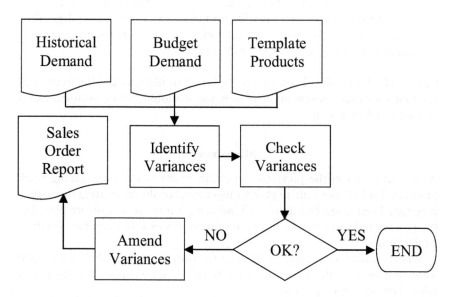

Figure 10.2 Activity flow for variance analysis.

Clearly, Sales has its part to play with the third item, but the effective responsibility for ensuring that the sale goes through is often up to Customer Service. If the item does not appear on the sales order, then it will not be shipped.

Where arrangements have not been put in place, Customer Service can look to sell part packs to customers, perhaps with appropriate incentives (for both Customer Service and customer), with the cost offset by the cost that would otherwise be incurred in having to deal with the part pack within the organisation (e.g. disposal).

Error spotting

As with all other functions and roles, Customer Service staff will undergo training in order to carry out the role. However, as with other roles, once the training has been completed, there will be little further training unless there is a change in the process – for example, the introduction of a new business system.

Rather than assuming the staff are alert to errors, routines should be developed to help Customer Service staff spot errors:

- Ongoing training in error spotting. This is similar to an IT department sending out fake phishing emails in order to train users what to expect and how to spot non-standard emails.
- Have a well-displayed list of typical errors and typical miscreant customers. This will alert Customer Service staff to look out for issues relating to certain customers. Having a list will also reduce the risk of being dependent on certain staff who normally deal with certain customers, but might, for example, be away on holiday (vacation).

Case Study 8.2 (in the chapter on Sales) serves to illustrate the importance of spotting errors and, where an error is made, it should not be assumed that a customer will pick it up.

Measures

As we have seen in the previous section, there are ways of developing work practices that help not only in preventing errors, but also in spotting them once they have been made. In Figure 10.3, we can see how these tools are placed in the process and form part of the suite of measures used to keep the system in equilibrium.

When creating any budget or general forecast, the data can be used to give some indication of the impact on level of activity, for example, the number of sales orders processed per day.

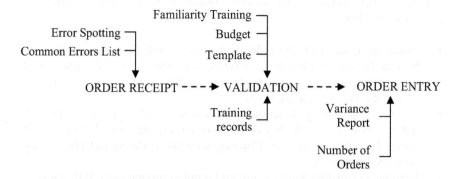

Figure 10.3 Sales order receipt and entry.

Comparing the actual number of orders processed against the historical average can be a flag to assess whether systems are being put under any strain. The logic here is that any deviation from a plan represents a change, and any change can increase the risk of an error occurring. The organisation could look to use the daily average as a benchmark or use the historical maximum as the standard against which to compare the current level. For example, if the daily averages number of orders per day were 76, 42, 58, 93 and 67, the maximum would be 93. Anything above this, or below 42, would warrant a review.

The type of benchmark used will determine the scale of any caveats. For example, when using the historical maximum, the caveat might be that sales order errors are not significantly higher when the maximum number of orders are processed. If an organisation does not have an existing benchmark, the approach should be to just adopt an approach and, over time, review its usefulness and make alterations as required.

Summary

Customer Service has a clear role to play in ensuring that the data being used by Planning is 100% correct. Sales order entry drives the planning process and subsequent manufacturing activity.

The impact of an error can be very real with potentially serious consequences impacting not just inventory, but also the organisation's reputation and balance sheet (where payments are made against claims).

Actions

Clearly, Customer Service has an important part to play in the inventory management process, and this is not limited to correct processing of customer orders.

Ensuring that accuracy is maintained throughout is vital, and the following are recommended:

- Count the number of sales orders and compare to the benchmark. This can be a useful way of identifying potential resource issues. If the number of orders is forecast to increase significantly, will Customer Service be able to cope with existing staffing levels?
- Create a report to pick up any potential sales order variances. Spotting differences is one of the key methods of picking up issues before further action has taken place (e.g. Planning scheduling the manufacture of an unwanted product).
- Introduce error-checking systems and training programmes. Training is an ongoing process, and routines need to be in place to help staff, not just Customer Service staff, refine their skills.
- Use Customer Service as a means of dealing with problems such as the creation of part packs. Arguably, having more contact with a customer than the Sales team, Customer Service can be viewed as an asset and used as a means of creating value.

11

MARKETING

In many people's eyes, Marketing is the function that both develops a company's image and promotes the company within the markets that it is active in. Whilst these activities will have little or no impact on inventory, there are two areas where Marketing has a more direct impact, namely promotional activities specifically related to a product, or products, and market research. The former has a more immediate impact on demand and can sometimes drive a fairly sharp increase in sales of the product(s) concerned. The latter (having already been touched upon in the chapter on Sales – Figure 8.5) provides Planning with a long-term view of market trends which are especially useful when assessing future capacity requirements.

It is important to recognise how both activities can impact inventory.

Product promotion

Whether promoting existing or new products, a successful marketing campaign will be expected to lead to a change in demand for those products. In some instances, new product introduction can be at the expense of existing products, and Planning need to be aware in both instances.

Whenever there is a change in demand, several aspects (production plan, lead-times, raw materials etc.) will be impacted, and careful consideration needs to be given to each. Figure 11.1 illustrates how an area can be impacted by any change in demand. Clearly, the bigger the change, the bigger the impact. This 'impact assessment' is not prescriptive and will include other areas depending on the nature of the product where a change of demand is encountered.

New product introduction, if successful, will lead to an increase in demand. The Sales Change – Impact Assessment diagram in Figure 11.1 can be used to point out which areas of the business need to be both aware of, and involved in, any new product introduction.

From a Marketing perspective, promotional activities should be scheduled around the forecast demand. Ideally, forecasts will be accurate, but either way, they need to be communicated to Planning and Production. The organisation

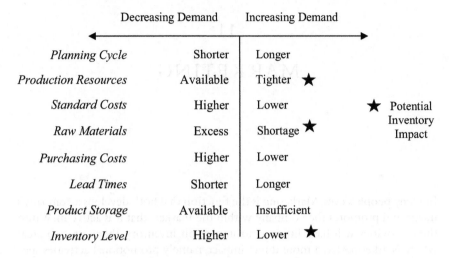

Figure 11.1 Sales change – impact assessment.

does not want to be caught out by rapid growth in demand, as there are likely to be several consequences.

- Constantly modifying the production plan
- Longer lead-times
- Raw material shortages
- Failure to ship customer orders on time and in full
- Damage to the organisation's reputation

Communicating effectively is key and involving all functions early in the process is vital in enabling an organisation to take on the challenge with the minimum of fuss.

As I write this, there is a good example of what can happen when a new challenge is taken on, but not sufficiently thought through – see Case Study 11.1.

Case Study 11.1   KFC and DHL

A failure to properly understand how your systems work can have catastrophic consequences when preparing to take on new business. Early in 2018, DHL took over the distribution of chicken for KFC in the UK. Their inability to anticipate the consequences on their business and properly define what was needed resulted in the temporary closure of several hundred KFC outlets.

The issues were resolved, partly by reverting back to their original supplier, Bidvest, but that the problem arose in the first instance serves to illustrate the importance of:

1   *Fully understanding the customer's requirements.*
2   *Understanding exactly what was needed and how the process would work.*

No doubt much will be written about this and many lessons learnt. Of course, these things are not easy, but perhaps attending to detail might have lessened the impact of taking on the challenge in the first place.

Understanding customer requirements

When looking to trigger new product development, it is essential that critical criteria are precisely understood and defined.

Not fully understanding the criteria related to the use of a product can result in products being developed that do not meet market requirements.

In general, understanding market requirements is done by means of discussions with direct customers and/or end–users.

Where they are one and the same, then it is likely that little will be missed. However, if the end-user is detached from the organisation, then there is the potential for a knowledge gap to appear.

Figure 11.2 illustrates the types of relationships that exist. The end–user is the ultimate customer and the one who drives the final performance criteria, but

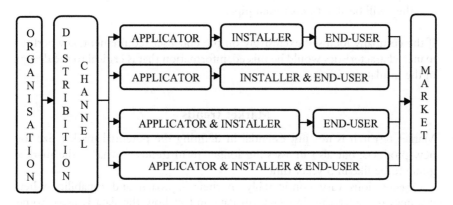

Figure 11.2 Channel gap analysis.

it should not be forgotten that the applicator and installer might also have their own specific set of requirements. In other words, each will have knowledge in relation to the product's performance requirements.

Speaking to the end-user alone risks missing out on understanding requirements that the applicator and installer might have. Failure to recognise this can lead to a poorly designed product and, when trials start, unsuitable inventory being manufactured that will have no value and need to be disposed.

An example of end-user requirements not giving you the complete picture is the insulation of offshore oil pipelines:

- *End-user*
  The end-user or field operator will have specific requirements relating to the insulation coating. They will have defined key performance criteria – what temperature the insulation coating will have to withstand and their requirements in relation to heat loss. These represent the final and key performance characteristics of the insulation coating.
- *Installer*
  Amongst the criteria specific to the installation phase are flexibility, structural integrity and adhesion.
  Flexibility – the coating will need to be sufficiently flexible to allow the coated pipe to be bent. In other words, it should not crack.
  Structural integrity – the coating will need to be strong enough to withstand the pressures exerted when the coated pipe is gripped during the lay process.
  Adhesion – during the lay process, the coating needs to have sufficient adhesion so that the steel pipe does not slip when the coated pipe is gripped by the lay vessel's tensioners.
- *Applicator*
  The applicator will have their own requirements relating to the ease of application of the coating onto the steel pipes and the speed with which they will be able to coat each pipe.

If the company focussed exclusively on the end-user requirement, key performance characteristics would be missed, information that is critical to the design of the insulation coating.

Market trends

Market research is not just essential in defining the potential market size for new products, but also in assessing longer-term trends – what is the market going to be like in 5 years' time?

Organisations vary considerably in their approach and capability when it comes to generating longer-term data and in how the data is used. Some will rely totally on a third-party organisation to collate data and report to the organisation, whilst others will look more closely at various third-party data sources and process raw data internally so that it can be tailored more closely to the organisation's needs.

Longer-term analysis is often strategically important to an organisation as it will impact not only on manufacturing resource decisions but also on product development decisions. Confidence and reliability in longer-term data is vital in enabling an organisation to make the best decisions.

As with any process there needs to be a clear structure in place, and everyone must understand how the data is to be used and how conclusions have been derived. In the first instance, an organisation needs to define what it is looking for and what it sees as the key driver(s) for the market. For example, is the correlation going to be with a country's GDP (gross domestic product) or is it some other factor like the price of oil.

Having defined exactly what it is looking for, the organisation then needs to select a data source. From the data source, various algorithms can be applied that help the organisation to see more clearly how its particular market or products are going to be affected. Underpinning the algorithms will be a set of assumptions. It is essential that these are not only agreed but validated. If some uncertainty exists, then work needs to be undertaken to establish how the assumptions can be validated.

The process of preparing longer-term market research data tends to be an ad hoc exercise, being undertaken every few years.

The problem with this is that people might forget which assumptions were made, why they were used and how they were applied, making it difficult to have complete confidence when comparing new forecasts with previously prepared long-term forecasts.

This means that, ideally, the process of preparing a long-term forecast needs to be standardised and structured with clearly defined processes and assumptions. One option is to obtain data from a third-party source; this is a fairly straightforward process, as illustrated in Figure 11.3.

To get the best out of a summary from a third-party provider, the organisation's requirements need to be clearly defined. Without clear definition, all that

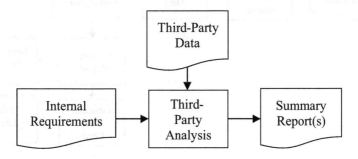

Figure 11.3 Sourcing market analysis from third parties.

173

an organisation might get are summary reports that provide overviews and are difficult to relate to the organisation's markets and products.

If assumptions are to be applied by an organisation, then the data being provided needs to be at a level of detail that makes the assumptions relevant. Otherwise, the reports will never have real value and the organisation will be unlikely to advance its understanding of the markets it operates in.

Of course, third-party summary reports are not necessarily the only option that an organisation has. For example, in the oil, gas and energy markets there are project data sources that provide access to more detailed data, and it is here that value can sometimes be extracted. Not only can this be more useful to an organisation, but it can also be advantageous over the longer term.

By clearly defining its requirements and understanding how to use the data, a company can develop a structured approach to converting the data into more useful product-specific information.

An example of the type of a structured approach is shown in Figure 11.4.

By adopting such an approach, data can be tailored to meet an organisation's specific requirements and, in some instances not just provide long-term forecasts, but also specific sales leads.

Project data sources are used extensively for their news feeds, but the raw data is rarely used. Project data analysis is a tool that harnesses detail available in project data sources for projects in the oil, gas and energy sectors. Using project data analysis can translate raw data into useful product-specific forecasts. The tool harnesses an organisation's knowledge and expertise in a bespoke manner and is a way of consolidating organisational learning.

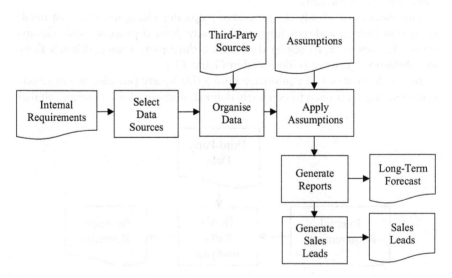

Figure 11.4 Internal data analysis process.

The keys to the process are the assumptions being used to effectively filter and convert raw data into usable information. Each assumption needs to be validated and, over time, as forecasts, assumptions and sales leads are tested against real market data and feedback, they can be refined, thereby improving the quality of the output.

When well established, the tools will be seen for what they are – an exceptionally useful resource that not only provides an insight into the market that cannot be achieved directly from third parties but that also provides the organisation with a source of competitive advantage.

From an inventory perspective, having confidence in such tools means that market trends – as predicted by the tools – can be viewed with a higher degree of certainty and will prove of real value in helping both Planning and Production anticipate upturns and downturns in demand and act accordingly.

Measures

Clearly, whether short term or long term, accuracy of forecasting is vital. We have already seen that both short- and long-term forecasts are relevant to an organisation from a Planning perspective, with the emphasis being on identifying changes in demand.

The key is that Marketing have a structured approach for the process of generating data from external sources.

One approach to developing a structured approach is to have a checklist, as illustrated in Appendix 20.

Checklists and validation will be the main features of measures designed to improve the quality of inputs into the process (Figure 11.5), whilst continuous reviews using feedback will enable assumptions to be tested and improved.

Summary

It could be argued that market research by its very nature is never going to be absolutely precise. However, rigour and attention to detail will ensure that confidence levels can be as high as possible. It is also clear that, over time, refining

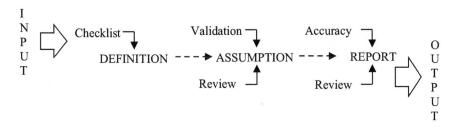

Figure 11.5 Market research elements.

assumptions and challenging the data being reported will result in continuous improvement and, consequently, develop even greater confidence in the data.

Using inventory management as one of the drivers for improvement in the quality of the data and market research process will not only benefit Planning's and Production's decision-making processes which, in turn, will have a positive impact on inventory, but also improve the organisation's understanding of the market and market dynamics – another potential source of competitive advantage.

Actions

A recurring theme is the need to have structured approaches for many of an organisation's processes. Whilst the emphasis is on inventory management, structured approaches clearly benefit an organisation in other, often significant ways, and Marketing is a good example.

- Develop a checklist (Appendix 20) to ensure a structured and consistent approach to market research. Using spreadsheets as the main tool for processing the data is very much to be recommended. Few people in an organisation will be familiar with a database tool such as Microsoft Access, but everyone will be familiar with Microsoft Excel.
- In the oil, gas and energy industries, tools such as project data analysis (developed by Cadnant Consulting Ltd.) can harness data from subscription sources and create easy-to-update, product-specific market forecasts.
- Set up regular communication meetings with Planning and Production to review new product and long-term data. It is essential to anticipate not only increases in demand, but also decreases in demand.
- Ensure that knowledge gap analysis is undertaken as part of new product development. It is essential that the target specification for a new product is well understood and defined not only for the end-user, but also for the applicator and installer, especially when these are discrete and separate activities. When this is not the case, unwanted inventory will inevitably be created, and time will be wasted.

12

RESEARCH AND DEVELOPMENT

Research and Development (R&D) is a key function in any organisation, with responsibilities ranging from developing new products to supporting production and helping resolve product-related customer complaints.

Each of these activities impacts inventory management directly or indirectly, either lessening or raising the risks associated with product manufacture.

New product development

The basic activities involved in New Product Development are shown in Figure 12.1.

As with other functions within the organisation, the basic approaches are still the same. When defining a formulation, it is vital that the target specification is both accurate and precise. Without accuracy and precision, it is likely that any product developed will fail with regard to one or more of its performance characteristics.

Channel gap analysis (referred to in Chapters 8 and 11), is a useful way of ensuring that all key stakeholders have been identified and interviewed in order to establish any criteria that will be specific to their part of the process.

For example, an organisation might want to develop a product with an end-user or end-use market in mind and accordingly interview several end-users. This will enable an organisation to understand what is ultimately required and set an appropriate performance specification for the new product.

However, where the application and installation stages are separate and undertaken by different organisations, there might well be criteria specific to the application and installation stages that the end-user will not be familiar with. If the applicators and installers are not involved in the market analysis, then additional criteria might be missed. Consequently, product design might be flawed, and this can result in an unsuitable product being developed.

It might well be that the organisation is lucky, and applicators and installers are happy with the new product, but in the worst-case scenario, much time and resource can be invested in a product that ultimately is unsuitable, thereby risking the creation of unusable inventory (both product and raw materials).

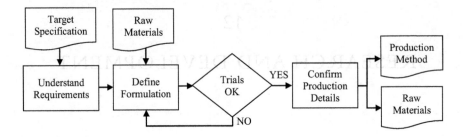

Figure 12.1 New product development.

Another aspect in the development of new products are the raw materials used. Depending on the nature of the product, R&D staff will either use raw materials currently used by the organisation or introduce one or more new raw materials.

Clearly, there can be sound technical reasons for the inclusion of a new raw materials, but there will be instances where staff will have been tempted by various promotional information to use new raw materials. Some control is desirable as, otherwise, the number of different raw materials used will continue to rise and place increased pressure on warehousing and production systems and risk spiralling out of control.

Including new raw materials will trigger a change in inventory equilibrium, introducing risks in several areas:

• New storage requirements
• New raw material handling procedures
• New packaging
• New supplier(s)

As we have already seen, any change has the potential to increase the risk of an inventory issue.

When a new product is to be introduced that utilises a new raw material, a smooth introduction can be ensured by using a checklist that covers all aspects of the process. An example is given in Appendix 21.

Production support

Either when new products are being introduced or when normal products are being produced, there will be occasions where R&D needs to provide expertise and support to the production plant.

Figure 12.2 shows some of the typical steps involved when Production requires R&D support.

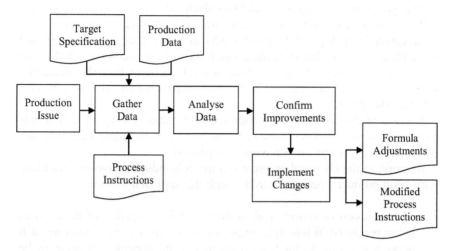

Figure 12.2 Production support.

As can be seen, potential outputs of the process are changes to either the formulation or process instructions, or both.

When any change is made, whilst ultimately delivering improvements, there is a risk that an issue will arise in the short term because the impact of the change was not fully appreciated.

Many organisations have change management systems in place with processes designed to not only ensure effective implementation of the change, but also to minimise the risks associated with the change.

Misunderstood changes or changes incorrectly applied can cause serious issues and clearly need to be avoided. Paying attention to detail is critical, and a structured approach (as with other functions) will help ensure a smooth change with minimal or zero risk.

Again, a checklist will prove a useful tool, and an example is given in Appendix 22.

Quarantine inventory

An organisation's production process can, at some point, end up creating inventory that is either outside the required specification or cannot be sold.

In the first instance, an organisation will clearly need to undertake a thorough analysis in order to understand the cause of the problem in order to prevent further issues. Equally though, the organisation has the challenge of dealing with quarantine inventory that has been created.

In some instances, dealing with the inventory can be quite straightforward. However, on many occasions some technical expertise will be needed, and this is where R&D plays a part.

The type of process requiring R&D involvement is illustrated in Figure 12.3.

The worst-case scenario for an organisation is that quarantine inventory will be designated for disposal. Disposal results in a direct impact on profit, and the only question is that of timing which, in turn, depends on whether the organisation has chosen to apply a provision at the point where the quarantine inventory is created or whether the financial impact is only felt when disposal actually takes place.

R&D (and this includes production technical support staff) has a clear role in helping to prevent this outcome. As can be seen from Figure 12.3, there are two main recovery options – rework or reprocess.

Rework, in the chemical industry, can mean blending quarantine inventory with good product. Points to consider with this approach include:

- The inclusion of rework will slightly modify the quality of the product being produced. Whilst this might not be deemed to be significant, it is nevertheless a deviation from normal, and the organisation needs to be aware of this.
- If a product is not manufactured very often, a rework level of 10% might mean that it would take several years to deal with it. This might be considered acceptable by an organisation, but it is easy to see that product quality is going to be affected for a long period of time. Prolonged storage might also result in further deterioration of the quarantine product and/or its packaging.

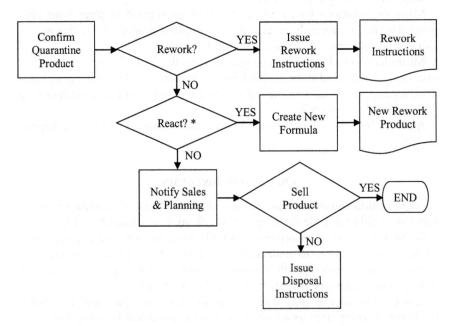

Figure 12.3 Dealing with quarantine inventory.

The risk with having a deviation from the equilibrium has already been discussed in previous chapters and, even when controlled, the risk will prevail until the product designated for rework has been completely recovered.

From this perspective, it is preferable to complete the recovery of quarantine inventory as quickly as possible. This might require a modification to the standard product but is preferable to a prolonged recovery.

In terms of storage, it is also preferable to deal with the problem quickly, as this will release storage space for standard products and reduce the 'clutter effect' of quarantine inventory.

If rework is not possible, then a reformulation approach should be considered. In other words, can the quarantine product be easily transformed into another product that can more easily be sold? Where an organisation has several types of quarantine inventory, a blend can also be considered.

Obviously, this aspect of R&D's involvement in inventory management is very much problem driven. The issue has already occurred and now the consequences have to be dealt with. As an organisation improves, the number of occasions that require R&D involvement should diminish. But in the meantime, R&D's active participation will help emphasise how important inventory management is and how every detail needs to be attended to.

Customer complaints

Involvement in dealing with customer complaints is an opportunity to enhance understanding of not only the product, but also how a product is used by customers.

The basic activities that involve R&D are illustrated in Figure 12.4.

The process is basically that of any problem–resolution process. Whilst a customer's own processing is often the likely cause of the problem, it will, in certain instances, be due to the product.

Where the product is at fault, it becomes even more important to establish the precise cause. If the root cause is within the organisation, it is likely to be a weakness in the inventory management system – be that material charging (see

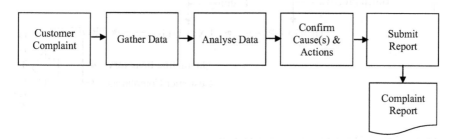

Figure 12.4 Customer complaint support.

181

Case Study 4.4), inventory management (see Case Study 5.1) or poor formulation (see Case Study 4.6) and so on.

Validated customer complaints are therefore a useful measure of how well the whole process is working and can provide valuable insights – often challenging an organisation to better understand the relevant system and bring about sustainable improvements.

Measures

Actions taken by R&D can impact inventory well down the line. It is important to ensure that the development of new products, whilst not constraining innovation, follows clear guidelines designed to ensure that attention to detail is maintained at all times.

Figure 12.5 illustrates the types of aspects that require measures such that risk associated with both the introduction of new products and maintaining consistent production are minimised, if not eliminated.

Summary

R&D can be considered to be at the beginning of the product process – effectively triggering change in the system. This makes it not only vital to exercise control using a structured approach, but also to have an effective change management process.

In some organisations, R&D is not actively involved in supporting initial manufacture of new products (merely transferring data etc. over to production staff) which makes it vital that planning and preparation is structured and takes account of previous experience.

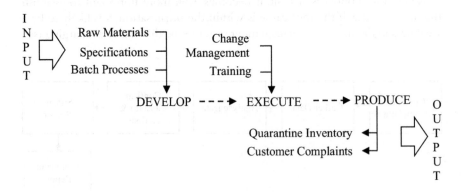

Figure 12.5 R&D activities and associated measures.

Actions

The actions are similar to those adopted in other chapters, and all will impact inventory in a positive way:

- Undertake knowledge gap analysis prior to all new product development to ensure that the all performance criteria are thoroughly understood.
- Develop a checklist for the introduction of new products along the lines of the example shown in Appendix 21, ensuring that it covers aspects such as storage, raw materials handling, new packaging, new suppliers etc.
- Develop processes and procedures that ensure that all production issues and customer complaints are thoroughly investigated and understood. A structured approach to problem solving is an important part of the overall process of improving inventory management.

13

ERROR MANAGEMENT

'The world as we have created it is a process of our thinking. It cannot be changed without changing our thinking'.

– Albert Einstein

When reviewing complaints or dealing with issues arising within an organisation, you will often hear the frustrated comment, 'No matter what we do, we never seem to stop making mistakes'. The same mistakes seem to be made time and time again, and the goal of zero complaints seems to ebb further away. Few organisations can claim to be immune to this.

As part of their efforts to resolve problems, organisations will often have processes and procedures in place to deal with internal issues and customer complaints. The better processes will follow a structured problem-solving methodology where the desired outcome is some form of preventive action that can be put in place to prevent a recurrence of the problem. That some problems recur suggests that, despite the best of intentions, sustainable improvement is not as easy to achieve as it might seem.

The obvious question is 'Why?' and often the reason will be put down to 'human error'. Such human error can typically be ascribed to one of three types – skill gap, knowledge gap and not following a process correctly.

Skill gap

An individual or team does not have the skill(s) required to carry out a task or activity. For example, they have not been trained to drive a car or carry out a plumbing repair or enter a purchase order.

Knowledge gap

An individual did not have sufficient knowledge to properly carry out a task or activity. For example, having learnt to drive a car, the individual does not have sufficient experience to deal with certain driving conditions or when a customer makes a special request.

Not following a process correctly

Despite having both the skill and knowledge, an individual can sometimes not follow a procedure correctly. For example, having learnt how to drive a car and acquired the knowledge to deal with different conditions, a driver can drift into adopting bad practices such as driving too close to the vehicle in front or using a cell phone whilst driving. They might also be distracted whilst driving or become tired from having driven for too long.

Being able to classify an error does move things on, but as has already been said, despite best efforts, human error sometimes seems stubbornly resistant to elimination.

Much work has been undertaken to try and understand why this should be the case, in particular from a psychological perspective. Whilst the focus tends to be, quite understandably, on safety and accidents, there is no reason why the concepts and approaches can't be applied to all errors.

James Reason and others suggests that, despite having robust systems, organisations and people should accept that errors are going to happen, and that they should look to develop ways of dealing with them when they arise.

Of course, accepting that errors are going to occur should not detract from efforts to eliminate them – or rather efforts to manage errors. By this, I mean that organisations might want not just to accept that errors will happen, but that errors are there waiting to happen and that they will pop out or 'escape' given the right conditions.

If we use criminals and prisons as an analogy for errors, then in much the same way that we use prisons to contain prisoners and prevent escapes, one can consider that errors are there waiting to escape and that efforts should be made to contain errors and prevent them from breaking out.

Viewing errors in the same way suggests a different perspective on error management, and that in addition to existing efforts we should consider the factors that are critical to containment.

As a starting point we can use the prison analogy and consider the attributes of a prison that aid in the containment process. Typically, the effectiveness of prison containment is a function of:

- Building design
- Equipment
- Control procedures
- Qualified staff

Taken as simple descriptors, merely removing the word 'prison' provides a structure that should be immediately familiar to all organisations. Of course, organisations might well say that they have all aspects covered. However, it is in how they are approached and how they are applied that the differences emerge.

Visualisation

The management of errors is one area where a visualisation approach can be useful. If we consider that there are key features present in error management, we can apply a visualisation structure to error management, leading to the creation of an error containment ring (ECR), as shown in Figure 13.1.

The perspective is on recognising that errors exist, and the ring is about containing those errors. Key to preventing 'error breakout' will be the integrity of the ring and of its individual components.

The next step, having recognised that errors are looking to break out and that they need to be contained, is to consider each of the main elements of the error containment ring:

- Equipment
- Process
- Training
- Focus

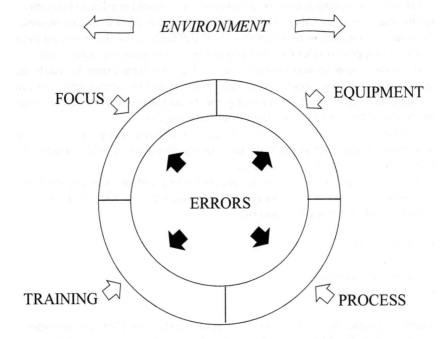

Figure 13.1 Error containment ring.

Equipment

There are two aspects to consider – suitability of the equipment for the product to be manufactured or activity to be undertaken and reliability.

It is sometimes the case that whilst manufacturing equipment is initially designed to perform one type of function, over time it ends up being used to manufacture a different type of product for which it might or might not be suitable. This can equally apply to software systems designed to facilitate administrative activities like order processing.

Clearly starting from scratch enables an organisation to design in all the required features as well as having all appropriate safeguards. In most instances, though, an organisation drifts into making do with what it has, perhaps introducing the occasional tweak or modification. Providing the equipment, process and product are well understood, then all should be OK. However, there will be instances where something that appears to work for most products might not be quite as suitable for others.

Ensuring that equipment is able to perform consistently with minimal risk of failure typically requires three types of actions to be undertaken. Firstly, checks and adjustments as recommended by equipment manufacturers should be adhered to.

This might be considered as similar to following the POWER checks for your car:

- **P**ressure – Check your tyre pressures and inflate as required.
- **O**il – Check the engine oil level and top up as required.
- **W**ater – Check the water level and top up as required.
- **E**lectrics – Check that all light bulbs are working and replaced as required.
- **R**adial – Check that the tyre tread depths are above the legal minimum.

Secondly, routine and preventive maintenance should be undertaken in line with the equipment manufacturer's recommendations. These should be supplemented by the organisation's experience. This can be considered as similar to a car's annual service or checking tyre pressures at regular intervals.

Thirdly, some equipment will need to be recalibrated so that it is functioning accurately and consistently. This would be similar to tuning your car and applies to equipment such as weigh scales, volumetric dispensers etc.

Process

Processes and procedures, most often in documented form, set out the sequence of activities required to complete a particular task (whether in the manufacture of product, or the creation of a sales order).

Either prescribed as part of a tool being used in the organisation (e.g. software package or piece of equipment) or developed over time, procedures and processes should reflect the best understanding of the steps required to undertake a task and undertake it correctly (i.e. deliver the same outcome each and every time).

Process-related errors are likely to arise for two reasons – firstly, they are not followed correctly, and secondly, they have an inherent weakness because they have been developed without having a complete understanding of the activity to which they relate to.

Many organisations will have instances where established procedures are not being followed correctly. There will be examples where staff will say 'but we've always done it this way'. This may seem an innocuous comment, and appear to have some merit, but a practice that has developed over time can, in truth, lead to small, but significant issues over time. An example of such an issue is given in Case Study 13.1.

Case Study 13.1   Pre-charging

Background

A production facility manufactured a vinyl acetate emulsion product used in the production of water-based vinyl silk and vinyl matt paints. Two vessels were used to manufacture a PVA (polyvinyl acetate) emulsion, each having a large hopper into which vinyl acetate monomer was charged.

The target solids content was 55% and, over time, it was noticed that the first two batches were always towards the bottom end of the specification (54–56%).

Review

As the production unit had two vessels, each of which was dedicated to the manufacture of the single product (PVA), there was the nagging question – 'Why did the first two batches each week always have lower solids content?'

An investigation showed that procedures were followed each and every time. Interviewing all operators revealed that, where the working week was Monday to Friday, having completed manufacture on Friday, the monomer hoppers were pre-charged ready for Monday morning.

By coincidence, the production chemist's desk was located in a building opposite to the PVA manufacturing unit that looked down on the roof of the unit. Jokingly, over the years, people working in the opposite building referred to the emulsion manufacturing unit as 'The Good Ship PVA.'

The reason why the unit was called 'The Good Ship PVA' was due to the vent lines coming through the roof of the unit and the vapour that could, on a still day, be seen to be coming out of these vent lines.

The production chemist realised that this vapour was in fact vinyl acetate monomer that was evaporating from the monomer hoppers. As the vent lines were open to the atmosphere, the 'chimney effect' meant that material was being lost from the monomer hopper. If material was lost, then the solids content of the batch being produced was being reduced.

The production chemist realised that this was not only affecting every single batch being produced but two batches in particular. These were the batches where the monomer was pre-charged on a Friday for Monday production. This meant that the chimney effect was left unchecked for nearly 60 hours, resulting in a greater loss of material, and therefore lower solids content than normal.

Outcome

The first action taken was to immediately stop pre-charging of batches on a Friday for Monday production. Secondly, pressure relief valves were fitted on both monomer hopper vent lines.

The first action eliminated the incidence of two low solids batches immediately. The second action resulted in slightly higher solids content (54.9% from 54.7%) being achieved. Whilst only a slight adjustment, the combination of the two actions increased yields by 20 tonnes per annum, all at the cost of fitting two pressure relief valves and changing a procedure.

This serves to illustrate not only how trying to be efficient had an unintended consequence, but also how investigating a procedural issue pointed to a design flaw in the equipment being used.

It also showed that a result that deviated from the norm (i.e. average solids content for the majority of production) hid the fact that the norm itself was a deviation. In many ways, this was a classic example of the saying – 'the devil is in the detail', and this is something that you should always be alert to.

That a procedure has inherent weaknesses is also something that might not be obvious and often reflects aspects of a process that are perhaps not well enough appreciated or understood. An example is given in Case Study 13.2.

Case Study 13.2   Process control

Background

Amongst a range of alkyd resins being produced by an organisation were a number of short oil, castor oil–based resins. Processing instructions directed a processing temperature of 210°C.

By its very nature the polymerisation process (condensation reaction) accelerated quite rapidly towards the end of the reaction and always risked going too far, resulting in a product with a tail (Figure 13.2).

Whilst not a frequent problem, it was a recurring one and affected all short oil resins manufactured by the company.

Review

Initial review of the data showed that processing instructions were followed in every instance and that materials were also accurately charged. Reflecting on the data, the production chemist noticed that during the processing of problem batches, the temperature drifted down from the prescribed 210°C towards 200°C and was brought back to 210°C by the operator – completely in line with the manufacturing instructions.

Where batches processed in line with expectations, no such drifting occurred, and therefore no adjustment was required.

It seemed as if bringing the temperature back up to the prescribed level injected energy into the reaction sufficient to cause it to accelerate almost uncontrollably.

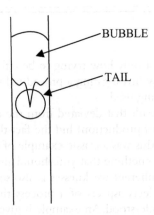

BUBBLE

TAIL

Figure 13.2 Bubble with tail.

Following this finding, the manufacturing instructions were modified to instruct operators that if the temperature drifted down they should not bring the temperature back up.

Outcome

The change in manufacturing instructions eliminated all further problems and proved so successful that it was extend to all similar products. This had the effect of increasing right first time to 100%.

Case Study 13.2 serves to illustrate that it should not be assumed that procedures and processes (manufacturing instructions in this instance) are correct and without fault.

It also showed that improvements made in one process can be extended to other similar products. Another lesson to take from the study is the importance of having confidence in operators to carry out procedures as they are set out or instructed to do so. This removes a potentially significant variable when investigating a problem.

When procedures are developed and documented, they rarely refer to the types of issues that an individual or team should look out for. Clearly, procedures set out the correct way of doing things, but they can also be used as a way of highlighting the types of situations to avoid and errors that can occur.

It is important for staff to be not just capable of following a procedure, but they should also be aware of the context within which the activity takes place and of the risks associated with the process. I would add that engaging staff in the investigative process is essential, not only because it avoids finger-pointing, but it encourages everyone not to be afraid of occasionally questioning what they do not being afraid to make what can appear to be innocuous, and potentially insightful, observations.

When looking to contain risks, a process user should always be aware of the types of risks that are likely to pop-out if the containment ring forms a gap or an element is weakened in any way.

Training

The third part of the containment ring bridges the gap between the equipment, associated procedures and the individual's level of skill and knowledge.

In most instances, training usually takes place when an individual is looking to acquire the skills to be able to carry out a task or set of tasks. The most obvious scenario is when an organisation has a new employee. Whether training is completed within days, weeks or months is dependent on the nature of the activities involved and the organisation's approach to training.

Typically, though, this training is often an activity that takes place once, and when the trainee has completed the training satisfactorily, they will be deemed to be competent enough to undertake the task. There will then be a period where the trainee will develop experience in carrying out the tasks involved.

Having acquired a skill, driving further improvement only comes through further and ongoing training. This is very much the approach in sport, and as we have seen in Table 5.1, some professional athletes can spend more than 90% of their time training with only a small percentage of their time actually carrying out the task. This does vary from sport to sport, and at one end of the scale a 100-metre runner might spend less than 1 minute per week actually competing, having spent many hours training for each race. At the other end of the scale, a professional road cyclist will spend considerably more time competing (Tour de France over 1 month, La Vuelta and Giro d'Italia also taking many weeks) and proportionally less time training. However, even in the latter case, they still spend a considerable proportion of their time training.

The entertainment industry is another industry where it can be argued that training makes up a high proportion of an individual's time when compared to time spent on the actual performance of the tasks being trained for.

Sport and entertainment are two examples. Firefighting and emergency services are further examples where training constitutes a high proportion of an individual's time relative to the time actually carrying out the task(s) involved.

In the business environment, the time spent undergoing training is considerably less than the time spent carrying out the tasks for which individuals have been engaged:

- 'Yes', an organisation will train an individual in the task(s) required to carry out the role for which they have been employed.
- 'Yes', training will be given to carry out tasks and follow procedures.
- 'Yes', further training will follow when new tasks are introduced, changes are made to an organisation's systems and for safety-related training.

However, once trained, individuals are unlikely to have refresher or follow-up training sessions designed to maintain and improve their skills.

People within an organisation will often have training records that demonstrate commitment to ongoing training, often covering a wide range of subjects. The assumption, though, behind all of this training is that once trained, an individual will know how to carry out the tasks from day one through the end of their tenure in that particular role. In other words, it is assumed that achieving 100% at the end of training means that 100% will be achieved 6 months later, 1 year later, 5 years later. The problem is that an organisation, unless it retests individuals, cannot know with certainty that this will always be the case. Often, the only way that deteriorating performance is identified is when an issue arises.

Clearly, the only conclusion one can draw from this is that some form of checking and/or refresher training needs to be undertaken. In other words, training cannot be deemed to end when training has been given together with any end-of-course testing. It is essential to check that the skills acquired are being used just as effectively after 5 years as they were after 1 week. This can only be determined by some form of regular testing or checks, which means that, in truth, training never ends.

This is what we see in sport where, for a professional athlete to maintain a level of performance, their training needs not only to be ongoing, but also closely monitored. We expect it of our athletes and emergency services, and we should equally expect it of ourselves and colleagues at every level in an organisation.

From the ECR perspective, good and effective training is about developing a strong training segment – a barrier that errors cannot breach – whilst refresher training is about maintaining the strength and integrity of the barrier over time. This can be viewed as training's preventive maintenance, but it recognises that the strength and effectiveness of every segment, training included, has to be maintained, and that this cannot be done without some effort being applied.

The timing and frequency of refresher training will vary according to the nature of the tasks, but there is no reason why they cannot become part of a daily routine. For example, training in the handling of materials delivered on pallets might involve a test to recognise different types of pallets. A score of 100% might be considered as the only acceptable pass rate.

If regular retests were undertaken and scores recorded of less than 100%, it might be that they point towards performance becoming weaker. Action can be taken to get the score back up to 100% and, again, in so doing maintain the strength of the process segment (in the ECR) and prevent errors from leaking through.

Focus

Of the four segments that make up the ECR, organisations will be familiar with and have systems in place to deal with equipment, process and training. The effectiveness of their systems will vary, but few will have given as much thought to the fourth segment – focus.

Focus is defined as 'paying particular attention to', and the risk of errors occurring is increased when focus is weakened through distractions, tiredness, boredom, monotony, stress etc. We all know how prevalent such things are in our daily lives and how easy it is to lose concentration, and therein is the challenge. The ease with which focus can be lost is why this segment can be the weakest one in the ring and the one through which errors will find their way out.

Strengthening this segment is key to maintaining the integrity of the ECR.

At first sight, this could a difficult segment to make progress in, and it would not be unreasonable to ask the question, 'Where exactly do you start?'

As with any problem, the key is not to view the challenge as a whole but to break it down into more manageable bits. Some of the factors that cause a loss of focus have already been mentioned, and they are a good place to start:

Distraction

Most people will be able to recall instances where they have been distracted from doing something. This can be whilst driving a car or at work or at home. The distraction will usually be either a visual one, a sudden or unexpected movement, a constant sound or a sudden or unexpected noise. Both types of distraction will cause an individual to possibly stop the task being undertaken and/or move away in the middle of the task they were performing. Whatever the type of distraction, it results in an interruption to the process that, in turn, means a disturbance to the equilibrium. Disturbing the equilibrium might not directly result in an error, but it weakens the focus segment, leading to an increase in the risk of an error breaking out.

Of course, visual and auditory distractions are sometimes deliberate, being used as either alerts or as a means of informing people, of which road signs and alarms are typical examples.

Using a crime metaphor, among the measures police recommend as deterrents to burglars are security features like an alarm and CCTV. Of course, whilst useful as a deterrent, CCTV is typically used when a crime is under way or after it has occurred. Other recommendations include ensuring that windows are closed and that objects are removed from around the property that could be used by a burglar, for example, a ladder.

These actions, in relation to crime, effectively assume that burglars are present in the area and are just waiting to spot a weakness. A further aspect that can be considered is that of reviewing the environment around the facility or home and looking to use design to reduce crime. The Design Council in the UK published a booklet on designing out crime that includes several examples of the use of design to prevent crime.

The Design Council demonstrated that the design process can go beyond the types of locks and doors being used, and that adopting a broader perspective can lead to new and very effective solutions to crime prevention.

In much the same way, whilst most organisations will not have the benefit of designing from scratch, consideration can be given to the layout of a working environment and how visual and auditory distractions can be minimised. Some typical examples include:

- In open plan offices, white noise being used to mask distracting sounds.
- The use of screens, again in open plan offices, to both provide some degree of privacy and limit what the eye can see and be distracted by.

The part that working environment can play should not be underestimated. How we are influenced, subconsciously, by our environment is the subject of much study. What we cannot doubt though is that we are influenced by our environment. You need only consider the work of Derren Brown, a mentalist and illusionist who has demonstrated how triggers in the environment can subconsciously influence how people act. Approaching the problem from a psychological perspective and working on the design of the environment can and will influence people in a positive way, especially in their decision making (Thaler & Sunstein, 2008).

One application is the use colour as a visual cue. A manufacturing organisation will have areas where certain safety precautions need to be taken. In addition to signs, one approach might be to use door colours to differentiate between entering a low-risk environment and entering a higher-risk environment where safety precautions need to be taken. For example, the side of the door designating entry into a high-risk area can be painted red, whilst that for entry into a low-risk environment can be painted green. Applying this across the whole of an organisation's facilities will effectively create a visual cue through repetition.

Organisations will often use colour to designate walkways, but rarely is colour used to designate access points (doors).

Such approaches can be used to find ways of reducing or controlling distractions. From an error management perspective, this means that the pressure on the interface of the environment with each segment is reduced, thereby maintaining the integrity of the segment.

Tiredness

Dealing with tiredness is a constant issue for people in general and organisations in particular. There are many ways of dealing with tiredness, some of which include:

- Avoid sugar – Sugar delivers a sudden rush of energy, but once the effect wears off, you'll be left feeling more tired than before. This means that sugary drinks and snacks should be avoided.
- Caffeine – Contrary to what you might expect, the Royal College of Psychiatrists recommends that anyone feeling tired should cut down on the amount of caffeine. This means that tea, coffee and some soft drinks, unless decaffeinated, should be replaced by water.
- Hydration – A little dehydration is known to be a contributory factor in making someone tired. Maintain hydration by drinking plenty of water.
- Get moving – Sitting at the desk for prolonged periods of time is not good. Get up and move around. If possible, everyone should also allow time for some exercise during the day, for example fitting in a brisk 10-minute walk during the lunch break.
- Plan the day – Where possible, try and plan the day and set time aside to deal with outstanding tasks.

Boredom

Boredom usually arises when someone is insufficiently stimulated by the tasks being undertaken. Aside from using psychological tricks to motivate yourself, speak to your supervisor or manager. Lack of motivation can lead to focussing on the end of the day, for example, counting the minutes to go. This neither benefits the individual concerned nor the organisation in which they are employed.

Effectively, a person's mind can drift away from a task, leading to a weakening of the focus segment and, again, increasing the risk of an error breaking out.

Monotony

Monotony is defined as 'lack of variety and interest; tedious repetition and routine'. When finding tasks to be monotonous, the mind can easily drift. An example is where during a car journey, as the driver, you find that you are unable to recall how the last 5 kilometres have been driven. Such instances are clear evidence of a loss of active focus, which can only lead to the weakening of the focus segment and an increased risk of an error breaking out.

In many ways, it is similar to boredom, and some of the approaches that are used to tackle boredom can be used to tackle monotony. One technique to reduce monotony is to break up routine and repetitive tasks.

Environment

Comfort is vital to the successful completion of a task. The workplace being too hot or too cold, an uncomfortable chair, the air having an odour, the colour scheme, lack of sunshine – these are all aspects of the environment that can bring about discomfort, resulting in a loss of focus and consequent weakening of the focus segment.

Examples of actions to address this aspect are:

- Reset air conditioning (if available).
- Purchase fans or heaters.
- Undertake an ergonomic review.
- Use light bulbs that more closely mimic sunlight.
- Consider a more calming colour scheme.

Stress

Stress is a serious enough condition such that in certain countries the need to tackle stress is recognised in law. Recognising and tackling stress is extremely important, as not only does it affect an individual's performance, but more importantly, it adversely affects their health and wellbeing.

Generally, stress is a reaction to excessive pressure and demands which are not necessarily work related. The first step in dealing with stress is to recognise the symptoms – usually seen as changes (deterioration) in performance, relationships and workplace attendance (sickness absence), to name but three.

Much has been written about stress and stress management, and many organisations provide help and guidance in dealing with stress. The full subject is beyond the scope of this book but suffice to say that stress is clearly a contributory factor in triggering errors. Some of the causes of stress include:

- *Workload*
  Individuals being asked to do more work than they can cope with.
- *Control*
  Individuals feeling that they do not have any control over what they are doing.
- *Relationships*
  Either a failure to build good relationships or having problems with discipline and bullying.
- *Change*
  People always find change difficult and challenging. It usually brings about uncertainty which contributes to stress.

Dealing with stress-related issues involves approaches such as:

- Reviewing the tasks an individual is being asked to do and the deadlines that they might be required to achieve.
- Providing training in tools used to organise work and manage time.
- Involving individuals and/or teams in the decision-making process.
- Ensuring that the organisation has effective policies for handling grievances, discipline and tackling bullying and harassment.
- Change rarely happens out of the blue. Plan ahead, involve and consult with individuals as part of the change management process.

Techniques such as mindfulness are very useful in helping individuals deal with stress, and many organisations are developing support mechanisms that include training in mindfulness.

Dealing with errors

Along with existing systems, adopting an ECR approach to preventing errors can further reduce the risk of an error breaking out. However, it is important to recognise that, despite great effort, errors might still sometimes occur.

It is therefore essential to have systems in place to deal with those errors speedily and effectively. Using the prison analogy, when prisoners escape, speedy recapture is essential. A prisoner on the run for several days will suck in more resource and increase the risk of either further escapes or more serious consequences. This is often the case with errors. The longer they remain unresolved, the more resource they consume until they are resolved. It's a case of asking the questions:

- Has it happened before?
- What did we do?
- Was it effective?
- Can we use that experience to set out what to do in the future?

Recognising the conditions that give rise to errors can be a useful skill and organisations should train staff to spot certain types of errors. A good example is where an organisation sends out fake phishing or scam emails to give their staff practice in spotting such emails.

Maintaining a strong ECR within an organisation is essential because when product has been shipped to a customer the likelihood is that the product has been moved to an environment where the ECR is much weaker.

Of course, before setting out on a programme to strengthen each segment of an ECR, the organisation needs to know where the gaps and weaknesses are. Assessing the strength of the organisation's ECR can be done by considering the attributes of each segment of the ECR. An example is given in Appendix 23.

You could say that an organisation is simply being pragmatic but, assuming that errors are just waiting to break out offers a different perspective on error management, and one that can provide a structured approach in the battle for improvement.

As James Reason says – *Error management is about managing the manageable.*

References

Design Council. (2015). *Designing out crime – a designer's guide.* London: Home Office.

Reason, J. (1990). *Human error.* Cambridge: Cambridge University Press.

Thaler, R.H. and Sunstein, C.R. (2008). *Nudge: Improving decisions about health, wealth and happiness.* New Haven, CT: Yale University Press.

14

SUMMARY

'If you always do what you've always done, you'll always get what you've always got'.

– Anon

Cash is considered to be the lifeblood of any organisation, and financial controls are something that all functions are aware of and impacted by. You need only look at a company's annual report to appreciate the prominence and importance of cash, and as the saying goes, 'cash is king'. By comparison, inventory is given relatively little prominence, usually only mentioned in relation to the value of the inventory held by the company with comments explaining any significant change from the previous report.

However, in terms of what people can relate to, inventory is something that people can see, touch and understand. Inventory in the form of product is what an organisation is all about. It is what the organisation produces and ships, what its customers buy and use. The organisation does not make and ship cash, and neither do their customers buy and use cash. Product, not cash, is what the organisation develops and promotes. This is why product, or rather inventory, matters and why inventory management is so important.

For an organisation, part of the problem is that inventory is often seen to be the responsibility of very few functions, typically just Planning and Production. Most of the other functions do not see themselves as playing a part in the management of inventory. Of course, modern technology has not helped in this regard as many people become increasingly detached from inventory.

The preceding chapters have, hopefully, helped to brush aside this misconception and have shown that all functions and everyone within them have a part, however small, to play in the management of inventory.

As the saying goes, 'the devil is in the detail', and it is one that is particularly relevant to inventory. Small, seemingly insignificant decisions made by R&D, Purchasing, Sales etc. have an impact on inventory, and appreciating this fact will make a difference.

When it comes to issues or errors, an incorrect price on an invoice, whilst an irritation, is easily dealt with. A product issue on the other hand can be much more difficult to resolve and consumes resource, manpower and time.

Preventing and dealing with such issues and errors is no easy task, whether inventory related or not. If it was easy, all organisations would have zero issues and their inventory processes would be perfectly aligned to the organisation's strategy.

Preventing issues is a challenge, and as you will have seen, there are a number of approaches that can be taken:

- Paying attention to detail.
- Aligning functional strategies and objectives to the overall strategy.
- Appreciating that processes need to be managed and that individual responsibility cannot be abrogated.
- Measures should be introduced that act as leading indicators for processes and procedures.
- Understand the context within which errors occur and creating an environment where errors are contained.

Paying attention to detail

When people ask what differentiates an ordinary restaurant from one that has a Michelin Star the answer is often down to paying attention to detail. The detail is not just about the quality of the food, but extends to all aspects of the location, staff, facilities and general experience.

And so, if an organisation wants to set itself apart from its competitors, it needs to pay attention to detail in absolutely everything it does. When it comes to inventory every function has a part to play.

Accreditation standards such as ISO9001 and BS5750 are valuable in giving businesses confidence in an organisation's capabilities, but they are not quite the guarantees of excellence that is the case with Michelin Stars.

Aligning strategies

All organisations and businesses talk of having a strategy, but as organisations grow, strategic gaps open up and functional strategies and objectives can become detached both from each other and, critically, from the organisation's strategy. Indeed, there can be instances where the detachment allows functions to develop strategies that conflict with each other.

You can also find that, quite often, individual performance goals focus on what individuals feel they should strive for rather than goals dictated by the strategy. These performance goals can seem very worthwhile and challenging, but they are not necessarily always aligned to the overall strategy.

200

Purchasing strategy is an interesting example. It is easy to focus on what are classed as 'strategic' raw materials, when in fact they are the ones that account for the majority of the spend. The '80:20 rule' is often the guide, and whilst an important part of Purchasing's role, it does not necessarily mean that purchasing activities are perfectly aligned to the organisation's strategy.

The purchasing strategy in Chapter 7, Part 2, shows how activities can be set out to ensure perfect alignment.

Processes

As with all aspects of an organisation's operations, processes feature prominently in the management of inventory. Some will be informal, often described as 'it's the way we do things', whilst many will be documented.

Often, processes will describe how manual activities interact with the organisation's business system. Over time, many tools will have been developed to support processes, which, in turn, have given rise to complex ERP (Enterprise Resource Planning) systems. Whilst varying in size and scope, most organisations nowadays use some form of ERP system.

The risk with ERP systems is that individual users become slaves to the system and merely interact with the system, rarely understanding how it works and what its' core requirements and limitations are. From the perspective of trying to improve inventory management it has to be recognised that processes and procedures are dynamic. They represent best practice at the time they were developed, but this does not mean that they cannot, and should not be improved upon.

Of course, the difficulty is that procedures and processes become institutionalised with imperfections becoming programmed into the organisation's method of working.

A good example of how adept, or not, organisations are is shown in Case Study 4.8 (Density and Drum Filling). Having made changes in pack weight, the improvement was shared with two suppliers, both large multi-national organisations that supplied virtually identical products, each having the same opportunity to increase the pack weight. One supplier adopted the idea very quickly and increased the pack weight from 225 kilos to 240 kilos. The other supplier did not want to know and seemed unwilling to adopt the idea. Whilst it is difficult to know precisely why the second supplier was unable to make the change, there is no doubt that internal procedures and processes had reached the stage where they were now barriers to progress and improvement. It should be remembered that where such barriers exist, an opportunity is created for competitors to develop competitive advantage through improved inventory management.

Of course, we should not forget that the effectiveness of procedures and processes are often dependent on the quality of information being fed into them.

Chapter 1 introduced a control loop (repeated in Figure 14.1) as a very useful tool describing the critical elements of a process.

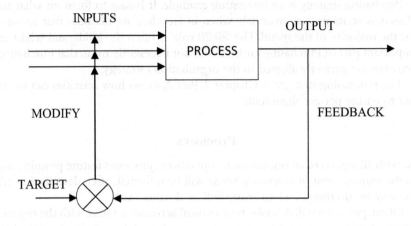

Figure 14.1 Control loop.

When a process is perfectly balanced and in control, it is likely to be thoroughly understood, such that where an organisation is looking to bring about improvement(s), the process owner(s) will know exactly which inputs to modify and by how much they should be modified. When an organisation has reached this stage, it will have recognised that not only is a balanced control loop the goal, it has also become the tool that enables improvements to be made.

Measures

Understanding and controlling processes requires data, and this will come in the form of measures. Without measures you cannot understand what is going on, and if you do not understand what is going then you cannot control what is going on.

Of course, measures are used extensively within every organisation, be they financial or operation related. However, the challenge with measurement is that they need to be relevant.

Many organisations, particularly public ones, misunderstand measures and how to use them. Quite often you will see measures being used to rate performance, which in itself is not a bad thing, but the consequence is often that institutions are rated as succeeding or failing and people and organisations risk being stigmatised as a consequence. Measures, when used correctly, are a tool that help organisations better understand a system and determine the gap between actual output and the target output, this being the first step in bringing about improvement.

When looking to introduce measures to tackle a problem, organisations must also be prepared to appreciate that the measure that is introduced might not actually be the most appropriate measure and will need changing. Case Study 14.1 illustrates this point.

Case Study 14.1 Expired inventory management

Background

An organisation had considerable inventory of expired product and needed to address it.

When setting out to tackle the problem, the goal was set to have zero expired inventory.

Review

The organisation produced a report that listed all expired items, and a team worked on trying to understand the causes. The data gathered revealed that the expired inventory was made up of full drums of product as well as part packs of product.

During the course of the exercise, it became evident that the team could only deal effectively with full drums of product and that expired part packs needed to be dealt with separately.

Having better understood the problem, the original measure was replaced by two measures – one for full drums and one for part packs.

Outcome

Splitting the measure meant that the team had a new goal of zero inventory of expired product in full drums – one which was considered achievable as it was a measure that could be controlled.

A separate approach was taken with part packs and this, in turn, resulted in progress being made that otherwise might have not been possible.

The focus of many measures (as illustrated by a control loop – Figures 1.7 and 14.1) is on the output part of a process. It is vital however, that an organisation looks to adopt measures that shift some of the focus onto the input part of the process. Sometimes described as 'leading indicators', input-related measures can point to instances where activity is deviating from the norm and place individuals or teams in a position to prevent an inventory-related issue from arising.

An example would be where damage occurs when handling materials. An investigation is likely to take place and actions taken to prevent a recurrence. If training had been given to the relevant staff, an input measure could be something like a regular test to check that the training was and continues to be effective. If 100% was the only acceptable outcome of such a test and someone was getting 90%, it might point to an increase in the risk of an error occurring well before an incident actually happens.

Technology is also offering new ways of measuring activities in such a way as to monitor and assess performance (e.g. telemetry in cars). Consideration can be given to developing similar measures and combining the activity level in order to create measures that monitor departmental performance trends or 'tiredness'.

An example might be to count the number of sales orders processed per day, the number of order lines, the number of customers, the quantity of materials, the number of materials, the number of staff involved, etc. Clearly, from development and introduction it will take time to determine the best correlation between activity and performance/tiredness.

The use of checklists as a proactive means of error prevention has been mentioned often throughout the book, and they are especially useful. There will

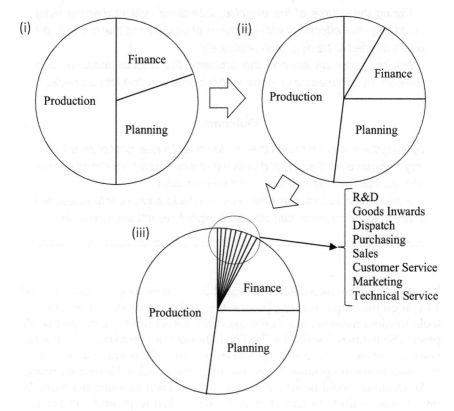

Figure 14.2 Inventory influence diagrams.

be instances where an infrequent task is being undertaken and a checklist can prove a vital tool in ensuring that the task-specific issues are highlighted and addressed. Without a checklist, people not familiar with the task may miss something that is critical, and the result could be the creation of unwanted inventory.

Using pie charts to show the degree of influence on inventory of the various functions, Figure 14.2 illustrates how the degree of influence is shown to change from initial perception, '(i)', to the reality of the situation, '(iii)'.

All functions matter and have a part to play. Understanding this point will enable you to turn inventory management and control into a sustainable source of competitive advantage. It is said that travel is more about the journey than the destination, and so it is with inventory management. More will be learnt during the journey, and the destination of competitive advantage will be a natural conclusion.

Well, dear reader, enjoy the journey, good luck and don't forget to send me a postcard when you get there!

Appendix 1

INVENTORY COUNT CHECKLIST

The following checklist is an example of an inventory count checklist. This should not be looked upon as prescriptive, but rather as a typical checklist that might be used for an inventory count.

Inventory count date:			
Count Controller (CC):			

STAGE: PRE-COUNT PREPARATION

	Action	Who	Due Date	Complete?
1	Access inventory count procedure document			
2	Cut-off point agreed			
3	Document processing completed?			
	Goods received			
	Batch cards			
	In-process adjustments			
	Dispatch notes			
	Inventory transfers (laboratory)			
	Inventory disposal			
	Inventory losses			
	Location transfers			
	Quarantine inventory classification			
4	Location maps	CC		
5	Teams			
	Size of inventory counting team established			
	Number of teams confirmed			
	Data entry teams confirmed and assigned			
	Number of auditors confirmed and assigned			

6 Timetable	CC		
7 Milestones	CC		
8 Documentation			
Inventory count paperwork			
Central register for document control			
9 Marking method			
10 Briefings scheduled			
Inventory counting team			
Data entry team			
Auditors			
11 Reconciliation methods			
12 Performance measures	CC		
13 Auditor validation methods			
Count validation			
Paperwork tracking			
Data entry validation			

STAGE: THE COUNT

Action	Who	Due Time	Complete?
1 Count validation	Auditors		
2 Location checked – validation	CC/Auditors		
3 Data entry validation	Auditors		
4 Inventory count progress checking	CC		

STAGE: RECONCILIATION

Action	Who	Due Date	Complete?
1 Confirm tolerances			
Percentage			
Value			
Quantity			
2 Physical reconciliation			
Items confirmed			
Investigation			
Adjustments applied			
3 Financial reconciliation			
WIP account reconciliation			
Provision level confirmed			
Final variance agreed			

4 Inventory count review

5 Update checklist with:

    Best practice

    Improvements

6 Update stock count procedure with:

    Best practice

    Improvements

Appendix 2

ANALYSIS TEMPLATE

The following below is an example of a form that might be used to detail each item being investigated. This should not be looked upon as prescriptive, but rather as a typical of a form that might be used to record the analysis undertaken.

Inventory variance analysis

Inventory count date   _____
Item to be reconciled   _____
Inventory counted   _____   Theoretical inventory   _____
Inventory variance   _____   Value variance   _____
Percentage variance   _____

Analysis

1   Double-check the inventory count data. Has the data been recorded correctly?

2   Has the data been entered correctly onto the business system? Has any data been transposed? In other words, are there any keystroke errors; '39' typed in when it should have been '93'? This can apply not just to quantities, but also to any item and batch references.

3   Have all batch cards been processed? Have raw materials been 'consumed'? Has the product inventory been updated?

4   Has any material been taken out of inventory for samples or for laboratory use?

5   Has any material been damaged, and the loss not recorded?

6   Was the correct quantity received into inventory? In other words, was there an error when the business system was updated upon goods receipt or confirmation of the quantity of product manufactured?

7   Was a raw material used that went un-recorded? This can occur when adjustments are made during the manufacturing process.

8   Was some un-saleable inventory used in the manufacture of the product? Was the use recorded?

CONCLUSION/ADJUSTMENTS MADE etc.

Appendix 3

SAFETY STOCK

The following template is an example of a form that might be used to determine whether Safety Stock should be set for a particular material. This should not be looked upon as prescriptive, but rather as a typical form that might be used to record the criteria used and factors to be considered.

Safety Stock application

Item description:	_____	Pack size	_____
Request date:	_____	Requested by:	_____
Safety Stock quantity	_____	Unit of measure	_____
Safety Stock value	£ _____		

Production

Minimum batch/production run:	_____	Units	_____
Maximum batch/production run:	_____	Units	_____
Process time:	_____	Units per batch	_____

Strategic justification – classification

Comfort	
Systematic	
Scenario	
Commitment	

NOTE: 'SYSTEMATIC' AND 'COMMITMENT' RAW MATERIALS SHOULD **NOT** BE CONSIDERED FOR SAFETY STOCK AS THEY DO NOT FIT WITH THE COMPANY'S STRATEGIC GOALS.

Product life cycle position

Introduction
Growth
Maturity
Decline

NOTE: RAW MATERIALS MOVING FROM MATURITY TO DECLINE AND FIRMLY IN DECLINE SHOULD **NOT** BE CONSIDERED FOR SAFETY STOCK AS THEY DO NOT FIT WITH THE COMPANY'S STRATEGIC GOALS.

Detail the full strategic justification for the Safety Stock proposal below:

Raw materials

Record any issues related to raw materials below:

Technical

Shelf life: _____ (days/months)
Special storage conditions:

Commercial

No. of customers: _____
Nearest _____ Km_ Shipping lead-time _____
Farthest _____ Km_ Shipping lead-time _____

Sales forecast

Record historical sales and forecast sales in the table below:

	Sales History		Sales Forecast	
	Month/Yr.	Quantity	Month/Yr.	Quantity
1				
2				
3				
4				
5				
6				
7				
8				
9				
10				
11				
12				

Record the evidence for the forecast – data sources used etc.

Safety Stock calculation

Basis used for determining the Safety Stock.

Inventory Days equivalence: _____
(i.e. the number of days the inventory should typically last)

Demand pattern justification

Commercial justification

Detail the full commercial justification for the Safety Stock proposal.

INVENTORY LEVEL TO BE SET AT: _____ Units: _____

Approval / Rejection

Safety Stock has been: <u>APPROVED/REJECTED</u> (Circle as appropriate)
Approved/rejected by:
Date:
Approval/rejection reasons:

Note: This might seem a long form to complete, but it should be remembered that when setting a product up to have Safety Stock, the organisation is making a financial investment, and all investments need to be justified.

Appendix 4

SAFETY STOCK REVIEW

The following template is an example of a form that might be used to review Safety Stock for a particular product. This should not be looked upon as prescriptive, but rather as a typical form that might be used to record the criteria used and factors to be considered. The review should be product specific and looks to assess whether any changes have occurred since the Safety Stock was set up or since the previous review.

Safety Stock review

Item:	_____	Pack size:	_____
Review date:	_____	Reviewed by:	_____
Safety Stock quantity:	_____	Unit of measure:	_____
Safety Stock value:	£ _____		

Review all sections in the original setup document to determine whether any of the data/criteria have changed. If any change has occurred, assess whether it has had an impact on the Safety Stock level set for this item and implement any change

	CHANGE?		
Data/Criteria	*YES*	*NO*	*ACTION?*
Raw materials			
Technical			
Commercial			
Sales forecast			
Safety Stock calculation			
Demand pattern justification			
Commercial justification			
Strategic justification			

Review comments

Data/Criteria	Comments

Safety Stock updated to: _____

Unit of measure: _____

Date of update: _____

Updated by: _____

Appendix 5

ANTICIPATED ORDER
PRE-APPROVAL

Anticipated order pre-approval

Item _____ Pack size: _____
Item _____ Pack size: _____
Item _____ Pack size: _____
Item _____ Pack size: _____
Request date: _____ Requested by: _____
Customer: _____ Date required: _____
Total order value: £ _____ _____

Customer credit limit: £ _____ Current level: £ _____

Invoices overdue?   YES/NO
Has customer received their order from their customer?   YES/NO
Will order be lost if we fail to supply?   YES/NO

Approval/rejection

Manufacture has been: APPROVED/REJECTED
(Circle as appropriate)
Approved/rejected by: _____. Date: _____
Approval/rejection reasons:

Appendix 6

DETAILED PRODUCTION PLAN

Whilst a firm plan will detail the sequence of products to be manufactured, scheduling manpower requires a more detailed approach. The following example is based on a very basic production plan (Figure A6.1) and the assumption that each process has three steps – charging, processing and discharge.

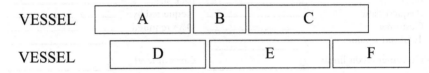

| VESSEL | A | B | C | |
| VESSEL | D | E | F |

Figure A6.1 Firm plan.

Step	Activity
1	Charge Product A
2	Charge Product D
3	Monitor Products A and D
4	Discharge Product A
5	Changeover from Product A to B
6	Charge Product B
7	Monitor Product B
8	Discharge Product D
9	Changeover from Product D to E
10	Charge Product E
11	Monitor Product E
12	Discharge Product B
13	Changeover from Product B to C
14	Charge Product C
15	Monitor Product C
16	Discharge Product E
17	Changeover from Product E to F
18	Charge Product F
19	Monitor Product F
20	Discharge Product F

Knowing the process time for each product means that the activities shown above would be expected to take place at specific times.

Each of the core activities of charging, monitoring and discharging will require a certain level of manpower. For example, Product A might need one person to charge the vessel, Product D, two people etc. whilst the monitoring might only need the equivalent of half a person.

Factoring the required resources levels in would create a resource profile. Taking the example given, each product has a resource requirement for each core activity, as shown in Figure A6.2.

Resource Level Requirement (Number of People)

	Charge	Monitor	Discharge
Product A	1	0.5	1
Product B	2	1	1.5
Product C	1	0.5	2
Product D	1	0.5	1
Product E	1	1	1
Product F	1	0.5	1

Figure A6.2 Resource level requirement.

We can take this information and create a resource profile, as shown in Figure A6.3.

Staff Required

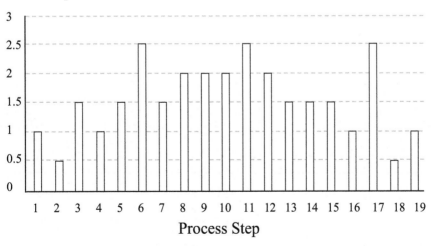

Figure A6.3 Manpower requirement (number of staff).

If there are 3 people available at any time, then the plan can be easily achieved, as the maximum requirement is for the equivalent of 2.5 people.

However, if only 2 people are available, then the plan will probably slip. Such situations can easily arise during, for example, holiday/vacation periods. In these instances, it is essential to communicate with Planning so that it can act accordingly when looking beyond the normal planning horizon.

Appendix 7

PRODUCTION BRIEFING AGENDA

Meeting date: _____   Start Time: 09:00
         (First day of the working week)   End Time: 09:30

Organiser: Production

Attendees: Production operators
            Production management
            Planner(s)
            R&D (where new products are being introduced)

Purpose: Review the upcoming production plan and identify key challenges, critical milestones and new products

Key challenges

Item	Line/Vessel	Challenge	
1			
2			
3			
4			

Milestones

Item	Line/Vessel	Critical Milestone	
1			
2			
3			
4			

New products

Item	Line/Vessel	Product	
1			
2			
3			
4			

Actions arising

No.	Action	Who	Due Date
1			
2			
3			
4			

Note: This form is only an example. The actual design of the form for any given organisation will vary according to the nature of the production process – number of vessels, shift pattern, staff levels, product types etc.

Appendix 8

SHIFT HANDOVER FORM

Date: _____ Time: _____
Handover from _____ to _____

Production status

Item	Line/Vessel	Status	
1			
2			
3			
4			
5			
6			
7			

Upcoming events/milestones

Item	Line/Vessel	Event/Milestone	
1			
2			
3			
4			
5			
6			
7			

Handover complete: YES/NO
Signed: _____

Note: This form is only for illustration purposes.

Appendix 9

DISPATCH VARIANCE REPORT

A dispatch variance report should be used to compare the required shipping details – customer, dispatch note ref., product, lot number and quantity –against the actual. What is being looked for is a variance between the required and the actual.

The source of the report could be the business system, a reporting tool or a spreadsheet designed to show variances.

An example format is shown in Table A9.1.

Table A9.1 Dispatch variance report example.

Report date:			
Customer:			
Dispatch ref:			
Product:			
Lot number:			
Quantity/unit			
Variance			
Notes			

With regard to bulk shipments, there should be a tolerance within which a variance report will not be triggered.

Note: The actual layout of a report will vary, depending on the source and its construction. The above is less of an example of how it might look but more of a means of illustrate the variances that should be flagged – specifically, lot number and quantity.

Appendix 10

STANDARD SELECTION LIST

This is an example of a selection list where an option has been included (as part of the form design) to add modifications. The format is not prescriptive, but rather offers an insight into methods of reducing the risk of human error.

Selection list

CUSTOMER	DELIVERY ADDRESS

Sales Order Ref: Customer Order Ref:

DELIVERY DATE:

SPECIAL INSTRUCTIONS:

Item	Product	Lot Number	Qty	Actual
1	PRODUCT A	171003	5	
2	PRODUCT B	170818	6	
3	PRODUCT C	170922	2	
		170923	3	

ORDER AMENDMENTS

ITEM	PRODUCT	LOT NUMBER	QTY

The example layout is for illustration purposes and serves only to show the type of data that should be found on a selection list. The actual number of lines will vary according to the customer order.

The use of boxes helps to standardise the format of manual data entry and should be of a size that allows figures and/or characters to be entered so that they are clear to anyone who subsequently uses the data.

Appendix 11

DISPATCH INSTRUCTIONS TEMPLATE

LANGUAGE: ENGLISH

Q = Question; A = Answer; Inst = Instruction

HEALTH AND SAFETY INSTRUCTIONS

If you hear the alarm, please turn your vehicle engine off and proceed to the assembly point.

DO NOT ATTEMPT TO MOVE YOUR VEHICLE UNLESS INSTRUCTED TO DO SO.

DO NOT USE YOUR MOBILE PHONE WHILST DRIVING YOUR VEHICLE OR IN AN UNAUTHORISED AREA.

Q. What are you coming to collect?

A. I have to collect for . . . . (Customer Name)

(Please write down)

Inst 1. Please wait here. I will tell you when to proceed.

Inst 2. Tea, coffee and toilets are available as directed.

Inst 3. Please drive down as directed (person will be showing you).

Inst 4. Please wait whilst I pull together the items to load.

Inst 5. Please clear some space to load the goods. I need space for. . . . . . pallets

Inst 6. I have completed the loading.

Inst 7. Please sign this document where I am pointing.

Inst 8. Please PRINT YOUR NAME CLEARLY.

Inst 9. Please take these documents and give them to the customer.

Inst 10. Please note any special instructions.

Inst 11. You can now leave – please drive carefully.

Note: This form can be translated into various languages and the flag can help the driver pick the correct document. The questions and instructions should be tailored for each organisation and shipment type where appropriate.

LANGUAGE: WELSH/CYMRAEG

Q = Cwestiwn; A = Ateb; Inst = Cyfarwyddiad

CYFARWYDDIADAU IECHYD A DIOGELWCH
Os glywch y larwm, diffodd 'injan' eich cerbyd a symudwch ymlaen i'r bwynt cynulliad.

PEIDIWCH A SYMYD EICH CERBYD ONI CHAIFF EI GYFARWYDDO I WNEUD.

PEIDIWCH A DEFNYDDIO EICH FFÔN WRTH DREIFIO NAC MEWN ARDAL ANARDUWDODEDIG

Q. Beth ydach chi'n casglu?

A. Dwi yma i gasglu dros: .... (Enw'r Cwsmer)

(Ysgrifennwch i lawr)

Inst 1. Arhoswch yma. Dywedaf wrthych pryd i symud ymlaen.

Inst 2. Pannad, coffi a lle chwech ar gael yn unol a chyfarwyddyd

Inst 3. Dylech yrru fel y cyfarwyddi (bydd unigolyn yn dangos is chi)

Inst 4. Disgwyliwch yma tra rwyf yn hel at i gilydd yr eitemau i lwytho.

Inst 5. Gwnewch digon o le i lwytho'r eitemau. Dwi'n angen lle am. . . . . . . o baledi.

Inst 6. Dwi wedi darfod llwytho.

Inst 7. Llofnodwch y ddogfen yn y lle dwi'n dangos.

Inst 8. PRINTIWCH EICH ENW YN GLÎR os gwelwch yn dda.

Inst 9. Dylech gymeryd y dogfennau hyn ac yn rhoi iddynt i'r cwsmer.

Inst 10. Dalwch sylw ar unrhyw gyfarwyddiadau arbennig.

Inst 11. Cewch chi adael rwan – gyrrwch yn ofalus.

Note: It would be useful to include the flag of the nation concerned so that selection of the appropriate language might be easier and quicker.

Appendix 12

GOODS INWARDS
INSTRUCTIONS TEMPLATE

LANGUAGE: ENGLISH

Q = Question; A = Answer; Inst = Instruction

HEALTH AND SAFETY INSTRUCTIONS
If you hear the alarm, please turn your vehicle engine off and proceed to the assembly point.
DO NOT ATTEMPT TO MOVE YOUR VEHICLE UNLESS INSTRUCTED TO DO SO.
DO NOT USE YOUR MOBILE PHONE WHILST DRIVING YOUR VEHICLE OR IN AN UNAUTHORISED AREA.
Q. What are you delivering?
A. I am delivering from . . . . (Supplier Name)
(Please write down)

Inst 1. Please show me the delivery documents.
Inst 2. Please wait here. I will tell check what we are expecting.
Inst 3. Tea, coffee and toilets are available as directed.
Inst 4. Please prepare to offload the items.
Inst 5. Please move your vehicle here (as directed).
Inst 6. I have completed the offloading.
Inst 7. Where do you want me to sign for the delivery?
Inst 8. There is a problem with the delivery.
Inst 9. Please wait here while we contact the supplier.
Inst 10. We cannot accept these items (point out the items).
Inst 11. You can now leave – please drive carefully.

Note: This form can be translated into various languages and a flag added to help the driver pick the correct document. The questions and instructions should be tailored for each organisation and delivery type, where appropriate.

Appendix 13

PREFERRED PURCHASE QUANTITY APPROVAL

Introduction

There will be instances where Sales will not favour a purchase-to-make approach to procuring raw materials, as this will incur a much higher price than expected for one or more raw materials. There might well be instances where this is acceptable to an organisation, but rather than having an ad hoc approach it is preferable to have some form of control. This form suggests the type of approach that can be adopted to ensure that everyone understands the reasons for moving raw materials from a purchase-to-make classification to a preferred purchase quantity.

Preferred purchase quantity approval

Item: _____ Pack size: _____

Used in: _____ (Product)

Customer(s): _____

	RAW MATERIAL	Unit	Purchase to Make	Preferred Quantity
A	Quantity	Kilos		
B	Unit cost	£/kg	£	£
C	RM quantity to be used	Kilos		
D	Inventory Balance (A − C)	Kilos	0.0	
E	Balance value (D × B)	£	£0.00	£
	PRODUCT			
F	Product quantity	Kilos		
G	Product standard cost	£/kg	£	£
H	Product price	£/kg	£	£

I Product margin (H − G)   £/kg | £ | £ |

J Total margin (I × F)   £ | | |

K Net margin (J − E)   £ | £ | £ |

Other Comments

Reviewed by: _____   Date: _____
Approved by: _____   Date: _____

Appendix 14

MANUFACTURE WITHOUT PURCHASE ORDER

The following template is an example of a form that might be used to determine whether a product should be manufactured before a purchase order has been received. This should not be looked upon as prescriptive, but rather as typical of a form that might be used to record the criteria used and factors to be considered.

Manufacture request

Item: _____   Pack size: _____
Request date: _____   Requested by: _____
Quantity: _____   Unit of measure: _____
Inventory value: £ _____

Production

Minimum batch/production run: _____   Units: _____
Maximum batch/production run: _____   Units: _____
Process time: _____   Per batch/unit _____

Product life cycle position

Introduction
Growth
Maturity
Decline

NOTE: PRODUCTS MOVING FROM MATURITY TO DECLINE AND FIRMLY IN DECLINE SHOULD **NOT** BE CONSIDERED FOR SAFETY STOCK AS THEY DO NOT FIT WITH THE COMPANY'S STRATEGIC GOALS.

Detail the full strategic justification for the manufacturing proposal.

```
┌─────────────────────────────────────────────────────────────┐
│                                                             │
│                                                             │
│                                                             │
│                                                             │
└─────────────────────────────────────────────────────────────┘
```

Technical

Shelf life: _____ (days/months)
Special storage conditions: _____

Commercial

No. of customers: _____   Nearest: _____ Km
                                       shipping lead-time: _____
                                       Farthest: _____ Km
                                       shipping lead-time: _____

Sales forecast

Record historical sales and forecast sales in the following table.

	Sales History		Sales Forecast	
	Month/Yr	Quantity	Month/Yr	Quantity
1				
2				
3				
4				
5				
6				
7				
8				
9				
10				
11				
12				

Record the evidence for the forecast – data sources used etc.

```
┌─────────────────────────────────────────────────────────────┐
│                                                             │
│                                                             │
│                                                             │
└─────────────────────────────────────────────────────────────┘
```

Demand pattern justification

```



```

Commercial justification

Detail the full commercial justification for the manufacturing proposal.

```



```

Approval/rejection

Manufacture has been: <u>APPROVED/REJECTED</u>   (Circle as appropriate)

Approved/rejected by: _____ Date: _____

Approval/rejection reasons:

```



```

Note: This might seem a long form to complete, but it should be remembered that the risks of ending up with un-usable inventory usually carry a significant financial penalty. It should be no different from an organisation making a financial investment, and all investments need to be justified.

Appendix 15

CONSIGNMENT INVENTORY REQUEST

The following template is an example of a form that might be used to determine whether a customer should be given the opportunity to have a consignment inventory arrangement put in place. This should not be looked upon as prescriptive, but rather as a typical form that might be used to record the criteria used and factors to be considered.

Consignment inventory request

Customer: _____   Sales p.a.:   £ _____

Request date: _____   Requested by: _____

Products requested

	Product Description	Minimum		Maximum	
		Qty (mt)	Val (£)	Qty (mt)	Val (£)
1					
2					
3					
4					
5					
6					

Product life cycle classification and shelf life

	Product Description	Life Cycle Position	Shelf Life (days)
1			
2			
3			
4			
5			
6			

Classification selections

The standard life cycle positions are Introduction, Growth, Maturity and Decline.

NOTE: PRODUCTS MOVING FROM MATURITY TO DECLINE AND FIRMLY IN DECLINE SHOULD **NOT** BE CONSIDERED FOR CONSIGNMENT INVENTORY AS THEY DO NOT FIT WITH THE COMPANY'S STRATEGIC GOALS.

Detail the full strategic justification for the consignment inventory proposal.

Special storage conditions

Commercial

Shipping lead-time: _____ days

Sales forecast

Record historical sales and forecast sales in the table below.

	Sales History		Sales Forecast	
	Month/Yr	£	Month/Yr	£
1				
2				
3				
4				
5				
6				
7				
8				
9				
10				
11				
12				

Record the evidence for the forecast – data sources used etc.

Demand pattern justification

```
┌─────────────────────────────────────────────────────┐
│                                                     │
│                                                     │
│                                                     │
└─────────────────────────────────────────────────────┘
```

Commercial justification

Detail the full commercial justification for the manufacturing proposal.

```
┌─────────────────────────────────────────────────────┐
│                                                     │
│                                                     │
│                                                     │
└─────────────────────────────────────────────────────┘
```

Approval/rejection

Consignment inventory has been: APPROVED/REJECTED (Circle as appropriate)

Approved/rejected by: _____ Date: _____

Approval/rejection Reasons:

```
┌─────────────────────────────────────────────────────┐
│                                                     │
│                                                     │
│                                                     │
└─────────────────────────────────────────────────────┘
```

Note: This might seem a long form to complete, but it should be remembered that the risks of ending up with un-usable inventory usually carry a significant financial penalty. It should be no different from an organisation making a financial investment, and all investments need to be justified.

Appendix 16

CONSIGNMENT INVENTORY ADMINISTRATION

Critical to any consignment inventory arrangement is the administration of the scheme.

Risks

Setting up consignment inventory means that, whilst legal ownership of a product is retained until used, the control of inventory is effectively ceded to the customer. This means that the inventory will be subject to the control systems and process operated by the customer.

It is essential therefore that consideration should be given to aspects such as the following when designing an effective administration scheme.

In transit

An accurate record of in-transit shipments should be maintained. When a customer submits their monthly usage, it should be remembered that there may be goods in transit, which means that the organisation may have, within their systems, added the shipment to the customer's consignment inventory but it will not be in place when the customer submits their returns.

Any procedure should therefore take account of in-transit shipments.

Shipment arrival

It is essential that the customer confirms receipt of product in good, undamaged condition. This will avoid any issues that may arise later in relation to responsibility for dealing with damaged goods.

Storage

The organisation should validate storage arrangements for its product(s), ensuring that any special storage conditions, where required, are in place.

Inventory rotation

It is likely that multiple lot numbers may well have been shipped to a customer, and it is critical that they appreciate that responsibility for inventory management and rotation rests with them. Their understanding of the organisation's labelling with regard to shelf life should be thorough, and both parties should agree on the process for inventory rotation.

Where product is found to be 'out of shelf life', whilst the organisation will look to help the customer deal with the product(s) affected, the inventory should be considered as 'used' and invoiced accordingly.

Accountability for inventory rotation means the customer will deal, at their own cost, with the consequences – for example, disposal.

Reporting mechanism

The reporting mechanism should be in an agreed format. A typical process might have the following steps:

- The customer supplies, at the start of any new consignment year, the forecast demand for each product.
- At the end of a month, the organisation submits an inventory summary to the customer. This will detail the closing inventory levels from the previous submission, together with shipments made in the intervening period.
- The customer will confirm the closing inventory level and whether shipments have been received.
- The organisation will confirm the new opening inventory (previous closing inventory + confirmed shipment arrivals).
- The customer will confirm the current inventory level and confirm the usage for each product listed (at lot number level if required).
- The organisation will confirm the invoicing arrangements and new closing inventory to the customer.
- The organisation will compare the usage figures to the forecast demand from the customer. Any significant deviation (e.g. ±10%) should be referred back to the customer so that the reasons for deviation can be understood.

Inventory count

At agreed intervals (e.g. 6 monthly or annually), the customer will agree to have the consignment inventory validated by having it counted by a representative of the organisation. This will help bring any discrepancies into line, triggering agreed adjustments to inventory.

Customer responsibilities

When setting up a consignment inventory arrangement, it is essential that the customer understands their responsibilities for managing the process and that there are consequences when their part of the agreement fails.

Appendix 17

CUSTOMER TRIAL CHECKLIST

A customer trial is not just an opportunity to get business established with a customer, either with existing or new products, but it is also an opportunity to promote a positive image of the organisation, not only in terms of the products that it sells, but also in terms of the way it goes about its business (organisation, planning etc.). Customer trials need to be planned, and it should not be a case of Technical Service staff turning up at the same time as the product and saying, 'OK, shall we start?'

Customer trial checklist

Customer: _____ Trial date: _____
Start time: _____ Estimated end time: _____
Product(s): _____ Requested by: _____

Pre-trial checklist

Topic	Item	Date
Product	Technical Data Sheet sent to customer	
	Material Safety Data Sheet sent to customer	
	PPE list sent to customer	
Equipment	Recommended equipment notes sent to customer	
	Recommended operating manuals sent to customer	
Audit	Equipment audit undertaken	
	Health & Safety audit undertaken	
Training	Training materials (manuals) prepared	
	Training materials (other media) prepared	
	Training resources confirmed	
Sessions	On/offsite preparatory session required?	
	Session completed? (if necessary)	

Trial checklist

Detail the trial objective below:

The objective should detail the trial outcome – for example, number of parts to be produced, target run time(s), people to be trained etc. The purpose needs to be clear.

Attendees	Name	Role
Organisation		
Organisation		
Organisation		
Customer		
Customer		
Customer		

Trial resources

Resources	Note	Date
Equipment	Does the organisation need to bring any other material (e.g. cleaning materials)?	
Product	Has the product required for the trial been manufactured and delivered?	
	Is the product within the targeted specification?	
People	Are all desired attendees able to be present at the trial?	
Training	Are all materials available for the trial?	
Process	Troubleshooting manual	

Post-trial checklist

Aspect	Notes	Comment
Objective	Was the objective achieved?	
Equipment	Did the equipment function as expected?	
People	Were all planned attendees present?	
Operation	Were issues identified during the trial?	
Process	Does the process require any modification in the future?	
	Does the equipment need to be modified for the future?	
Training	Was the training successful?	
Follow-up	What are the next steps?	

Notes: The above checklist is an example only and serves to illustrate the type of aspects that need to be considered when conducting a trial. As can be seen, the trial has been split into four parts – pre-trial, trial, trial resources and post-trial. The value of the pre-trial and post-trial stages cannot be understated, as they are critical not only to the success of a trial, but also to the success of future trials (where an organisation's experience can be used to promote good practice and improve on weaknesses).

Appendix 18

INITIAL USE CHECKLIST

Following on from a trial, certain customers will require support during their period of initial use. This can be due to either an element of confidence building on the part of the customer or that they have used the product infrequently and need support as their staff might be new to the product.

Whilst similar in certain regards to the trial checklist in Appendix 18, a certain degree of familiarity can be assumed, if for no other reason than certain of the customer's staff will have had some training in the product's use or with similar products.

Customer initial use checklist

Customer: _____   Initial use date: _____
Start time: _____   Estimated end time: _____
Product(s): _____   Requested by: _____

Pre-visit checklist

Topic	Item	Date
Product	Technical Data Sheet sent to customer	
	Material Safety Data Sheet sent to customer	
	PPE list sent to customer	
Equipment	Recommended equipment notes sent to customer	
	Recommended operating manuals sent to customer	
Audit	Equipment audit undertaken	
	Health & Safety audit undertaken	
Training	Training materials (manuals) prepared	
	Training materials (other media) prepared	
	Training resources confirmed	
	Have all users been trained?	

Visit checklist

Detail the visit objective below:

| |
| |

The objective should detail the visit outcome – for example, number of parts to be produced, target run time(s), people to be trained etc. The purpose needs to be clear.

Attendees	Name	Role
Organisation		
Organisation		
Organisation		
Customer		
Customer		
Customer		

Visit resources

Resources	Note	Date
Equipment	Does the organisation need to bring any other material (e.g. cleaning materials)?	
Product	Is the product within the targeted specification?	
People	Are all desired attendees able to be present at the initial use visit?	
Process	Troubleshooting manual	

Post-visit checklist

Aspect	Notes	Comment
Objective	Was the objective achieved?	
Equipment	Did the equipment function as expected?	
People	Were all planned attendees present?	
Operation	Were issues identified during the visit?	
Process	Does the process require any modification in the future?	
	Does the equipment need to be modified for the future?	
Follow-up	What are the next steps?	

Notes: The above checklist is an example only and serves to illustrate the type of aspects that need to be considered when supporting a customer's initial use of a product. As can be seen, the visit has been split into four parts – pre-visit, initial-use visit, visit resources and post-visit. The value of the pre-visit and post-visit stages cannot be understated, as they are critical not only to the successful use of a product by the customer, but also to the success of future initial use visits (where an organisation's experience can be used to promote good practice and improve on weaknesses).

Appendix 19

ONGOING USE CHECKLIST

The need for Technical Support during ongoing use is likely to be in response to a problem that the customer is experiencing. Often, the user of any product, when encountering a problem, will blame the product, whilst in most instances, the process is to blame. Of course, apportioning blame should not be the objective. Rather it should be seen for what it is – helping a customer resolve a problem and learning from the experience. In so doing, it is another opportunity to present the organisation in a positive light.

Of course, Technical Service might be the first to be made aware of a customer issue though it might already be the subject of the organisation's complaints procedure.

Indeed, with the visit likely to be part of a complaint, a record will to be added to the organisation's CRM database.

Customer ongoing support checklist

Customer: _____   Complaint ref: _____
Visit date: _____
Product(s): _____
Nature of issue (enter details below):

Pre-visit checklist

Topic	Item	Date
Product	Check batch numbers reference by customer	
	Check retained sample condition	
Equipment	Recommended equipment notes sent to customer	
	Recommended operating manuals sent to customer	
Training	List customer staff who have been trained.	
Process	Prepare copy of troubleshooting manual	

Visit checklist

Detail the visit objective below:

The objective should detail the visit outcome(s) – for example, problem(s) to be resolved, number of parts to be produced, target run time(s), people to be trained etc. The purpose needs to be clear.

Attendees	Name	Role
Organisation		
Organisation		
Organisation		
Customer		
Customer		
Customer		

Visit resources

Resources	Note	Date
Equipment	Check equipment operating correctly	
Product	Check product(s) reported to have been used by customer (reference codes and lot numbers)	
People	Have equipment users been trained?	
Process	Has customer attempted to resolve any problem, and if so, how?	

Post-visit checklist

Aspect	Notes	Comment
Objective	Was the problem resolved?	
Equipment	Did the equipment function as expected?	
People	Were all planned attendees present?	
Operation	Were issues identified during the visit?	
Process	Does the process require any modification in the future?	
	Does the equipment need to be modified for the future?	
Follow–up	What are the next steps? Training, manuals etc.?	

Notes: The above checklist should not be seen as prescriptive, but only as an example illustrating the types of aspects that need to be considered when responding to a customer issue. As can be seen, the visit has been split into four parts – pre-visit, initial use visit, visit resources and post-visit. The value of the pre-visit and post-visit stages cannot be understated, as they are critical not only to the successful resolution of a customer's issue, but also to the success of future issue resolution visits (where an organisation's experience can be used to promote good practice and improve on weaknesses).

Appendix 20

MARKET RESEARCH CHECKLIST

Whenever market research data is being used for decision making (whether over the short or long term), it is essential that users have confidence in the data. Consideration should be given to the data sources and how both data and assumptions have been validated. Quite often, market research might only be undertaken on an ad hoc basis, and maintaining consistency in the structure of the data is not always easy to achieve. Often people will forget why certain assumptions were made and what was used to validate the data. A checklist can be a useful way of working towards consistency.

Market research checklist

Definition/scope

Requirement defined?
Is market-related view required?
Is regional-related view required?
Is product-related report required?
Primary and/or secondary markets included?
Type of data required?

Data sources

External sources for data that has been defined as a requirement?
What internal data source is available?

Assumptions

List each assumption
Define each assumption
Validate each assumption
Create algorithm for use in data analysis spreadsheet

Reporting format

How should data be reported?

As a database?
By product?
By region?
By market?

Sales leads

Style of sales lead(s)
Data that should be presented.
Frequency of reporting

Feedback

Are systems in place to refine assumptions?
Are systems in place to refine data presentation?
Are systems in place to refine sales leads format?

The above is not prescriptive but is an illustration of the types of issues that should be considered when looking to undertake market research.

Appendix 21

NEW RAW MATERIAL
INTRODUCTION

Whenever a new raw material is introduced there is a risk of an inventory issue being triggered. Minimising, if not eliminating, this risk requires all aspects to be considered and appropriate action taken.

New raw material introduction

RM description: _____

RM code: _____   Supplier: _____

Used in: _____   _____

Aspect	Comment	Y/N
Packaging	Is RM in new packaging type?	
	What is packaging similar to?	
Purchasing	Who is the new supplier?	
	New supplier added to business system?	
	Typical order quantities required to meet forecast demand?	
Technical	New codes added to business system	
	Confirm RM shelf life?	
	Review Material Safety Data Sheet (MSDS)	
Planning	Is Safety Stock required?	
	What are the supplier lead-times?	
	Shelf life requirements?	
Goods Received	Where will RM be stored?	
	How will the RM arrive on site?	
	When is first delivery due?	
	Inventory rotation criteria.	

	How should the RM be handled?	
	Health & Safety requirements	
	Personal Protective Equipment (PPE) requirements	
Storage	What type of storage is required for the RM?	
Production	Where is RM stored?	
	Handling methods?	
	PPE requirements?	

The checklist is not prescriptive, but illustrates the types of aspects that need to be covered when introducing new raw materials.

Appendix 22

FORMULA AND PROCESS CHANGE MANAGEMENT

Whenever a change is made to a production process, be it a formulation change or process instruction modification, it is essential that the change has been well managed. This means that consideration should be given to four key aspects:

1   Staff awareness of change.
2   Resource/equipment change.
3   Has the change affected the product adversely in any way? (e.g. made it more unstable)
4   Has the processing change been tested and communicated?

These do mimic one of the classical tools used to analyse problems – Man, Machinery, Method and Materials.

Formula and process change management

Product description: _____
Type of change (describe in detail):

Aspect	Comment	Y/N
Staff	Have staff been involved in the process?	
	Are staff aware of the reasons for change?	
	Have staff been briefed on the change being introduced?	

Resource	Is equipment capable of accommodating the change? *(If 'No', then ensure further change management process initiated to deal with fitting, testing and training.)*	
Product	Has the product been assessed for any change?	
	Has a further review been set up regarding product quality?	
Process	Has the process changed significantly?	
	Have new instructions been issued?	
	Have staff been trained in new instructions?	

The above provides insight into factors that need to be considered when making any change, no matter how small. The change management process should be applied equally to minor manufacturing-related changes as well as to major changes.

Appendix 23

ECR SEGMENT ATTRIBUTES

Ensuring the integrity of each segment of the error containment ring is an essential part of preventing the breakout of an error or errors. Examining the key attributes of each segment is a useful approach to assess the integrity and strength of the segment concerned.

ECR segment attribute analysis

Segment	Positive	Negative
Equipment	Designed for product	Not designed
	Unmodified	Modified
	Preventive MTCE	No preventive MTCE
	Restricted products	Uncontrolled number of products
Process	Documented operating procedures and evidence of use.	Assumed that process is easy to learn.
	Documented and detailed manufacturing instructions and evidence of use.	Little guidance provided
	Troubleshooting document available.	Need to rely on intuition or local expert.
	Variances recorded	No formal process
	Documented process records	Poor records
Training	Induction	No formal training
	Ongoing to maintain skill level	Poorly organised training
	Reviews	No reviews
	Tests to maintain skill level	No ongoing tests
	Variety of techniques (computer based, classroom, one-to-one, offsite etc.)	
Focus	Quiet	Noisy
	Visually calming	Visually clashing
	Controlled movement	Random movement
	Ergonomics well understood	Poor ergonomics
	Time management in place and practiced.	No time management

Segment	Positive	Negative
	Controlled workload	Tiredness
	Involved in decision making	Stress and tension
	Well organised with planning and preparation	Poorly organised

The above is not prescriptive, as there will be features that are specific to each function. However, the above list provides a basis for assessing the integrity of each ECR segment.

INDEX

For Product Safety Concerns and Information please contact our EU representative GPSR@taylorandfrancis.com Taylor & Francis Verlag GmbH, Kaufingerstraße 24, 80331 München, Germany